ALL ON SHOW
The circus in Irish literature and culture

All on Show

The circus in Irish literature and culture

ELEANOR LYBECK

First published in 2019 by
Cork University Press
Youngline Industrial Estate
Pouladuff Road, Togher
Cork
T12 HT6V
Ireland

British Library Cataloguing in Publication Data
A CIP record for this book is available from the British Library.

ISBN 978-1-78205-294-4

Printed in Poland by HussarBooks
Print origination & design by Carrigboy Typesetting Services,
www.carrigboy.com

www.corkuniversitypress.com

For Marianne

Contents

LIST OF FIGURES   viii

ACKNOWLEDGEMENTS   ix

INTRODUCTION   Circusing Ireland   1

CHAPTER 1   Joyce's Family Circus   16

CHAPTER 2   Imagined Communities at the Irish Circus   49

CHAPTER 3   Irish Circus History and Ireland's Theatrical Heritage   94

CHAPTER 4   Revisioning the Circus   131

CHAPTER 5   Conclusion: 'All tales of circus life are highly demoralising.'   175

ENDNOTES   187

BIBLIOGRAPHY   203

INDEX   217

List of figures

1.1 Artist unknown, Programme for Hengler's Grand Cirque, 1892, Poster,
The Mitchell Library Theatre Collection © CSGCIC Glasgow Libraries
Collection. All rights reserved   17

1.2 Artist unknown, Front cover of *Johnny Patterson's Great London Circus
Songster*, DeWitt's Song & Joke Book Series Number 241, 1878, New York
Public Library of the Performing Arts   20

1.3 Jack B. Yeats, *The Singing Clown*, 1928, Oil on canvas, Sligo Municipal
Collection & Model Arts and Niland Gallery © Estate of Jack B. Yeats.
All rights reserved, DACS 2017. Photo © The Model Arts & Niland
Gallery Limited   29

1.4 Artist unknown, *Metempsychosis*, c.1880, Poster, Evanion Collection,
British Library © The British Library Board   32

2.1 Robert Lynd, 'John Bull's Famous Circus', *The Republic*, vol. 1, no. 15
(21 March 1907), n.p.   57

2.2 John Tenniel, 'Two Forces', *Punch*, 29 October 1881 © *Punch*   58

2.3 Constance Markievicz, 'Comic Cosgrave', 1922, Etching, National
Library of Ireland. Image courtesy of the National Library of Ireland   76

2.4 Artist unknown, 'Fianna Fallacy Puppet Show', 1932, Poster, National
Library of Ireland. Image courtesy of the National Library of Ireland   78

2.5 Artist unknown, 'Devvy's Circus', 1932, Poster, National Library of Ireland.
Image courtesy of the National Library of Ireland   78

2.6 Edward Seago, 'Paddy O'Flynn', 1934, Reproduction of pencil sketch,
in *Sons of Sawdust* © The Estate of Edward Seago, represented by the
Portland Gallery, London   80

3.1 Jack B. Yeats, *The Double Jockey Act*, 1916, Oil on canvas, National
Gallery of Ireland © Estate of Jack B Yeats. All rights reserved, DACS 2017.
Photo © National Gallery of Ireland   102

4.1 Bruce Davidson, *IRELAND. 1967. James Duffy and Sons Circus*, Gelatine
silver print, Collection of the artist © Bruce Davidson/Magnum Photos   132

4.2 Bruce Davidson, *IRELAND. 1967. James Duffy and Sons Circus*, Gelatine
silver print, Collection of the artist © Bruce Davidson/Magnum Photos   133

5.1 Paul McErlane, 'Tumble Circus Perform in Belmont Park during the 2013
Ulster Bank Belfast Festival at Queen's', 2013, Digital image © Paul McErlane   179

Acknowledgements

Research for this book began in 2012 when I entered the Faculty of English at the University of Cambridge as a doctoral candidate. This phase of research was generously supported by the Arts and Humanities Research Council (AHRC). I was encouraged and productively challenged by many members of the faculty as I developed the thesis that is fundamental to the present work: my special thanks are due to Steven Connor, Sinéad Garrigan Mattar, Roderick Mengham, Jenny Bavidge, Alex Houen and Hope Wolf. The continuing interest and counsel of my thesis examiners Colin Graham and Zoë Svendsen has been, of course, exceptionally valuable. During my time at Cambridge, I benefited a great deal from the Cambridge Group for Irish Studies: I must acknowledge John Kerrigan, Eamon Duffy, Kenneth Madden and Peter Hession, who gave me the opportunity to present my work-in-progress to the group in April 2015. I am sincerely grateful to the British Association for Irish Studies (BAIS), who recognised the potential of this research with the BAIS Postgraduate Essay Prize in 2014. This prize allowed me to begin to establish myself as a recognisable voice within the field of Irish cultural criticism. More recently, I have thoroughly enjoyed opportunities to share aspects of this research with its largest audiences to date as one of ten AHRC/BBC Radio 3 New Generation Thinkers for 2017: many thanks are due to Robyn Read, Zahid Warley and Matthew Sweet for their expert advice and curiosity. At Cork University Press, it has been a pleasure to work with Mike Collins and Maria O'Donovan.

The quality of this book derives in significant part from the wealth of archival material that I have been fortunate enough to recover at institutions in England, Ireland and the United States. I am grateful to archivists and librarians at the following institutions for generously sharing their expertise and resources over the past five years: the National Fairground Archive at the University of Sheffield, the National Gallery of Ireland Yeats Archive, the National Library of Ireland Department of Manuscripts, the Trinity College Dublin Manuscripts & Archives Research Library, the British Library, the New York Public Library Berg Collection, the New York Public Library for the Performing Arts, the New York Public Library Manuscripts and Archives Research Division, and the University Library, Cambridge. Visits to archives would not have been possible without funding from the AHRC, the Faculty of English at the University of Cambridge, and from Girton College, Cambridge. I am especially grateful to Girton and to Trinity College Dublin for jointly awarding me the Luker-Cobbe Bursary in 2014. Images made by Jack B. Yeats and Edward Seago are reproduced by kind permission of their estates. Photographs by Bruce Davidson and Paul McErlane are featured in chapter four and the conclusion with their kind permission. I must also thank *Punch* magazine, the National Library of Ireland, and curators of the British Library's Evanion and the Mitchell Library Theatre Collections for granting me permission to reproduce the posters and cartoons discussed in chapters one and two. Details of Stewart Parker's composition process are provided in chapter one with the kind permission of Marilynn Richtarik, and references to the Dublin Players' 1974 production of *The Circus Animals' Desertion* are made in chapter three with the kind permission of Patricia Goldstone. I have learnt much from less formal correspondences with Lynne Parker, Ellen Cranitch, Hélène Montague, Gerald Dawe and Tina Segner. I am indebted to Martin Dyar for his assistance in comparing translations of Ó Conaire and for his generous response to the book as a whole. And I would not attempt to estimate the value of the interviews with Owen Roe, Neil Jordan, John Banville and Paul Muldoon that are represented here.

Finally, my thanks are due to old friends and relations Mark Doggett, Albert James and Florence Peile for their inspiration and guidance. They are due to new friends, too – especially to James and Edith Mateer for their companionship and engagement. Best thanks go to my family: to the Lavan troupe, to Eric, and to baby Marianne, who keeps me entertained, enthralled and enchanted.

June 2018

Circusing Ireland

This is a book about the circus as it appears in twentieth-century Irish literature and culture. It is a book about how the idea of the circus has been conceived in the minds of Irish writers, artists and filmmakers, and how real personalities, troupes and events from Irish circus history have been reimagined in prose, poetry, play and visual art forms. Its major concern is how the circus has become an icon – often a frustrated and disruptive icon – of certain normative ideas of Irishness across a century of literary and cultural history. By looking in this way at representations of the circus, we can then look back at the circus itself to ask what the circus is, and how it is distinct from other kinds of performance.

In this book, historical narrative weaves in and out of the literary and cultural criticism. This narrative has been constructed in significant part from material held in archives in Ireland, Britain and North America. Of all the archival sources I considered while writing this book, few were more compelling and complementary to my project than *Circus* magazine, which was published by the Circus Association of Ireland between 1990 and 2000.[1] The showman's periodical details trade secrets such as the latest developments in human physical performance styles; state-of-the-art designs in circus machines, apparatus and architecture; and the skills of world-class acrobats and animal trainers working in Ireland. *Circus* is caught between looking forward and looking back, combining historical features with news and reviews. Magazine articles attend to the past and present practices of Ireland's two leading circus families, the Duffys and the Fossetts, as well as promoting those smaller Irish, European and international troupes that are 'ones to watch'. At the same time, developments in and beyond circus society throughout the 1990s are apparent across issues.

The November 1990 issue of *Circus* exemplifies the wide variety of material that the fanzine's editors selected for publication. The success of Fossett's summer season was headline news: audiences benefited from the 'usual efficiency' of famed ringmaster Edward Fossett Jnr, who is considered 'the epitome of traditional Irish circus'.[2] Teddy Fossett commanded his acts expertly, and the programme was complemented by animal actors including an African elephant, camels, llamas, zebras, and myriad horses: big and little, chestnut and Arab. Fossett's also presented 'exotic' acts to the people of Ireland including El Hakim the Fakir (played by familiar favourite Barry Walls) and their latest version of the ever-popular American frontier narrative, 'The Westerners with Chief Otaki: Ropes, whips, fire etc.' (p. 6). By contrast, Albert Courtney's Big Top Circus, based in Portlaoise, was evidently conscious of heightened animal welfare campaigns: they prided themselves on performing without 'wild' animals, seeking only native and domesticated acts to join Shetland ponies, Teddy's Tricky Terriers, and the American Riding Machine (p. 12). Listings of Chipperfield's fifteen-stop touring route from Cork to Carlow for the 1989/90 season demonstrate that Irish circuses such as Fossett's and Albert Courtney's Big Top had to compete against established English companies to win over the imaginations of their audiences (p. 16). This was an historic competition: the article 'Operation Circus Train' details Bertram Mills' 1964 tour, which was billed as 'the most glamorous show ever to visit Ireland' (pp. 18–22). Extensive descriptions of changes made to the Irish rail network in the 1960s are given in the article; such descriptions exemplify the ways in which interactions between the Irish circus and Irish society are apparent throughout all issues of *Circus*. These interactions are clearly revealed in the paratextual elements of the magazine: Ireland the country appears through this record of circus history and current affairs, its photographic illustrations and advertisements. For instance, trends in Irish consumerism are seen on back covers of *Circus* in promotions for Clairol hair colour or adverts for Irish agricultural financiers such as Woodchester Farm Finance.[3]

Pen portraits chronicling major events in the personal family histories of Ireland's leading show families – births, deaths and marriages – are prominent in the magazine. The summer 1998 issue of *Circus* carried an obituary for Teddy Fossett: the man who was considered, in 1990, 'the epitome of traditional Irish circus'. Significant space is given over to Fossett's regrets:

> Teddy regretted many of the social changes he witnessed during his lifetime (1927–1998) – the loss of traditional sites, increasingly hostile local authorities, bureaucratic regulations, competition from new forms of entertainment (although he made effective use of television to keep the Fossett name before the Irish public), the inability to use flyposting

because of 'tidy town' campaigns, the regular visits to Ireland of circuses from elsewhere in Europe and so on.[4]

As with the advertisements sponsoring the production of *Circus*, readers glimpse aspects of twentieth-century Ireland through Teddy Fossett's obituary. Changes impacting on his way of life are wrought at local, national and international levels. Furthermore, it is notable that Fossett's death occurred in 1998: a momentous year for Irish national and international politics, as the Good Friday Agreement was signed at Stormont and the Republic qualified for entry into the European Union's Economic and Monetary Union. The tone of the article suggests that, in Fossett's passing, certain elements of the Irish circus community were subject to the palpable sense of an ending.

It is unclear whether or not editors realised that the autumn 2000 issue of *Circus* would be the final edition of the magazine; however, its contents seem an appropriate valediction for the enterprise. 'Irish Circuses Y2K' details the Russian and Polish acts working with Duffy's, and the Romanian acts working with Fossett's; the article gives notice of Wayne Courtney's Planet Circus and of CBC International's American Three Ring Circus, which had been pitched at Dublin Airport for two weeks in January.[5] Issue 17 also includes, rather poignantly, a feature by Agnes Sullivan entitled 'The End of the Strolling Players' that looks back to the small shows and circuses touring Ireland in the 1930s and 1940s: the McCormacks, the Bells, the Radio Stars, Ernie Clegg's dramatic company, the Bailies, the Daniels, Ray Mirth and his Merry Scamps (an all-girl variety show), Harry Lynton's Hippodrome, and Dusky Dan and his Christy Minstrel Show.[6]

Circus represents an attempt to materialise and memorialise the ephemeral world of the Irish circus through text and image. The magazine co-ordinates the past and present of popular entertainment in Ireland, identifying key events and recognisable personalities within circus history and current affairs. Incidentally – perhaps unconsciously, but most importantly – *Circus* reveals for its readers changes in Irish culture and society across the twentieth century. The magazine is an inspiration. Throughout, this book is engaged by texts like *Circus* that consolidate and narrate performance history. Evidence from a wide variety of sources proves how the circus has participated in and been affected by major political events in Ireland since the eighteenth century. Wolfe Tone's revolutionaries were parodied in a brutal pantomime at Astley's Dublin Amphitheatre.[7] World-famous Irish clowns apparently died in the ring for their political beliefs at the end of the nineteenth century.[8] Contemporary international troupes rivalling traditional circuses like Fossett's take on 'the darker themes' of the Northern Irish Troubles in their hybrid shows of circus theatre.[9] However, it must be stated again that this book is predominantly a work of literary criticism, throughout which cultural history is weaved. It is remarkable that forgotten and familiar fictional sources use the circus similarly to talk about events in Ireland. A wealth of under-explored texts deserving of critical attention has been recovered through detection of the recurrent circus motif, from Pádraic Ó Conaire's curious novel in the Irish language, *Deoraíocht*, or *Exile* (1910), to Neil Jordan's little-known film *The Miracle* (1991). Moreover, approaches to over-determined authors, including James Joyce and Seamus Heaney, are refreshed by historicising their work within the context of a marginal cultural practice.

The Circus in Theory

The incidental benefit of looking at representations of the circus in this way is the opportunity to reflect upon the nature of circus. The model of Helen Stoddart's *Rings of Desire: circus history and representation* (2000) is, then, an influential precedent for this book.[10] A dispute central to her argument as to what the circus is in itself, and to her suggestions as to how and why it is co-opted and represented by non-circus artists, is whether or not the popular form should be classified in terms derived from Mikhail Bakhtin's theories of the carnivalesque. Stoddart states from the outset of *Rings of Desire* that, 'far from being a carnivalesque space in which disorder, illegitimacy and inversion reign, [the circus is] rather one in which there is an incorporation but also a hierarchical ordering of both the forces of chaos and inversion and those of order, ascendancy and power in which the latter inevitably maintain the upper hand' (p. 5). Later in the study, she works to clarify her position: 'circus and circus texts may *perform* or represent some of the inversions and mésalliances which Bakhtin identifies as features of carnival processions, but they do so as carnivalesque art rather than as (temporarily) socially subversive carnival' (p. 38). Arguably, this attempt at clarification is unsuccessful. Of course, the circus is not carnival; it is circus. However, Stoddart's acknowledgement of the circus' carnivalesque potential is essential to this book. The episodes and events in circus history cited in brief above and detailed at length subsequently might even serve to counter Stoddart's refusal of the (temporarily) subversive potential of the circus itself.

   Crucially, it is limiting and imprecise to restrict the meaningful potential of circus texts. Stoddart undoes herself when analysing, most instructively, the impact of relocating the circus within other formal or generic frames. Discussing the staging of circus performances within theatre spaces, she writes, 'when resituated and newly contextualised in the theatre before spectators more accustomed to narrative (if not necessarily realist narrative) drama it is argued that they acquire a certain novel and indeed shocking quality' (p. 92). The disturbance, or shock, caused by situating the circus within alternative frames is the essence of its subversive potential. Quite rightly, Stoddart realises from the outset that, over time and through this process, 'a gap emerges between *the* circus and circus' (p. 28). The present book is energised by such shocking acts of relocation. It minds that gap between the circus itself and the idea of circus by coining the adverbial and adjectival concepts of 'circusing' and 'circused' to signify the transposition of an individual, an event or, indeed, an entire nation into the conceptual space of the circus.

The celebrated Irish painter Jack B. Yeats offers these concepts their best illustration in *The Circus has Come* (1952). This late work centres upon a single figure – a woman, apparently – who stands on the headland of an unknown shore and looks down to a circus that has pitched itself at the water's edge. The circus is small and indistinct as it blends into the streaks of blue, yellow, green, white and black that loosely mark out the land from the sea and sky. The woman, too, dissolves into her background: at once, she is integral to her natural surroundings and composed of the same tones as the circus she meditates upon. Art historian Róisín Kennedy appreciates from this canvas Yeats' ability to 'represent the world of possibilities and indicate the boundless limits of the human imagination'.[11] Certainly, the woman appears to be contemplative, suggesting that her thoughts roam beyond what is immediately in front of her and towards the personally metaphoric potential of the circus that she sees. The mood Yeats creates encourages the viewer of the painting to respond to the entire scene – to the landscape, the seascape, the sky, the circus, and the woman herself – in the same way. Her whole environment and she herself have been changed, and changed utterly, since the circus has come.

Yeats' metaphysical painting introduces a discussion of what is surely one of the most intriguing – and, at times, frustrating – aspects of many of the primary texts to which this book attends. The absence of texts by women or from a woman's perspective is remarkable. Instead, I have taken the conscious decision to focus upon texts by male authors that pose the most compelling and, indeed, urgent set of questions within Irish culture and for Irish cultural studies. In these texts, circus women or circused women figure as icons expressive of individual or collective male concerns and anxieties. They are not composed, like Yeats' female figure, in solitary contemplation; most often, they are placed by their creators within a hyperactive circus context to become passive icons for men's thoughts, feelings and experiences. Frequently, these thoughts, feelings and experiences are sexualised, politicised and violent, and the image of the circus woman thereby serves to perpetuate certain types of femininity which are troublingly familiar.

Only on rare occasion do the male artists and writers considered here endeavour to achieve more complex points of identification with the women they create. The effect is to suggest explicitly that the circus is the ideal setting within which to explore gender as synthetic, socially constructed and performative. James Joyce offers one such example. The circus as it is seen in *Ulysses* (1922) is the subject of the first chapter of this book. In 'Calypso', Bloom worries over child and animal welfare as he considers excitedly the supposedly fetishised pulp-fiction body of *Ruby: the Pride of the Ring*; in 'Circe', Bloom himself becomes both a patriarchal civic guardian and Ruby the circus girl. Two works detailing circus life in the west of Ireland in the early twentieth century are similarly preoccupied with women's roles in the circus setting. In Ó Conaire's *Exile*, the circus freak Michael Mullen proposes a sham marriage to another curiosity, the Fat Lady, who personifies at a literal level all that is grotesque in the circus venture; at a metaphoric level, she represents all that is exploitative and infantilising in the colonial venture. Conversely, the English artist Edward Seago shows in *Sons of Sawdust, with Paddy O'Flynn's Circus in Western Ireland* (1934) how women preserve the circus family in various ways: his focus is often on Amy, the 'knock-about, good-hearted slut' who acts as a sustaining maternal substitute, or Derry, a juvenile trick rider who performs in drag to pull in the punters with his nimble turns and pretty head of curls.[12] Degrees of disrespect for women are measurable in the dramatic works considered in the third chapter. Fox Melarkey cares little for the collateral damage his self-destructiveness inflicts upon his wife Crystal in Brian Friel's *Crystal and Fox* (1968); in the mind of Dion Boucicault, as he is resurrected in Stewart Parker's *Heavenly Bodies* (1986), no woman ever quite lives up to the apparently false idol that is his adulterous mother. In the final chapter of this book, Neil Jordan's Renee Baker, protagonist of *The Miracle*, and Seamus Heaney's circus cowgirls in 'Wheels within Wheels' (*Seeing Things*, 1991) are idolised as explicit revisions of Catholic iconography, while the circus women imagined by John Banville in *Birchwood* (1973) and Paul Muldoon in 'Duffy's Circus' (*Mules*, 1977) are significant as consciously created versions of Ireland 'herself'.

There is a difference between how these women appear in texts as themselves, and how they are perceived by the men who created and narrated them, but such a doubling effect is not only seen in relation to circus women. Split personalities and alter egos are also common to many of the protagonists and voices who appear in the primary works considered. These are made sensible within the circus: a fantastic space within which audiences expect quick shifts, character changes, and the doubling of seemingly incompatible roles. Readers must try to keep pace with Bloom's metamorphoses throughout 'Circe'; they must try to find sympathy with Michael Mullen as he is faced with his family and with 'what might have been' from inside the circus sideshow booth. Friel makes the split life of his performers very clear in the stage directions and production notes for *Crystal and Fox*, marking out the metatheatrical performance space from the spaces back- or offstage within which Fox's troupe perform unconsciously. The boundary separating these distinct locations is placed under stress before finally collapsing. Parker matches his melodramatic Boucicault with a cynical rendition of the world-famous nineteenth-century Irish clown Johnny Patterson in order to diminish conventions that place theatre above popular entertainment forms. Notably, the 2004 Rough Magic production of *Heavenly Bodies* at the Abbey's studio theatre, the Peacock, used stage-craft to effect this diminishment mischievously. During the run of Parker's play, Boucicault's *The Shaugraun* (1874) played nightly on the Abbey's main stage. *Heavenly Bodies* director Lynne Parker arranged for an audio transmission from the main auditorium that interrupted her company of live actors at certain significant moments to identify just what she and her uncle Stewart Parker wished to undermine.[13]

Related to the frequent exploration of doubled or split personalities seen in texts central to this book are the interventions of voices 'off', or those coming from elsewhere, much like those at play in Lynne Parker's production of *Heavenly Bodies*. Perhaps the most preoccupying example of such an intervention occurs in Heaney's 'Wheels within Wheels', when W.B. Yeats is made to echo around the circus ring. Interviews with Banville, Muldoon and Jordan reported in the final chapter identify the major influences shaping their circus worlds, including Yeats' poetry. In interview, Banville talked of literary influences – chiefly, Yeats and the magic realists – but he also cited an enduring fascination with circus performances he attended as a child:

> The circus has a strange erotic potential, an erotic energy, and that was what the authorities, Church and State, feared and discouraged: passionate energy of any kind. We were forced into meekness and quietude and a sinister sort of compliance. But energy, such as one encounters in the circus, encourages rebellion, resistance, and a Marx

Brothers sort of anarchy. In the circus it looks as though real violence is being done – think of the clowns, how wild and uncontrolled they seem – how *rebellious*. And then there are those girls, in their corsets and sequins: posing and spinning in the powdery spotlights, what a dream-like eroticism they created. I know the circus didn't have any real similarity to our history of violence, of course. The circus was a life outside life. Yet it felt, for the duration of the performance, as uncontrollable, as makeshift, as potentially and gloriously anarchic as life itself.[14]

Throughout, this book considers the transposition of the actual circus into textual form. It removes Banville's 'life outside life' into a central position as it examines representations of the Irish circus and circused Ireland.

This is not by any means the first study to be curious about the ways in which popular culture has shaped Irish literature and identity. Luke Gibbons' *Transformations in Irish Culture* appeared a year after Declan Kiberd's critical landmark *Inventing Ireland* (1995). A forceful statement in that work's introduction might well serve to counter Stoddart's definition of the circus and circus texts as 'carnivalesque art', as Gibbons writes, 'Culture, for the most part, is limited to "artistic" works, and refined out of existence, while historians and social scientists get on with the business of studying the facts, and determining how society really operates.'[15] Graham is engaged in a comparable project throughout *Deconstructing Ireland: identity, theory, culture* (2001). In his examination of the cultural value of irish ephemera, he argues persuasively that: 'we need to begin to look again at popular culture as a source for the representation of Ireland in and beyond the colonial metropolis.'[16] The theoretical bent of *Deconstructing Ireland* is apparent from this quotation: it disturbs the stability of the signs 'Irish' and 'Ireland' in much the same way as Gibbons upsets the coherence of the sign 'artistic' in *Transformations in Irish Culture*. Both Gibbons and Graham identify performances and representations of Ireland within an expanded field of material and visual culture. This study aims to pitch the circus within that field.

There is a special case to be made for the circus as a peculiarly apt theme, trope or sign in texts produced since the turn of the nineteenth century that are concerned with the transmission or frustration of the concepts 'Ireland' and 'Irish culture'. In *Strange Country: modernity and nationhood in Irish writing since 1790* (1997), Seamus Deane explores parallels between revolutionary France and rebellious Ireland in the eighteenth century that are suggested in the philosophical writings of Edmund Burke. Deane considers the legacy of the thinker:

For over a century after Burke, the same ambiguity prevailed – between the representation of a country that is foreign and unknown, in which the conditions are phantasmagoric especially to the English reader, and a country that is, at the same time, part of the British system, perfectly recognizable and part of the traditional world that the French Revolution had overthrown. Reality will be restored to that phantasmal country only through the introduction into it of that kind of civic stability which is characteristically British.[17]

This image of the eighteenth-century Irish cultural, intellectual and political landscape, as it is described by Deane after Burke, is located somewhere between the weird and the familiar – or the barbaric and the civil. What the circus offers writers and artists subsequently is an opportunity to resist the civilising process explained by Deane, and thereby contest the formation of modern Ireland in the image of an external force. In both a personal and a political sense, the circus transforms the landscape around it in texts as different as Seago's *Sons of Sawdust* and Muldoon's 'Duffy's Circus'. Graham, meanwhile, has conceived of the country as antithetical and fragmentary. 'Ireland is everywhere and nowhere,' he writes, while discussing the work of nineteenth-century Irish American writer Ignatius Donnelly, '"broken in pieces", enveloped in a story in which its particularity and therefore its definition will never be resolved.'[18] A gap emerges between Ireland itself and Ireland as we see it in diverse forms, including popular culture, in much the same way as a gap opens up between '*the* circus and circus' in Stoddart's assessment. The appeal of the circus depends upon the paradox of its unreality and its recognisability. Fragmentation and narrative discontinuity, presented without any sense of existential anxiety or self-consciousness, are what we expect from the circus show. This book aims to demonstrate how the circus adds these dimensions to texts produced in modern Ireland which turn to it as a theme or device.

But the circus brings something else too: nostalgia and anticlimax emanate from that sign. Nostalgia, in Deane's strange country, is fundamental to the modernising project in Irish literature and culture. Irish romanticism, he asserts:

needed the spectacle of ruin to stimulate it to an imaginative intensity that would be the more impressive precisely because it derived from a history that had been lost, displaced, a history that had no narrative but the narrative of nostalgia. Nostalgia was the dynamic that impelled the search for the future.[19]

The Oxford English Dictionary defines nostalgia as 'a sentimental longing *for* or regretful memory of a period of the past, esp. in an individual's own lifetime' (original emphasis). The stress placed by *OED* editors upon the preposition in this definition indicates something of the personality of nostalgia, much like Yeats' use of the past tense in titling his painting *The Circus Has Come*. It is a feeling which belongs to an individual, but its most precise articulation is eternally beguiling and might thereby capture a collective mood of longing or regret. Graham identifies, in approximate terms, that there have been both 'radical fulfilments and disappointments' in the search for a nation-narrative in Ireland.[20] In turn, this accords with the concept of triumphant failure that is developed by circus theorist Paul Bouissac in *Semiotics at the Circus* (2010) – a theoretical text that is influential throughout the present work. Bouissac's concept of anti-performance is synonymous with anticlimax, as he tests 'how far it was possible to push the limits of an anti-performance, and still qualify as a performer, that is, being successful with an audience'.[21] In the end, it is the nostalgic, anticlimactic atmosphere of the circus that I find most compelling. Ultimately, this book evaluates the circus as seen in modern Irish culture in order to consider how and why artists strive to recreate its promise and stage its failures.

The Circus in Irish Literature and Culture

The opening chapter, 'Joyce's Family Circus', reconsiders ideas of the father in Joyce's writing by examining in detail those ideas as they are elucidated through circus anecdote and imagery. The focus rests decisively on *Ulysses*, but references to Joyce's earlier writing and to *Finnegans Wake* (1939) demonstrate the enduring resonance of the circus for the author. Declan Kiberd asserts in *Ulysses and Us* (2009) that '[i]t is time to reconnect *Ulysses* to the everyday lives of real people'.[22] Following the lead of critics including Cheryl Herr and John McCourt, and in concert with emerging voices in Joyce studies such as that of Ronan Crowley, the chapter works broadly to make that reconnection, contextualising hitherto overlooked circus references within the history of nineteenth- and early twentieth-century popular culture.[23] Through this history, it appears that Joyce imitates others in placing male authorities within both actual and invented circus rings to question legitimate influence in domestic and wider social settings. The argument cites evidence from the biography of the nineteenth-century circus clown Johnny Patterson, as well as the content of his most popular songs. Following Barabbas Theatre's stage

biography *Johnny Patterson the Singing Irish Clown* (2009), theatre critic
Patrick Brennan described Patterson as 'arguably Ireland's greatest clown', an
opinion that echoes contemporary publicity material and the performer's self-
promotions which were distributed to potential audiences in Ireland, England
and North America in the 1800s.[24] Subsequently, and by way of records of
circus performances attended by the artist Jack B. Yeats and his creative partner
John Millington Synge, this chapter returns to *Ulysses* and compares the place
of the circus in paired episodes 'Calypso' and 'Circe'. Ultimately, the argument
moves from local settings to the international scene to assess the disquieting
consequences of Joyce imagining political authority within this particular
performance space in the fraught period of world history from 1904 to 1939.

Concepts of the family and diverse representations of family life are common
in – indeed often central to – the texts selected for detailed analysis, including
works of cultural theory. The notion of 'family' in Ireland is constitutionally
sacrosanct, guarded by the state as: 'the natural primary and fundamental unit
group of Society, and as a moral institution'.[25] When Fintan O'Toole looked
back in *The Ex-Isle of Erin* (1996) on dramatic – at times traumatic – changes
in Irish society since the 1950s, he commented that: 'With politics in flux and
the church in crisis, the family seems to many people to be the only institution
that can offer a refuge from uncertainty.'[26] This book is particularly keen to
consider texts that seem to desecrate that Irish institution through co-option
of the circus. A sense of dislocation from family, community and modernity
in early twentieth-century Ireland is crucial to the second chapter, 'Imagined
Communities at the Irish Circus'. Ó Conaire's Irish-language novel *Exile* is the
earliest literary text to be given sustained attention in the book. Written in 1910
while the author was living in London and actively participating in the mission
of the Gaelic League, *Exile* reconsiders in novel form ideas of nation formation
contemporaneously explored in political literature by cultural nationalists.
His protagonist Michael Mullen is, in some ways, typical of Irish narratives as
both fated economic migrant and dislocated returnee. In other ways, Michael
appears to be an innovation: as Ireland entered a decade of seismic political
and social change, Ó Conaire personifies a collective sense of disablement
and disempowerment in the body of a dismembered circus freak. *Exile* is, in
part, a harrowing relay of emigrant experience in London. At the same time, as
protagonist Michael Mullen travels Ireland with an English circus, the author
offers an equally unforgiving portrayal of life in the otherwise lyricised west.

Intriguingly, Ó Conaire's narrative, as it is mediated through Gearailt Mac
Eoin's 1994 translation, echoes Victorian and Edwardian English literature
and journalism. The aim in suggesting possible sources for Ó Conaire, or Mac

Eoin, is to realise the potential of postcolonial criticism as defined by Colin Graham: 'Postcolonial criticism, as it currently exists, has the capacity to undertake exactly this critical project – to produce readings of Irish culture which stress its dependency on "Englishness", on rhetorical formations, on defining its "other", and which will simultaneously comprehend the ironies of cultural interchange in a theoretical framework that is both rigorous and precise.'[27] In order to illustrate this cultural interchange, *Exile* is read alongside Seago's travel journal *Sons of Sawdust* – a lively account of his journey westward with an Irish circus troupe. Both *Exile* and *Sons of Sawdust* are, more or less obviously, travel writing of a kind. Tim Youngs characterises the genre in late nineteenth-century England by stating:

> First, that there were still, in the last quarter of the century, large uncharted parts of the world. Second, that a motivation of travel was to fill in those blanks (though they were not, of course, blanks for those who lived there). Third, that once 'discovered', many of those places would be exploited for their commercial potential. Fourth, that ideologies of race impacted on the representation of those places, as well as on dealings with those who inhabited them [...][28]

This chapter concentrates on the first two characteristic elements identified by Youngs as they are evidenced in the writings of Ó Conaire and Seago. However, Youngs' word 'uncharted' could well be replaced with 'untranslated', since what both authors offer their audiences is an account of hitherto unknown worlds in a language they might better understand. While Ó Conaire shows readers the destitution of turn-of-the-century London in the Irish language, Seago shows readers the west of Ireland in establishment English. Throughout the chapter, these quasi-documentaries of Irish life are set against another kind of travel writing: the contemporary findings of the Harvard Irish Study (1931–6). Under the leadership of Conrad Arensberg and Solon Kimball, waves of archaeologists and social anthropologists travelled from east coast America to west coast Ireland in search of a better sense of community. Their conclusions were ultimately published by Arensberg and Kimball in 1940 under the title *Family and Community in Ireland*, thereby constituting another imagined community.

We move from imagination to invention in the third chapter, 'Irish Circus History and Ireland's Theatrical Heritage'. Shortly after the publication of the *Inventing Ireland*, Gerald Dawe questioned the absence of the Northern Irish playwright Stewart Parker from Kiberd's survey in his essay 'A Hard Act' (1998).

Dawe wrote: 'I cannot think offhand of another playwright who, in the space of roughly a decade between the mid-1970s to the late 1980s, offered more light *specifically* on the various historical Irelands which inhabit the country called Ireland.'²⁹ Dawe analyses the last of Parker's so-called history plays, *Pentecost* (1987), which, together with *Northern Star* (1984) and *Heavenly Bodies* (1986), dramatised national history since 1798 through pastiche, parody and allusion to leading cultural figures. Dawe argues that, in creating such plays, Parker met drama's constant demand in the context of the Northern Irish Troubles: 'that we re-invent it, that we transform it with new ways of showing, to cater adequately to the unique plight in which we find ourselves'.³⁰ Drama is less reinvented in Parker's *Heavenly Bodies* than it is subjected to a not uncommon, yet hitherto unfamiliar process of transformation that creates a hybrid of circus and theatre. This chapter examines the specifics of that hybrid by looking at how the circus has been written into mid-twentieth-century Irish dramatic arts that need not necessarily have been intended for the stage. The intention is to dismantle perceived boundaries between circus and theatre, and to give purpose to the historically co-dependent and continuing relationship between these forms. It is for this reason that Samuel Beckett plays a supporting role in the chapter. The moment at which Vladimir and Estragon appear to break through the fourth wall and confront audiences of *Waiting for Godot* (1952; 1956) with an evaluation of the quality, and formal qualities, of their performance is remarkable; the audience wonders: is *Godot* as bad as circus, or pantomime, or music hall? Estragon completes the exchange by settling on the circus.³¹ Poems, paintings and plays made by brothers W.B. and Jack B. Yeats mark out the fluctuating boundary between theatre, circus and other popular entertainments – a boundary which is subsequently traced in Brian Friel's *Crystal and Fox* and Parker's *Heavenly Bodies*, two theatre plays explicitly reliant on circus energy to heighten dramatic tension. Essentially, Friel and Parker mimic what is certainly the most famous and provocative question in Ireland's theatre history. Like the first stage Irishman, they ask: 'What is my nation?'³²

Graham returns a conflicted answer to that question in the introduction to *Deconstructing Ireland*. He writes that, 'in basic terms, Ireland's dissipation into a plethora of images and its formation of itself as a fantasy island are both aspects of a continually projected utopianism which acts as a bait and as a promise'.³³ Captivating concepts of utopia are central to the final chapter, 'Revisioning the Circus', which charts the development of a trend in contemporary Irish literature and film produced by male authors: Banville's *Birchwood*, Muldoon's 'Duffy's Circus', Jordan's *The Miracle* and Heaney's 'Wheels within Wheels'. This trend transmits the erotic potential of the circus through images that are, to varying degrees, peculiarly infused with political significance and confused with Catholic iconography. As in *Exile*, physical half-ness is taken as political metaphor in *Birchwood*, a novel which could be taking place at any moment in modern Irish history. Writing to Banville regarding the proposed adaptation of the novel for the screen, director Thaddeus O'Sullivan remarked upon the suggestion that the film ought to be fixed within the period of the Irish Civil War:

> No matter how stylised the film is, people will always look for that kind of gap in which they can 'ground' the film. If this were to happen to Birchwood the universality (that is to say, the 'Irish universality') of the theme might be more difficult to achieve: we would have less freedom as a result. I am in fact trying to preserve that very quality of non-naturalism which is of such concern to you.[34]

This chapter attempts to get to grips with exactly what such a time-place might look like by handling images of the circus set within the Irish universal, since the brilliance of O'Sullivan's parenthetical, paradoxical notion illuminates not only Banville's novel, but also Muldoon's poem 'Duffy's Circus', where the circus is represented as a vehicle for the sudden and crazy world of troubled Northern Ireland. By contrast, Jordan suppresses the local, political significance of *The Miracle* in favour of a widely familiar narrative that is nonetheless considered by the filmmaker himself as 'particularly Irish' in its representation of the male/female relationships staged at the seaside circus.[35] The concluding reading of Heaney's 'Wheels within Wheels', meanwhile, suggests a far more personal interpretation of the trend. Dennis O'Driscoll asked Heaney in an interview for the celebrated collection *Stepping Stones* (2008) whether he had been motivated to write about 'some of the most atrocious incidents in Northern Ireland' which occurred around the time of composition of the *Seeing Things* poems; Heaney quoted nationalist ballad 'The Wearing of the Green' in his reply: 'I was still involved with "the most distressful country that ever yet was seen", but as a subject it had just gone flat.'[36] Unwittingly, perhaps, Heaney's reply echoes Muldoon's 'Duffy's Circus', in which Secretary of State for Northern Ireland William Whitelaw is seen as Wild Bill dancing a rain dance that falls 'flat'.[37] But at the outset of *Stepping Stones*, Heaney deliberately invokes the mood of another circus poem, W.B. Yeats' 'The Circus Animals' Desertion' (*Last Poems*, 1939), by direct quotation: 'There's a paradox, of course, since the poems that provide the recompense are the very ones that turn your private possessions into images that are – as Yeats once said – "all on show".[38] In this way, Heaney unifies the poet with the poetic voice. It is to be understood that the authors attended to in this final chapter aim to recreate collective experience out of particular incidents, not only through setting their works within an 'Irish universal', but also through comparable instances of allusion and generative collapse.

The book concludes with two thick descriptions of performances given by circuses working in Ireland today: Ireland's National Circus, Fossett's and Belfast-based contemporary troupe Tumble Circus. Each company confronts national and international socio-political realities on their own terms, as each company consciously or unwittingly constructs their own version of an 'Irish universal'. The performances detailed at the end of this book are an excellent means of connecting its central themes of gender, the family, identity and national politics. Most importantly, they offer an opportunity to root the discussion of these literary texts firmly within the real circus ring.

CHAPTER I

Joyce's Family Circus

L eopold Bloom and Stephen Dedalus sit opposite one another at the kitchen table of 7 Eccles Street in 'Ithaca', the penultimate episode of *Ulysses*. Midway through their conversation, Bloom articulates in thought tensions that frustrate his ambition to act as Stephen's surrogate father. Remembered circus and remembered coin substantiate his abstract concerns with 'the irreparability of the past' and the 'imprevidibility of the future':

> What rendered problematic for Bloom the realisation of these mutually selfexcluding [sic] propositions?
>
> The irreparability of the past: once at a performance of Albert Hengler's circus in the Rotunda, Rutland Square, Dublin, anintuitive [sic] parti coloured clown in quest of paternity had penetrated from the ring to a place in the auditorium where Bloom, solitary, was seated and had publicly declared to an exhilarated audience that he (Bloom) was his (the clown's) papa. The imprevidibility of the future: once in the summer of 1898 he (Bloom) had marked a florin (2/-) with three notches on the milled edge and tendered it in payment of an account due to and received by J. and T. Davy family grocers, 1 Charlemont Mall, Grand Canal, for circulation on the waters of civic finance, for possible, circuitous or direct, return.
>
> Was the clown Bloom's son?
> No.
>
> Had Bloom's coin returned?
> Never.
>
> Why would a recurrent frustration the more depress him?
> Because at the critical turningpoint [sic] of human existence he desired to amend many social conditions, the product of inequality and avarice and international animosity.[1]

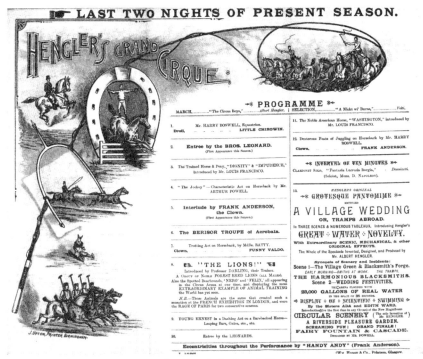

1.1 Artist unknown, Programme for Hengler's Grand Cirque, 1892, Poster, The Mitchell Library Theatre Collection

The step seen here between 'Never.' and the next question is massive. We begin with Bloom's immediate interventions in the life of an individual (Stephen), then move to his aspirational vision of a social action programme which might alter the course of human existence. The negative experience contained within Bloom's memory of the circus is a hindrance as his mind wanders towards good works on a grander scale.

Bloom's recurrent frustration, provoked in 'Ithaca' by a memory of Hengler's Circus, is, of course, his inability to act as a father – a personal preoccupation which is born out of his longstanding grief for the loss of his son Rudy, who died in infancy in 1893. That loss has proved definitive for Bloom; it punctuates his history and memory like the full stop in that desperately expressive phrase, 'Me. And me now.' (p. 168). In the Hengler's anecdote, the clown is a symbolic stand-in for Stephen, who has been associated with various clowns across the day and who represents initially a possible son substitute for both Leopold and his wife Molly Bloom. That possibility is denied conclusively in 'Ithaca', and this is disappointing. But then, by the time of this conversation with Stephen, Bloom has already concluded: 'All tales of circus life are highly demoralising.' (p. 431).

Hengler's Circus, a Glasgow-based troupe that played at the Dublin Rotunda annually between 1860 and 1924, first appears in *Ulysses* during 'Calypso'. There, Bloom fleetingly recalls the embarrassing memory that will be more fully explained in 'Ithaca'. In the earlier episode, a mob gapes and guffaws as performers generate the circus' peculiar kind of entertainment through the control of extreme pain. Further reference to Hengler's is made in 'Eumaeus' by pathetic drunken sailor W.B. Murphy as he re-enacts in the cabman's shelter what he thought he saw the all-Irish sharpshooter Simon Dedalus perform on tour with Hengler's Royal Circus in Stockholm a decade ago. Hengler's offered Joyce a circus motif that is repeated for comparable effect in *Finnegans Wake*. Murphy's elision of father failure with Royal Circus is enacted again in the later work at II.II, when the Earwicker children Shem, Shaun and Issy go over their essay assignments. Among a typically eclectic list of titles is 'Hengler's Circus Entertainment', a topic that surely provokes discussion of the role of the father seen under this curious guise.[2]

Primarily, this chapter reflects upon Joyce's situation of dubious male authority in circus settings through similar historical and literary contextual references. To do so, it recounts the biography of the Irish clown and nineteenth-century circus star Johnny Patterson, who wilfully confronted politics in the ring. Patterson's name is still widely known through the work of artist Jack B. Yeats, who painted the clown numerous times throughout his career. The Patterson–Yeats link enables discussion of the account given by J.M. Synge of the circus he saw in Dingle when touring County Kerry with Yeats in 1905. The climax of that circus in Dingle is a song, performed by another clown, which narrates the cuckolding of a husband and father. One cannot help but draw connections between the sentiments expressed by Synge's fool and the part played by circus acts in *Ulysses*: focus rests here on those represented by Joyce in paired episodes 'Calypso' and 'Circe'. Extended discussion of 'Circe' draws in evidence from the early reception history of *Ulysses* and makes greater reference to *Finnegans Wake* as it moves to consider further disquieting consequences of imagining political authority within this particular performance space in the fraught period of Irish, European and international history between 1904 and 1939.

Johnny Patterson Does His Best

Johnny Patterson, 'the Irish Singing Clown', strove to institute a politically responsive form of Irish circus action throughout his career. In 1859, he bought himself out of five years' service with the 63rd Foot Infantry and into John

Swallow's Circus. Patterson was billed at Swallow's first as the Irish Singing Clown and later as the Rambler from Clare. The latter stage name stuck, and is perhaps misremembered by a paralytic HCE in III.II of *Finnegans Wake*: 'the auspicious waterproof monarch of all Ireland' Roderick O'Connor disdains the 'ramblers from Clane' (pp. 380–1). (Incidentally, it is easy to imagine how an 'r' in Joyce's hand, or in that of his transcriber, might have become an 'n' in print.) At Swallow's, Johnny worked up an act which was delivered in a fluid mix of Irish and English colloquialisms, constantly renewed with the embellishments of local place names and characters. A decade later, he joined the Liverpool-based troupe of rope dancer Pablo Fanque. In England, he sought to develop a complex stage identity that celebrated his national heritage. This was in reaction to attitudes assumed by other Irish clowns on the English stage. Famed performers such as Tom Barry, Barney Brallaghan and O'Donnel replicated standard music hall sketches offering national stereotypes of 'rollicking Irishmen', while the Cork native Pablo Paddington obscured his nationality as the Coloured Rider, cantering around circus rings while balancing a quart bottle on his head.[3] Meanwhile, Patterson aimed, supposedly, for originality in a more thoughtful expression of his Irish origins. In prefacing the collection *Johnny Patterson's Great London Circus Songster: only original Irish clown* (1878), its editors celebrated the clown's intelligence and originality as proof that he possessed 'a proper knowledge of the English language, in addition to being able to discourse upon matters, men, and things apropos to the time and occasion'.[4] His talents were recognised beyond the British Isles. American circus owners were keenly aware of the potential revenue represented in the Irish emigrant population and constantly sought acts that would appeal to that mass market. Cooper and Bailey's Circus first secured Patterson on a one-year contract in 1876, where he proved a valuable asset to show businessmen exploiting homesick audiences. Lyrics in songs such as 'Castles in the Air' struck the sentiments and sentimentality of the newly hyphenated Irish-American:

> This world is all a bubble, no matter where we go,
> There's nothing here but trouble, hardship, toil and woe,
> Go where we will, do what we may, we are never free from care,
> And at best this world is but a castle in the air.
> And yet each being loves the land where he sported as a child,
> The very savage loves his plain, his woods and prairies wild,
> And I, with a true Irish heart, still wish in Ireland there
> To sit among her groves and build my Castles in the Air.[5]

1.2 Artist unknown, Front cover of *Johnny Patterson's Great London Circus Songster*, DeWitt's Song & Joke Book Series Number 241, 1878, New York Public Library of the Performing Arts

Other entries in this popular songbook appear to express Irish experience in plain terms. Possessive pronouns in ballads such as 'Acushla Machree' suggest that the clown's own political opinions motivated their composition:

> Oh Erin, my country, though thousands now leave thee,
> With suffering provocations that no tongue can tell,
> To see the pride of my country depart so does grieve me,
> And their sighs fill the souls as they bid thee farewell.
> Your foes they are smiling, whilst wealth they are piling,
> Our sons for them toiling by land and by sea.
> Oh, land of great plenty, there's your barns and stores empty!
> Oh, Ireland! Wronged Ireland! Acushla machree![6]

Reading this verse and considering the 'Oirish' cover image of Patterson reproduced at Figure 1.2, the tendency of the clown's biographer Harry Bradshaw to romanticise his subject can perhaps be seen as excusable.[7] However, such romanticism denies the force of 'Acushla Machree' and other ballads Patterson made popular in America which transmitted conventional images of wronged Ireland from the circus ring, keeping them fresh in the minds of emigrants through mass entertainment. At the same time, Bradshaw and others exclude instances in which Patterson transacted with his audience by reinforcing Irish stereotypes. 'Danny, Go After Your Father' – a comic treatment of failing fathers in which Danny the Irish son figures as intermediary between husband and wife – is a prime example:

> I'm Mrs O'Mally, Roger's Wife,
> He is very fond of drink;
> From Monday morning till Saturday night
> Of nothing else he'll think …
>
> Danny, go after your father,
> He is down in the corner store,
> Playing forty-fives with the Dutchman –
> Against it he often swore;
> Tell him to come home to his supper,
> I know it will save his life;
> So that's a good lad,
> Go after your dad,
> And tell him to come home to his wife.[8]

Joyce's Stephen Dedalus was familiar with a similar shirking of paternal responsibility. In *Stephen Hero* (*c.*1914), an early draft of Joyce's first novel *A Portrait of the Artist as a Young Man* (1916), Dedalus' father Simon begins to fall apart when the family falls in social standing. Simon is described as a man who 'knew that his own ruin had been his own handiwork but he talked himself into believing that it was the handiwork of others'.[9] In the course of this ruin, the narrator explains that 'this slight thread of union between father and son had been worn away by the usages of daily life and, by reason of its tenuity and of the [failure] gradual rustiness which had begun to consume the upper station, it bore fewer and feebler messages along it' (p. 101). In the 1944 edition of *Stephen Hero*, Joyce's editor Theodore Spencer maintains the original sense of the failed relationship between father and son: in a parenthesis of bitter memory, it haunts the published text in square brackets. The dull attack on his father's character concludes more broadly with: 'Stephen did not consider his parents very seriously' (p. 102). Notably, though Stephen idly watches the steady disintegration of this line of communication, he radically breaks from his mother through the course of the novel. Maternal convictions and the Catholic faith are taken as symbiotic, a binding dismissed with the equation 'It's absurd: it's Barnum.' (p. 121) in a procession of ridicule that goes on to refute the Christian origin myth of the Immaculate Conception. Joyce's invocation of the name of American circus proprietor P.T. Barnum to denote the ridiculous is its first recorded use in this sense in English, according to the *Oxford English Dictionary*, predating by some twenty years Harold Arlen's popular song 'It's Only a Paper Moon' (1933). And it would seem that Barnum remained an expressive insult for Joyce's Stephen and his peers who, in *Ulysses* at 'Circe', incoherently invoke the impresario as the sixth doubly buggered beatitude recited in a scene that comically collapses cultural distinctions: eight young Irishmen assume a teaching each and confuse Yeats with Keats as they goosestep past an orientalised John Eglinton, '*who wears a mandarin's kimono of Nankeen yellow, lizardlettered, and a high pagoda hat*' (p. 479).

Janet M. Davis describes the historical Barnum and Bailey in comparable, if somewhat more formal, terms: their 'ethnological congress of strange and savage tribes' were a 'colorful panoply of foreign animals and human performers [that] seemingly compressed time and space when the entire world appeared on Main Street'.[10] Johnny Patterson brought flashes of green to Main Street, USA, but it was in America that he also first complemented his Irish and Irish-American material with pieces that were more concerned with universal ideological notions of the Brotherhood of Man. The ballad 'Many Can Help One' is exemplary:

> A man may be wealthy one end of the year,
> The next may be wretched and poor;
> He's struggled his hardest to keep himself up,
> But has sunk down to poverty's door;
> Such men are those that deserve your support,
> So give it to them who most need
> For those who've experienced poverty know
> 'Tis a very hard battle indeed.[11]

The song – popularised whilst Patterson was performing with the Great London Circus throughout America in the late 1870s – is a treatise on social action emphasising the worth of labour undertaken to fight poverty. As such, its sentiment is relatable to Bloom's humanitarian desires as they are expressed in the catechism of 'Ithaca'. However, Bradshaw suggests that when Patterson returned to Ireland in 1885, national political upheaval affected a performer who became grave rather than remaining romantically wistful. The clown continued to perform songs expounding a universal socialist vision, but this expression of economic, social and political concerns was without commercial appeal. Circus owners such as James Lloyd and circus audiences felt that the materialisation of anxieties for Ireland's future in song form had no place in the ring. Lloyd, who contracted Patterson for his Belfast-based circus, describes in his autobiography a fractious incident instigated by a hostile and inebriated Patterson:

> he began to run me down and told the audience that I was Protestant and ought not to be in Ireland. Those of the clown's faith got up from their seats and were halfway into the ring when I asked Patterson what was the cause of all this. [...] I stood firm and told the audience that they had not paid their money for this unseemly conduct.[12]

Undeterred by critical responses, Patterson and his sons forged a succession of unhappy business partnerships that ensured that the clown could compose and perform political material. He first performed the ballad 'Do Your Best for One Another' at a stand in Tralee on 28 May 1889. The clown was dressed in his standard costume: green tweeds embroidered in gold with the national symbol of the shamrock. But for this performance, Patterson apparently accessorised with two flags: one flag was green, embroidered with a harp; the other red, embroidered with a crown. The flags were waved in a semaphore of ideological unity – two fractious symbols brought together to demonstrate the possibility of peaceful coexistence without the need for explicit political statements from the clown. News reports published in the evening edition of the *Clare Journal* on Thursday 30 May 1889 told of heckling from the stalls that was soon quelled. But when Patterson died just three days after his performance, versions of that night became more extreme. Certain eyewitness claims state that a violent riot broke out, in the course of which Patterson was struck on the head by a circus tent pole. An influential subscription to this sequence of events came from Patterson's son, Johnny Junior, who was thirteen at the time. He would argue that this politically motivated injury precipitated his father's death on 31 May 1889.[13]

Perhaps it was the sight of Patterson dressed to personify religious and political union that led the audience to behave as they did during 'Do Your Best for One Another' that night in Tralee – especially those members of staunch republican movement the New Irelanders, who were present. Others cite incendiary lyrics as the cause of Patterson's death. Although Bradshaw states in his biographical article 'Johnny Patterson, the Rambler from Clare' (1986) that nothing survives of the ballad but a few disjointed and unquoted lines, he believes that this performance was motivated by Patterson's ardent support for the fated Irish Parliamentary Party leader Charles Stewart Parnell.[14] In 1976, Bradshaw presented an RTÉ radio programme on Patterson that was similar in content to the article published a decade later. The radio programme was a major source for Stewart Parker while he was writing the character of Patterson into his play *Heavenly Bodies*, which focuses on the playwright and performer Dion Boucicault. Parker shows us Boucicault on the night of his death and enquires into the facts of his life through the mouthpiece of a Mephistophelean Patterson. In Marilynn Richtarik's deft condensation of Parker's aims in the play, parallels appear between 'Boucicault's ambiguous parentage and his ambivalent relationship with Ireland', as Parker draws an analogy 'between Boucicault's lost father and his lost Fatherland'.[15] Legitimacy is, then, the play's central concern; its questions over paternity, political integrity, originality and authorship are raised most often by Patterson.

Parker includes lyrics for 'Do Your Best for One Another' in *Heavenly Bodies*:

> As I was climbin' one fine spring mornin'
> On high Slieve Gullion and the air so sweet,
> I spied above me a poor old woman
> With most of Ireland spread at her feet –
> Upon that vision she was a-gazin'
> Whilst from her eyes there sprang a tear,
> Yet could I hear from that wither'd bosom
> A young girl's voice proud and clear –
> Do your best for one another,
> Not for Erin or the Queen;
> Make your peace with one another,
> Sure we all love our isle of green.
> Though my family be divided,
> Still this land we all must share,
> Do your best for one another –
> 'Tis your mother's dying prayer![16]

This version of the ballad would perhaps accord with Bradshaw's postulation that the song was explosive because of its political sentiment. However, its authenticity is dubious. There is no indication in the published text of *Heavenly Bodies* as to who wrote these lyrics; only Jim Parker receives a credit for his musical compositions. This differs from credits listed in Parker's other published plays such as *Spokesong* (1975), where Parker is named as author of the play's original lyrics, while Harry Dacre and Madlyne Bridges are credited with words and music for music hall favourites 'Daisy Bell' and 'The Spinning Song' respectively.[17] In *Stewart Parker: a life* (2012), Richtarik records that in reconstructing Patterson, the playwright relied on 'patchy information' and 'on his own imagination, using bits of the clown's story that suited his purposes and making no attempt to find out more about the historical Patterson'.[18] Elsewhere, Richtarik has suggested that these lyrics for 'Do Your Best for One Another' were penned by Parker himself as another means of representing his own ideas about and critique of Boucicault.[19] As the image of a divided family and the call for devotional acts to an iconic mother precede taunts from Patterson which strike at Boucicault's cuckolded father and cosseting mother, the song might then operate as a mirror to melodramatise major themes in the play.

The real Johnny Patterson's originality appears to be somewhat limited. Evidence from *The Great London Circus Songster* shows that many of his songs were borrowed from other performers and composers: at page forty-nine, we read that 'Danny, Go After Your Father' was also performed by an untraceable singer, James Bradley; at page twenty-nine, we read that 'The Old Log Cabin in the Dell' was written by C.A. White; and it seems from pages twenty-six and thirty-one that the Original Irish Clown borrowed considerably from the repertoire of vaudeville entertainer Gus Williams. Therefore, another historical song can legitimately be considered as a possible contender for that which Patterson performed at Tralee in May 1889. 'Pulling Hard against the Stream' was popularised by its prolific composer 'Handsome Harry' Clifton in Britain and Ireland in the 1860s. Clifton is credited with having written or revised over 500 songs in his career. Like Patterson, he showed skill at setting topical verses to familiar tunes responding to current affairs. Others also wrote songs for Clifton to perform, including the Galway poet D.K. Gavan, who penned him 'The Rocky Road to Dublin' (date nk). In *Ulysses*, Joyce would have Stephen recall Gavan's lyrics in 'Nestor', as schoolmaster Garrett Deasy attempts to draw a straight lineage back from himself to Ireland's kings with his family motto '*Per vias rectas*' (p. 31) – a phrase which is transposed into the fantasy world of 'Circe' in the pronouncements of Deasy, seen there in

Stephen's wild imagination as a postage-stamp-plastered, hockey-stick-wielding jockey flanked by mounted dwarves (p. 533).

Clifton was considered by music hall historian S. Theodore Felstead to be a 'pioneer' of a particular class of entertainment that appealed to a mass Victorian audience, with 'homelier types of songs, those embodying a moral sentiment'.[20] The *Sun* newspaper favourably reviewed Clifton on 8 July 1867 for the 'healthy spirit' which prevailed in exemplary songs such as 'Bear It Like a Man', 'The Family Man' and 'Never Look Behind'. The *Sun* also highlighted 'Pulling Hard against the Stream' as an excellent work; its lyrics were published the same year under the subtitle 'Do Your Best for One Another':

> In the world I've gain'd my knowledge
> And for it have had to pay,
> Though I never went to college
> Yet I've heard that Poets say,
> Life is but a mighty river,
> Rolling on from day to day,
> Men are vessels launch'd upon it,
> Sometimes wrecked and cast away.
>
> So then, do your best for one another,
> Making life a pleasant dream.
> Help a worn and weary brother,
> Pulling hard against the stream.
>
> Many a bright goodhearted fellow,
> Many a noble-minded man,
> Find himself in water shallow,
> Then assist him if you can;
> Some succeed at every turning,
> Fortune favours ev'ry scheme,
> Others too tho' more deserving,
> Heave to pull against the stream.
>
> If the wind is in your favour,
> And you've weather'd every squall,
> Think of those who luckless labour,
> Never get fair winds at all;

Working hardcontented willing,
Struggling thro' life's ocean wide,
Not a friend and not a shilling,
Pulling hard against the tide.

Don't give way to foolish sorrow,
Let this keep you in good cheer,
Brighter days may come tomorrow,
If you try and persevere;
Darkest night will have a morning,
Tho' the sky is overcast,
Longest lanes must have a turning,
And the tide will turn at last.[21]

Perhaps unsurprisingly, Clifton's 'Do Your Best for One Another' is empty of explicit reference to Irish affairs. Instead, an audience is invited into a utopian vision which is timeless and dislocated. The present of 'this world' is deliberately opposed to the future life of pleasant dreams, into which all may enter irrespective of class. The economic barriers structuring social order 'today' are removed by cross-community support. In Clifton's ballad, the present can be resisted and the future looked forward to if only we co-operate. Crucially, the unpredictability of future experience is emphasised, as is the role that luck plays in the art of living. This conviction is similar to that of Bloom, who sees in 'Ithaca' that dismantling social constructions cemented with inequality, avarice and international animosity is essential to securing society's return to a more human condition. 'Do Your Best for One Another' is a version of the imprevidible future, known also to Bloom through financial experience and the interrupted circulation of the florin, which is at once both problematic and full of potential as an unknown state. At that moment in 'Ithaca', Bloom transforms the supposed certainty of the capitalist economy and its objectification as hard currency into a game of chance in which loss and failure are understood as possible outcomes. In this sense, the play becomes circus-like: the labour of others producing popular entertainment relieves its audience from the everyday world of experience as narratives unfold within a dreamlike performance space where human and animal potential is pushed beyond imagined limits.

According to Paul Bouissac's 'science of the individual', the performer who creates that atmosphere of promise is also prepared to stage what he terms 'anti-performance' in manufacturing negative experience. He describes 'circus acts that represent failures or evoke the possibility of accidental death as an essential dimension of their meaning'.²² Performers who stage negative experience, then, trade in shock and depend on let-downs to intensify experience within the circus dream. The failure – a slip, trip or fall – serves to interrupt the easy progress of an audience's delight during feats of the apparently impossible. The concept of staged failure is of lasting consequence here. As biographers relay Johnny Junior's description of his father's death, Johnny Patterson's pathetic image is elevated posthumously to the status of tragic heroism. The clown becomes a man who died not of pneumonia (as the registrar recorded), but instead for his ideal of national and intra-national unity. Parker's confident ascription of *his* 'Do Your Best for One Another' to the clown who he invests with the authority to question claims to both paternal and literary-artistic legitimacy is further evidence of this. The construction of negative experience after performance is salvaged from and then retrofitted onto an irreparable past. Meanwhile, the possibility that Patterson was simply performing an unoriginal popular song written by an English music hall star, which accorded to his own pacific and universal outlook, is overlooked in favour of a nationed mythology that is easier to celebrate in its opposition of heroic leader and betraying mob. The idealistic clown is martyred through the collective action of illegitimate authority. In this way, Patterson's story might offer a tragic parallel to the lop-sided altercation between Bloom and the Citizen in 'Cyclops', where the appearance of reason – and a mischievous parting shot – incites an irrational attempt at comic violence. The Citizen hurls a biscuit tin after Bloom, who, in the eyes of the narrator, has become just some other 'bloody clown or other kicking up a bloody murder about bloody nothing' (p. 327).

Clowns and Cuckolds: Jack B. Yeats and J.M. Synge at the Circus

The romantic heroism identifiable in Johnny Patterson's public remembrance is perhaps most significantly informed by Jack B. Yeats' paintings of him. As a child growing up in Sligo in the 1880s, Yeats had seen him perform and the clown's influence was lasting. Yeats was among the first to institute Patterson as a folk hero in paintings such as *The Singing Clown* (1928). According to Donal Maguire, the clown came to personify 'man's tragic situation, both comical and courageous but yet pathetic and vulnerable'.²³ Significantly, Patterson is transformed in *The Singing Clown* (Fig. 1.3) from the 'Only Original Irish Clown', dressed in pompous national costume, to the universally recognisable figure of Pierrot, the white-faced clown. He thereby becomes symbolic not only of the artistic spirit, but of tragicomic loss that is without national limitations.

1.3 Jack B. Yeats, *The Singing Clown*, 1928, Oil on canvas, Sligo Municipal Collection & Model Arts and Niland Gallery

In 1905, Yeats was present alongside J.M. Synge to record a better-natured circus disturbance than that which preceded the death of Johnny Patterson in 1889. The writer and illustrator toured west Kerry together that year, and their collaborative journal of the trip was published in three successive editions of *The Shanachie* from summer to winter 1906.[24] Yeats and Synge attended a circus in Dingle, advertised as performing for one night only. There, Synge encountered a community that could well have provided models not only for his own writing, but also, perhaps, for that of Joyce. The playwright describes Dingle's population in a manner reminiscent of the simple country people cosmopolitan Stephen so disdains in the last few pages of *Stephen Hero*: the family above whose hearth hangs a chalk sketch of the circus actors who once came to town (p. 212). Synge was less derisive as he recorded motley rural types alighting the evening train while he waited to enter the tent: the 'wild looking fishermen and fisherwomen, gaily-dressed young women and half-drunken jobbers and merchants' (p. 79). Upon entering the circus, Synge noted that it was circus women that kept the order. There was a danger of the place being rushed as a 'strangely black and swarthy' crowd pushed into the rows of wooden seats, until:

in a moment three or four of the women performers, with long streaming ulsters buttoned over their tights, ran out from behind the scenes and threw themselves into the crowd, forcing back the wild hillside people, fishwomen and drunken sailors, in an extraordinary tumult of swearing, wrestling and laughter. These women seemed to enjoy their work, and shrieked in amusement when two or three of them fell on some enormous farmer or publican and nearly dragged him to the ground.

(p. 80–2)

This record of events is comparable to the brothel scene of 'Circe', where gaudy doll-faced women give the drunken, impotent local men a fantastically rough ride. The sight of these sturdy women play-fighting it out with their local patrons perhaps impressed Synge more than the 'usual' dirty white horse, 'gaudy' horsewoman, clown, gymnasts and horse people who put in repeat performances sporting different clothes and make-up to bolster the circus programme (p. 82). But Synge was somewhat more taken with the final act and his description is also worthy of comparison with Joyce's use of circus in *Ulysses*. A prolonged bout of fooling between the chief horseman and a clown – in which the 'medieval' jokes reminded Synge of little circuses on the outer boulevards of Paris – was followed by the horseman's song (p. 82). The song presents its own comedic inquest into paternity:

> Here's to the man who kisses his wife,
> And kisses his wife alone;
> For there's many a man kissed another man's wife
> When he thought he kissed his own.
>
> Here's to the man who rocks his child,
> And rocks his child alone;
> For there's many a man rocked another man's child
> When they thought he rocked his own.

(p. 83)

The scenario given in Synge's transcript of this particular song is converse to that which is humorously narrated in Patterson's 'Danny, Go After Your Father', thereby offering a precedent for Joyce. 'Here's to the man' gives a backhanded pat on the back to the family man who is, as we shall see, like Bloom, in that he is humiliated in the circus ring by forceful encounters with acts of adultery that upset order at home.

Reade's Ruby and Joyce's Rudy: Sources for the 'Calypso' Circus

In his disquieting essay 'Subjugation' (1898), Joyce cites the circus as a location where man betrays his 'desire to overcome and get mastery of things':

> Thus, in the swampy marshes of South America, the venomous snakes are lulled into deadness, and lie useless and harmless, at the crooning of the charmer and in shows and circuses before large crowds, broken-spirited lions and in the streets the ungraceful bears are witnesses to the power of man.[25]

Here, the circus is taken as a space in which the impotence and vulnerability of even the most fearful-seeming beasts are laid bare for the entertainment of the crowd. Violence and the control of violence are essential to the activities of the 'real' circus. When publicly exercised, they generate exemplary spectacles of control, thereby physicalising the rules that order the performance space. Without extreme demonstrations of physical control, it can be supposed that the spectacle will flop and fail. Potential humiliation immediately and indiscriminately attends the circus population – acts and audiences alike.

The embarrassing potential of the circus is first encountered in *Ulysses* in 'Calypso' during an exchange between Bloom and Molly. This is Molly's first appearance in the novel. The couple's conversation sets up themes and images which will recur throughout the text, most brutally in 'Circe':

> – Metempsychosis, he said, frowning. It's Greek: from the Greek. That means the transmigration of souls.
> – O, rocks! she said. Tell us in plain words.
> He smiled, glancing askance at her mocking eye. The same young eyes. The first night after charades. Dolphin's Barn. He turned over the smudged pages. *Ruby: the Pride of the Ring.* Hello. Illustration. Fierce Italian with carriagewhip [*sic*]. Must be Ruby pride on the floor naked. Sheet kindly lent. *The master Maffei desisted and flung his victim from him with an oath.* Cruelty behind it all. Doped animals. Trapeze at Hengler's. Had to look the other way. Mob gaping. Break your neck and we'll break our sides. Families of them. Bone them young so they metampsychosis [*sic*]. That we live after death. Our souls. That a man's soul after he dies. Dignam's soul …
> – Did you finish it? he asked.
> – Yes, she said. There's nothing smutty in it. Is she in love with the first fellow all the time?
> – Never read it. Do you want another?

(p. 62)

Home life is circused at 7 Eccles Street. At a basic and general level, metempsychosis is a concept associated with popular performance at this time; witness Figure 1.4, which suggests that it might be induced by the soon-to-be editor of *Punch* magazine, F.C. Burnand, and his Curried Prawns:

1.4 Artist unknown, *Metempsychosis*, *c*.1880, Poster, Evanion Collection, British Library

Meanwhile, at the synchronic mention of metempsychosis and the circus in *Ulysses*, the same synapse occurs in Bloom's head during this conversation with Molly in 'Calypso' as it does in the middle of the night during his conversation with Stephen in 'Ithaca'. The circus trope becomes a thought-space within which personal anxieties and popular concerns are played out. To order a physically strong family by extreme training ensures a lineage, which seems to mean for Bloom a kind of life after death. Bloom is acutely self-aware of his inability to impose order through such an exercise of dominance since the death of his son Rudy. Then the unfaithful wife asks her cuckolded husband hours before her latest infidelity with her manager Blazes Boylan: 'Is she in love with the first fellow all the time?' Bloom's reply, the taut 'Never read it', cuts off further discussion of this particular tripartite relationship, which is conceived of in 'Nausicaa' not as triangular, but as circus-ring circular. In the later episode, Bloom's thought process forces him to meet Molly and Boylan in the ring: 'Curious she an only child, I an only child. So it returns. Think you're escaping and run into yourself. Longest way round is the shortest way home. And just when he and she. Circus horse walking in a ring' (p. 360).

There is associated value in examining the explicit and implicit cultural references Joyce inserts into the exchange between the Blooms in 'Calypso'. Bloom sympathises, if not empathises, with the circus characters he imagines out of the fictional body of *Ruby* languishing on the bedroom floor. The memory of the Henglers' trapeze perhaps offers a premonition of a major transformation Bloom will undergo in 'Circe', as he becomes the anatomically fascinating 'womanly man' (p. 465). This transformation perhaps has its own historical precedent. An 'unfortunate accident' befell Hengler's chief attraction, 'The Beautiful Girl Aerialist and Circassian Catapultist' Lulu, during a performance at the Grand Cirque in Dublin during the 1878 season. Lulu was born Samuel Wasgate in Maine, USA, in 1855. He began performing at the age of ten to great acclaim in circuses in London and Paris under the stage name and male persona of El Niño Farini. It was in 1870 that Wasgate's gender switched and El Niño became Lulu. Lulu's true identity was exposed by Dublin doctors after a catapult malfunction badly injured the aerialist's legs, preventing the rehearsed landing on a plank suspended between two trapezes in the rafters of the Grand Cirque. The V&A biography of Wasgate mentions that 'there was much embarrassment amongst male admirers when it was revealed in 1878 that Lulu was in fact a man'.[26] Other historians suggest that the accidental re-gendering of Lulu was sensational – and lucrative. John Turner recounts newspaper articles from the following year when Lulu returned to Dublin with Hengler's. Reporters described how: 'The vast circus is nightly crowded from floor to ceiling with enthusiastic spectators eager to witness the extraordinary entertainment of LuLu.'²⁷ It might then be supposed legitimately that this astonishing revelation capitalised upon the idea of the staged failure, which Bouissac would later theorise as a beguiling element of dramatic tension common in circus performance.

The title of Molly's book refers more directly to turn-of-the-century culture. Mary Power was the first to identify Amye Reade's *Ruby: a novel founded on the life of a circus girl* (1889) as the likely ghost text for Joyce's *Ruby: the Pride of the Ring*.²⁸ Reade was an active child- and animal-welfare campaigner, and her novel won her cause sympathy and support from an influential circle of politicians and educators. In consequence, the book was reprinted the following year with a new title, *Ruby; or, how girls are trained for a circus life. Founded on fact* (1890). This edition is dedicated to (among others) the reformers Joshua and John Rowntree, and the High Sherriff of Wicklow Colonel D'Oyley Battley.²⁹ The front and back boards of this reissue are crowded with advertisements, as might be expected from this genre: Beecham's Pills are 'worth a guinea a box' since they nourish 'The Rosebud of Health'; Blenkiron's British Argory Braces are 'strongly recommended by the medical profession'; Holloway's Pills and Ointments capitalise on the fact that 'THEY are INVALUABLE for FEMALE COMPLAINTS'. These notices, and the many other examples printed in Reade's book, further illustrate the print cultural world in which Joyce was composing *Ulysses*.

In the text proper, heavy-handed pathetic fallacy tells Reade's late-Victorian story of betrayal, profligacy and child neglect through the language of flowers – this vocabulary sets protagonist Cynthia Dawson up for a fall from the first page. There, the narrator muses: 'Perhaps flowers breathe out longings, and cries of anguish for the homes of their birth before they droop and die. Perhaps man can never fathom the mysteries of the pure world which belongs exclusively to the flowers; so they know not' (p. 1). The ensuing tale of Cynthia's elopement from Kent with Oxford graduate and parish vicar's pupil John Hayward, her refusal to become his lawful wife, and her obstinate insistence upon a stage career after John's unwise investments push the family to the brink of financial ruin are all intended by Reade to prove her anti-heroine's villainy through resolute selfishness, coquettish ignorance and an unnatural lack of maternal instinct. Readers are given to understand that, from the first, Cynthia has been uninterested in the child Ruby, born out of wedlock. She finally abandons both Hayward and her daughter to pursue a lucrative marriage with the foppish Earl of Stanhope. The child is passed from the hands of cronish stage manager Dot

Dane and sold into the charge of circus trainer Signor Enrico. Ruby is put to work in the ring as a bareback rider, and becomes a circus sensation, but is forced to perform to the point of fatal exhaustion: she collapses during a performance that her father is (conveniently) just in time to attend, returned as he is from exile in Australia, without knowing that his daughter is the fading star. The novel draws to a close after a deathbed scene between Ruby and John, and an account of Cynthia's thwarted attempts to marry the Earl of Stanhope, resultant mental breakdown, and consequent committal to an asylum. It is not until after the death of their child that John reconciles himself to Cynthia, but their last meeting is complicated by her complete descent into madness. Her final thoughts are expressed in the floral language that the novel's narrator has used throughout to illustrate moral anxiety. But the deployment of this scheme of imagery at this moment associates Cynthia with other tragic literary figures: she becomes an echo of Ophelia in her ramblings about the great hills which tower up in her mind as 'one mass of flowers – white flowers!' (p. 398); through this allusion, Dot Dane's earlier suggestion that Cynthia should 'Get up an argument as to whether Hamlet was mad or not' (p. 220) as a means of demonstrating her social standing to the Stanhope matriarch, the Countess of Dunhoe, becomes tragically – if rather laboriously – ironic. Cynthia's dramatic death at the end of this scene frees John Hayward to marry champion rider Victoria Melton, Ruby's closest friend and ally at Signor Enrico's circus. When their child is born, history repeats itself: Victoria and John name their daughter Ruby.

It is easy to see the shadows of Reade's novel in *Ulysses*. At the moment of Cynthia's impetuous departure from the idyllic Kentish farmhouse, the narrator laments: 'Homes are few – but earthly hells are always gaping with open mouths to catch the sunbeams, which we call the young' (p. 33). This cluster of words is perhaps mimicked by Joyce to produce Bloom's memory of Hengler's: 'Mob gaping. Break your neck and we'll break our sides. Families of them. Bone them young so they metempsychosis. That we live after death' (p. 62). More broadly, Margot Norris comments: 'Joyce must have seen the metafictional possibilities of using a titillating come-on to lure readers (like Molly Bloom) into delving into a work with a serious intention.'[30] The morality of the parodied tale of circus life might demoralise Molly in her search through pop cultural texts for stimulation and sexual sensation, but Ruby's nakedness reveals social codes which manage (female) sexuality. Elsewhere, Jennifer Burns Levin examines at length the inversions of the foundation text's moralising tendency that occur in Bloom's imagination, emphasising the potential erotic charge contained within the circus girl.[31] However, Levin's analysis does not sufficiently complicate the ambivalent position assumed by Bloom within the circus metaphors that barely cover Molly's intended liaison with Boylan in 'Calypso'. His knowledge of their liaison and suppositions regarding Molly's past indiscretions at times gesture towards a wife's deliberate cruelty and her husband's subsequent humiliation. Joyce thereby repeats the dynamics of the Hayward/Cynthia relationship, while at the same time reversing the roles of dominator and victim reinforced by the circus episodes involving the child Ruby. In this way, Reade's social commentary is also injected into *Ulysses* with complicated and intriguing ambivalence.

Power's discovery of *Ruby* leads her to trace parallels and divergences between Cynthia Dawson and Molly Bloom that are then retraced by Norris and Levin. Originally, Power concludes that: '[n]either woman aspires to be the ideal wife or mother. Both are *artistes*. However, Cynthia is a desperate case [...] much less serious an *artiste* than Molly is.'[32] Following Power's lead, Levin tends to focus attention upon comparisons drawn between representations of female sexuality in the two texts. This is a legitimate practice and obviously valuable, but the extent to which Reade's work perhaps pervaded Joyce's writing might be considered even more expansively in reading the passage quoted from 'Calypso'. Bloom's interests lie not just in the circus girl, but in various human and animal constituents of the circus community. He repeats the sentiment of the young Joyce's essay 'Subjugation' when, significantly, he hears the laughter of the gaping mob at Hengler's. In this way, definite echoes of Reade's prose can be heard in 'Calypso', which exceed the gendered or sexual dimensions arresting the development of critical arguments made hitherto, to forge connections between *Ruby* and *Ulysses*.

Moreover, the tonal ambivalence of Bloom's reflections on circus family life in 'Calypso' also requires reassessment. Shortly after Power announced her discovery of *Ruby* to readers of the *James Joyce Quarterly*, Caroline Nobile Gryta placed her response in the same publication. Gryta was anxious to supplement Power's findings, acknowledging the potential wider significance of *Ruby* within *Ulysses* (not least in the audible similarity between 'Ruby' and 'Rudy') and demonstrating that Joyce's circus story was, in fact, a composite of popular fictions.[33] Gryta's argument ultimately suggests that Henry T. Johnson's *The Pride of the Ring: a world famous circus story of fun, frolic, and adventure* (1902) was the leading source, as Joyce compounded this morality novel of circus life with Reade's *Ruby*. She cites Johnson's conclusion – the 'fairy-tale ending' in which Athol the circus boy is reunited with the father he believed was dead – as crucial evidence for this.[34] But in fact, even more extensive correspondences between Joyce and Reade are revealed when the long-lost parent–child relationships central to their narratives are considered more carefully and at greater length.

In the course of his exchange with Molly, Bloom thinks fleetingly about the ethics of circus practice: 'Bone them young so they metempsychosis' (p. 62). The train of thought then leads on to phrases that consider death and conflate ideas of how the self or the soul might continue: through spiritual reincarnation or, less explicitly, the family line. Bloom casts recently deceased friend Paddy Dignam as a model upon which these ideas might be developed. En route to Dignam's funeral at Glasnevin Cemetery, Bloom thinks of his lost son Rudy, the child who died aged eleven days, as he regards Stephen's failing father Simon Dedalus in the funeral car:

> Noisy selfwilled [*sic*] man. Full of his son. He is right. Something to hand on. If little Rudy had lived. See him grow up. Hear his voice in the house. Walking beside Molly in an Eton suit. My son. Me in his eyes. Strange feeling it would be. From me. Just a chance.
>
> (p. 86)

Fathers become interchangeable with their sons at this moment. Like the circus families who bone their children young and thereby ensure that the name lives on in skilled performance, there is physical proof that these men have lived in the appearance of their heirs. There is a similar pause for reflection in Reade's *Ruby*. John Hayward anxiously contemplates his inability to act as a socially acceptable husband and father, and the impact of his elopement upon his relationship with his own father after Cynthia rejects his proposal of a proper church wedding: 'Don't turn religious Jack,' she derides, sounding more than a little like plain-speaking Molly Bloom. 'I hate people who put everything down to higher powers, and all that kind of cant …' (p. 121). Full of grief for the loss of paternal love and the family line, John Hayward turns to a photograph of his father for solace:

> with trembling hands he grasped his father's photograph. Yes! He could see by the dim candle light the face once so dear, the form so beloved, it seemed to him as if the great, grave eyes were speaking to him from the picture … As he gazed at the photograph, he knew the fiat which had gone forth would be absolute; that there would be no retracting from what his father decided as the right course to follow. The son had sinned – the father remained implacable, resolute, stern.
>
> (p. 125)

The father is literally in the eyes of the son as John Hayward looks at this photographic image. But there is a moment of realisation at the tragic climax of *Ruby* that is perhaps still more significant in this comparison of the ways in which Reade and Joyce express parent–child relationships. The final collapse of Reade's circus girl occurs in a chapter entitled 'Shame! Shame!', anticipating exclamations which are first heard from a 'manly voice in the stalls' and then taken up by the whole crowd as Ruby's exhaustion becomes apparent (p. 359). That manly voice belongs to her unwitting father John Hayward, who goes to enquire after the child at the close of her act. Only then does he realise that she is his child. Hayward seeks confirmation from circus clown Tom, who proves himself to be at least as intuitive as Joyce's parti-coloured clown in 'Ithaca'. Having discounted Hayward's relation to Ruby as brother or uncle, he understands from the gravity of his reaction to the girl's condition that this stranger is something more fundamental. In curiously familiar terms, he says: 'I half guessed you were her father … As I looked at you the eyes seem alike, and now and then you speak like her' (p. 367). Bloom might be as envious of John Hayward as he is of Simon Dedalus, since Hayward is so obviously in his daughter's eyes.

In 'Hades', the subjective position is that of the father: we see from his perspective. But it is an imagination of his Eton-suited son and not Rudy's concrete image that Bloom chooses to meditate upon. In that episode, he does not confront proof that the child has once lived: Rudy is buried alongside Bloom's mother Ellen in the family plot at Glasnevin, but Bloom does not visit the grave. Instead, the prospect of the lost boy punctures the present everyday and echoes through the home. Reade's narrator closes *Ruby* with a comparable explanation: Hayward and his new wife Vic Melton 'left two green graves behind […] their thoughts often wandered to the little churchyard where the mother and daughter lay sleeping' (p. 416). In *Ulysses*, the melancholy echo is the stumbling block for Bloom, who cannot fully express his masculinity to Molly in sexual terms. He has assumed debilitating responsibility for the misfortune that he believes resulted in Rudy's death. It is therefore sensible that Bloom is pleased to suffer the punishment later inflicted on himself as Ruby in 'Circe'. The episode's sadomasochism is a version of this unspoken statement of guilt burlesqued in fantasy fiction. Nowhere in *Ulysses* is violence more graphic; at no time are failure and humiliation more acutely felt. And nowhere in *Ulysses* is the circus trope more elaborately constructed.

Irreparable Pasts and Imprevidible Futures: The Fragility of 'Circe'

'Circe', in all its zoological intricacy, was Joyce's proudest boast. It is a deliberate aberration within *Ulysses*: an extreme literary anomaly that releases certain social tensions through the imitation of popular performance. Ronan Crowley has argued persuasively that the structure, or 'scaffold', of the episode is borrowed from various live performance venues and dramatic literary texts, including the music hall.[35] The proven exchange between that performance space and the circus has been made evident in this chapter through details of Johnny Patterson's performance of songs by music hall stars such as White, Williams and, possibly, Clifton. These details might then give historical licence to a reading which also identifies circus acts and circus behaviour in an episode entitled 'Circe'. There, the suggested adoption of the circus model, in which abhorrence and abjection often generate the spectacle, is terrifically effective.

Contained within dramatic form, the experience of reading 'Circe' is to be acknowledged as physically strenuous as eyes follow the rapid returns between lines; this physical experience is made explicit at the same time as the imagination becomes distinctly active. This can be paralleled to the experience of reading circus bills. A circus poster provides audiences with a one-page summary of events that demands physical labour on behalf of potential audience members to generate enthusiasm for what is promised. On the bill for Hengler's 1892 season (Fig. 1.1), images of acrobatic riders flying through whips, stirrups and horseshoes are shorthand fantasies which immediately associate mechanics – the tack required to subordinate the performing animal – with spectacle. The printed programme which details in words the real acts one will see make the same association, though less obviously, through the typesetter's play with font and formatting.

'Circe', the fifteenth episode of *Ulysses* and conclusion to Part II of the novel, similarly summarises action. The events of Bloom's day so far are recovered in brief but ingenious extravagance at a brothel in Dublin's red-lit Nighttown. As a tale of circused life, the episode deliberates that the absolute grotesque – the pure grossness of the real – is only possible in the surreality of the mind. Where the 'Sirens' episode begins with the texture of musical overture, 'Circe' features a chorus number: dozens of characters are regurgitated to play upon Bloom's mind. The result is a Joycean interpretation of Barnum and Bailey's 'ethnological congress of strange and savage tribes' as described by Davis: those foreign hum/animal bodies that seemingly compressed real time and space.[36]

There is a pantomimic exchange of volleyed farts between flatulent English knockabouts Private Compton and Private Carr, while Ireland's Cyclops, the Citizen, plays fire-eater; the reader is free to compute the combinatorial explosions which would occur were he to meet the Privates. Bloom's wife Molly is orientalised as the camel-training Sheikh, while the puckered face of the dead baby Bloom bears in mind on the way to Paddy Dignam's funeral in 'Hades' is seen in another dwarf. Signor Maffei the lion tamer returns as the master of Leo Bloom, the kisses' fancy. Parti-coloured Buck Mulligan jests with buttered scone in hand. Some prostitutes perform mask work behind Matthew Arnold's face; others are tufty-pitted snake charmers and reeking husbands to this menagerie of unmarried men. Bawd Bella's barking sowcunt and Bloom's moments of piggishness repeat not only Homer's story, but also popular nineteenth-century circus acts detailed by Davis as revealing, in both appearance and habits, the 'uneasy, liminal proximity of pigs to human beings'.[37] The 'Circe' circus is fleshed out with support acts: gargoyle-like ornaments to the activity include pigmies, gnomes, trick cyclists, hobbyhorse riders and bearded women.

Joyce remains attuned to the effect of the written circus procession in *Finnegans Wake*, where (as in *Ulysses*) domestic drama is positioned within a public spectacle. HCE recounts shenanigans 'round Skinner's circusalley [*sic*]' (p. 532). Socially unacceptable family relations steer the course of misadventure as he approaches a shiftless prostitute with the offer: 'let me be your fodder' (p. 551). Then comes a parade in which European political authorities on the left and right march past in military fashion for the 'pleashadure' of his 'lalaughing' female audience that is, quite literally, near-unspeakable and impossible to imagine outside the compound words of Joyce's creation:

> claudesdales with arabinstreeds, Roamer Reich's rickyshows with Hispain's king's trompateers, madridden mustangs, buckarestive bronches, poster shays and turnintaxis, and tall tilberys and nod noddied, others giggling gaily, some sedated sedans: my pricoping gents aroger, aroger, my damsels softside sadlled covertly, covertly and Lawdy Dawe perched behind: the mule and the hinny and the jennet and the mustard nag and piepald shjelties and skewbald awknees steppit lively (lift ye left and rink ye the right!)
>
> (pp. 553–4)

Like the real Hengler's riverside pleasure garden, which is described as the 'SCREAMING FUN! GRAND FINALE!' of the circus' 1892 show, this satirical sequence from *Finnegans Wake* presents a grotesque procession. Readers stand to attention when the terrible political realities of thirties Europe are invoked. 'Down with them! Kick! Playup!' cries a revolutionary voice after the Holy Roman Empire of the First Reich and the fallen Spanish monarchy march past in burlesqued military fashion, the pompous memorials to waned or waning state apparatuses (p. 554). It is more local characters who lead the political parade in 'Circe'; their representation as authorities within the satirical circus of *Ulysses* is ultimately and inevitably humiliating. Bloom's imagined audience celebrates 'the world's greatest reformer' (p. 455) when he first outlines his '*schemes for social regeneration*' (p. 462) to this maddest of crowds. Their celebration is an excessive parody of the style of politicised spectacle designed by the nationalist Inghinidhe na hÉireann (Daughters of Erin) who are later addressed by messianic Bloom. Fantastic political virtuosity has Parnell's brother John Howard driving a triumphal pageant of Dublin city officials, religious leaders, colonial forces and guildsmen into the new Bloomusalem – that is, the realm of Bloom's imagination. Political genius and rightful monarch Bloom Leopold the First awaits their arrival performing juggling tricks, sleights of handkerchief and mouth, and other '*grotesque antics*' (p. 459).

In her study of the cultivation of heroic figures during the Revival, Geraldine Higgins scrutinises satiric works by W.B. Yeats and J.M. Synge alongside rather more romantic laments for 'the lost opportunity of Parnell's uncrowned kingship', which ran 'like a vein of fool's gold through the biographies, histories, and literature that proliferated in the period soon after his death'.[38] In *Ulysses*, Bloom for one is familiar with the cult of the idol with feet of clay and believed without doubt in the Return of Parnell. 'You had to come back,' thinks L. Boom in 'Eumaeus' before his own homecoming, '– that haunting sense kind of drew you – to show the understudy in the title *rôle* how to' (p. 604). In 'Circe', he himself is Parnell's understudy, and 'Illustrious Bloom' is fixed up as Parnell's true successor (p. 456). The body natural of Leopold lets his imagined Other, a version of the body politic, down, while the verbal violence of his detractor Alexander J. Dowie derives rhetorical force from both religious and political schemes. In his appeal to The Mob of 'fellowchristians and antiBloomites', proof of how Bloom was brought low by Woman inverts the festive energy and incites political energy. Irish evicted tenants refuse to spare the past of Bloom – the lost king who, like mythic Ireland's Labhras, has ass's ears – while the urban mass cries: 'Lynch him! Roast him! He's as bad as Parnell was. Mr. Fox!' (p. 464). Political Bloom is, then, premonitory of scapegoated cinematic clown Charlie Chaplin in *The Circus* (1928), who when falsely accused of theft is 'forced to fly into the "maze of mirrors" where terror-stricken Charlies in their dozens stare at him from every side'.[39] Fugitive Bloom, who acknowledges the futility of self-escape through circus metaphor in 'Nausicaa', enters the 'Circe' circus through another maze of mirrors, only to become caught in the tangle of looking glass and watch psychic life reflecting his absurdity on every side.

Hounded and wounded, Bloom is then vivisected by male doctors who exaggerate the circus-suggestive beastly character traits of this degraded figure, who exhibits freaky traces of elephantiasis, ambidexterity and chronic exhibitionism. The man who was once successor to Ireland's uncrowned king, Parnell, is compelled by an unruly body politic feasting on his failure to regenerate his motivations and please himself with domestic ambitions which are more simply expressed. 'O, I so want to be a mother,' longs Bloom (p. 466). This wish looks forward to the seventeenth episode of *Ulysses*, 'Ithaca', and Joyce's deliberately ambiguous location of the clown who seeks a father at the Rotunda. Hengler's played annually in the Rotunda Gardens, Rutland Square. Joyce's deliberate lack of definition in 'Ithaca' is doubly effective: circus is instantly homonymous with Dublin's Rotunda maternity hospital, which sits on the west side of the same square. The impossibility of family life within this demoralising scheme is confirmed when Bloom is confined to the unproductive sexual role of prostitute. As mastery of this anomalous womanly man is passed from Sheikh Molly to Signor Maffei to belligerent pimp Bello, the re-gendered, depoliticised male renders himself totally impotent.

Christine Froula sees how the 'savage comedy and fantasy' of 'Circe' keeps us 'a leaf away from the real social and cultural violence, destruction, and madness to which it bears witness'.[40] Froula's metaphor of physical distance can be extended to Joyce's setting of the 'Circe' circus within distanced Nighttown. Temporary performance structures or dislocated performance spaces set the circus apart from the architectural stability and central action that give the everyday world the appearance of permanent order. The crowd of Bloom's memory sit with their mouths open, hungry for the relief of failure, waiting for the superhuman to break so that they can break themselves too. The circus is the site of the body politic purging itself, but those in control of the products brought up in this fantastic performance space ensure that it is kept at a safe distance from the real world. But Circean Bloom's negative experience is an exercise in soul searching, within both the individual body and the body politic. While discussing Synge's *The Playboy of the Western World* (1907), Seamus Deane reflects that between the late nineteenth century and the founding of the Free State – a period of rapid political and infrastructural change in Ireland – the national 'process of regeneration also involved a process of re-gendering'.[41] Active and passive, masculine and feminine, Bloom therefore comes to typify, as 'a finished example of the new womanly man' (p. 465), the ideological problems with authority that a masculine-feminine governing body might encounter.

Bloom the androgynous circus act is a being without proper limits or decidable contours, a physical space within which, at least in the popular imagination, anything goes. As we think about Bloom's body in this way, it is notable that Joyce's library records for the years 1904 to 1920 detail his reading of sixteenth-century French writer, scholar and doctor François Rabelais.[42] It was, of course, Rabelais' work that would found twentieth-century Russian cultural critic Mikhail Bakhtin's theories of heteroglossia and the carnivalesque. Through Rabelais, Bakhtin would prove that openness was a condition experienced not only by women, but by all of society as the grotesquery of real life appeared to escape bounds imposed by church- and state-organised calendars on high days and holidays. Bakhtin's classic definition of Renaissance festival would see the world turned upside down, as low cultural forms played upon and played with the low spaces of the human body.

Helen Stoddart refutes designations of the circus as 'a carnivalesque space in which disorder, illegitimacy and inversion reign', since at the circus, she argues, 'order, ascendancy and power […] invariably maintain the upper hand'.[43] Truly, the circus is carefully managed to reach the most effective and sensational climax. Convention fixes an authority at the centre: most often, a ringmaster dominates order, actors and audiences. Strict programming allows for brief moments when authorities internal to circus action are undermined. Externally, while the circus runs by its own calendar, economic considerations enforce limits on how long one show can disrupt a community's cultural life. However, it is necessary to take greater care in understanding the notion of the carnivalesque. Terry Eagleton defines that festive state as 'a *licensed* affair in every sense, a permissible rupture of hegemony, a contained popular blow-off as disturbing and relatively ineffectual as a revolutionary work of art'.[44] Crucially, Bakhtin's carnivalesque apprehensions invert social hierarchies and transform community leaders into subjects of ridicule as the body politic asserts its version of authority. This world would then be righted as society passed out of carnival and back into the standard time and locations of the everyday. Stoddart fails to appreciate in her apprehension of the theoretical carnivalesque that which she clearly discerns from actual circus performance: the significance of 'fantasies of liberation'.[45] The carnivalesque depends on such fantasies of liberation for its powerful and lasting effect – and Joyce is keenly aware of this dependency.

In her essay 'The Humanism of Joyce' (*c.*1931), Adrienne Monnier presents 'the true epigraph' for *Ulysses*: 'That which is above is as that which is below, and that which is below as that which is above.'[46] By Monnier's reckoning, this text – where the lesser reveals the greater – bears ribald resemblance to the charitable exchange of human sympathy which occurs in the co-operative verses of Johnny Patterson. More deliberately, this epigraph carries theosophical and humanitarian (if not socialist) overtones at the same time as consolidating a Rabelaisian inversion. French critics were quick to cast Joyce as Rabelais' heir when *Ulysses* first appeared in translation in 1929. P. Demasy reviewed the work for *Chronique de Paris* in the article 'Un Nouveau Rabelais' published on 14 February 1930:

> Rabelais et Joyce prouvent qu'on y peut joinder la liqueur séminale et la matière fécale. Le tout est d'avoir le génie. James Joyce en a. Quel malheur qu'il ne soit pas français! Il est Angais [*sic*]. Ou plutôt, il est Irlandais. L'Irlande est celtique. Un Anglo-Saxon eut été incapable d'écrire *Ulysse.*[47]

Forty years before the publication of *Rabelais and His World*, Joyce had revelled in the grotesque body throughout *Ulysses* and most graphically in 'Circe'. His hyperawareness of the circus body refutes the kind of artistic existence that ignores all the grossness of the real. As the pathetically ludicrous new 'Bloomusalem' is razed by those who refuse to do their best for one another along the lines of Clifton's ballad, Bloom is transformed into Ruby Cohen. But this re-gendered conversion goes beyond the stage whore contained within the scripted form of 'Circe'. The hyper-effluent spill of self-reflexive 'Circe' opens up the past of *Ulysses* through Bloom's nomination as Ruby. That name returns readers to 'Calypso', to *Ruby: the Pride of the Ring*, and thus to ideas of fathers and sons at the circus.

Bringing It All Back Home: Rudy's Apparition

Unlike *Ruby: the Pride of the Ring*, 'Circe' is not a morality tale. Instead, it is a string of demoralising fantasies. Burns Levin considers the positive value of Bloom's transformations, which she believes Joyce celebrated: 'Through the ensuing expressionistic performance of a marginalization not limited to gender but also including racial and class hierarchies, Bloom experiences the classic masochistic catharsis of pleasurable empowerment through martyrdom.'[48] This perspective on Bloom's perverse sense of 'empowerment' derives from present-day trends in literary criticism and preoccupations with passé identity politics rather than from the tone and content of Joyce's text. Arguably, Bloom does not experience any kind of catharsis in the episode; it is unclear who (other than the reader, perhaps) might be left at the end of his 'expressionistic performance' to martyr him for his own pleasure since, finally, he fails to represent any marginalised community. His continual transformations permit no kind of release and, ultimately, Bloom recedes into the background of action in Nighttown. In fact, 'Circe' turns protagonist and reader upside down and inside out through a satire that takes aim and fires to deliberate ineffect. There is no socio-political motive force other than the revelation of such motives as hypocrisies. The desire instead is for the shock of self-recognition and of immediate experience. It is the surprise of the gas leak from the smashed chandelier that results in '*Nothung!*' (p. 542). Although the character of End of the World is imagined in the political circus of 'Circe' as a two-headed Scotch octopus whirling across an infinite invisible tightrope, there is no final explosive purgation out of the present-time Boschian nightmare. The effect is much more subtle as principal actors shift out of Nighttown before disparately crossing St George's Circus towards 'Ithaca', and home.

In *Ulysses*, the popular performance art of circus is a guise under which critiques of Irish social politics are transmitted. Eagleton singles Joyce out from his Revival contemporaries as the exception 'who succeeded in exploding the whole genre of high fiction, transgressing the border between high and demotic art'.[49] Specifically, the circus offers Joyce the ideal model within which to transgress those artistic borders and to embody philosophies of the grotesque body politic. Eagleton sees that, as political revolution in Ireland gained in pace, 'barriers between fiction and reality gradually crumble to leave a set of surreal images lingering in the mind'.[50] The surreality of 'Circe' undoubtedly destroys barriers between fiction and reality, dreamscapes and waking life. After *Ulysses* was published in 1922, the defeat suffered by feminised socialist and pacifist Bloom perhaps became increasingly disturbing.

On 3 March 1928, Joyce was the subject of a feature article in French newspaper *La Gazette des Nations*. Marcel Brion's profile piece 'Les Grandes Figures Européennes – James Joyce, Romancier' appeared on page four of the paper, following articles on Franco-Belgian relations and the literary tastes of another 'great' European, Benito Mussolini.[51] Where Brion considered the verbal richness of *Work In Progress* as Rabelaisian, journalist Jean Carrère highlighted Risorgimento poet and novelist Alessandro Manzoni, whose robust masterpiece *I Promessi Sposi* (1827) was considered essential reading for Italian nationalists, as a favourite of Mussolini.[52] In literary-cultural terms, Jared Becker considers Italian proto-fascist Gabriele D'Annunzio as an influential inheritor of Manzoni and wider Risorgimento traditions.[53] D'Annunzio achieved new prominence after Lucy Hughes-Hallett's biographical interpretation of the life of 'the sex-crazed Italian demagogue', *The Pike*, won the 2013 Samuel Johnson Prize.[54] Reporting from the awards, BBC Radio 4 journalist Nick Higham commented on the Italian politician's exceptional foresight in 1919. According to Higham, D'Annunzio was among the first to realise that: 'In the age of mass media, politics is a performance art.'[55] Quasi-socialist and pacifist Joyce was contemporaneously aware of the changing spirit of his age. The rigorous physical control demanded for the routinisation of spectacle and the violence inherent to circus performance, which Joyce exploits throughout *Ulysses*, seems responsive to political events and actors on both national and world stages in the 1920s.

Desmond MacCarthy included a comparative study of Joyce and Rabelais within his analysis of *Ulysses* in 'Le Roman Anglais d'Après-Guerre (1919–1929)'. Of Rabelais, he wrote:

> Derrière la bouffonnerie et son grand talent de conter se cache la philosophie du sens commun est un stoïcisme enjoué. Au contraire, l'arrière-plan des torrents verbaux d'*Ulysse* est une tristesse hallucinée et une délectation morose. Le caractère essentiel de l'esprit de Rabelais est son intrépidité; il considère le corps avec amusement et non pas avec horreur. *Ulysse* me frappe, ainsi qu'il en a frappé d'autres comme un produit de la souffrance, d'un sentiment presque insupportable d'oppression [...] En dépit de la précision mordant de ses phrases, de ses éclairs de beauté dominatrice, de son rire sardonique – choses que tout le monde peut apprécier, – l'auteur d'*Ulysse* me donne l'impression d'un esprit asservi, bien plutôt que d'un esprit intrépide.[56]

Presumably, MacCarthy has Bloom in mind. But the extent to which *Ulysses* reads as a testament to '*un esprit asservi*', the enslaved mind of its author, is surely questionable: perhaps MacCarthy falls down in his appraisal of the text's tone when he equates the mind of the author with the body of the book. However, '*une tristesse hallucinée*' is, indeed, essentially conclusive in *Ulysses*. Davis rounds off her history of the American circus with the assertion that 'the circus endures because it beckons us to contend with our own fragility and potential'.[57] At the close of 'Circe', the saddest of hallucinations catches a shadow of the past that is cast throughout *Ulysses*, compelling its audience to contend with life's fragility and lost potential.

Having recovered from his trans-historical, international, ecumenical metempsychosis, Bloom the failed authority returns to the family and to Plato's cave for one final illusive allegory. There, he finds his son:

> (*Silent, thoughtful, alert, he stands on guard, his fingers at his lips in the attitude of secret master. Against the dark wall a figure appears slowly, a fairy boy of eleven, a changeling, kidnapped, dressed in an Eton suit with glass shoes and a little bronze helmet, holding a book in his hand. He reads from right to left inaudibly, smiling, kissing the page.*)

BLOOM

(*Wonderstruck, calls inaudibly.*) Rudy!

RUDY

> (*Gazes unseeing into Bloom's eyes and goes on reading, kissing, smiling. He has a delicate mauve face. On his suit he has diamond and ruby buttons. In his free left hand he holds a slim ivory cane with a violet bowknot. A white lambskin peeps out of his waistcoat pocket.*)

(p. 565)

Since 'Calypso', we have almost heard tell of Rudy, the Blooms' son, in tales of Ruby, the circus girl; almost, but for one stopped consonant. Now, only the child's ruby buttons remember the demoralising stories that have gone before. Rudy's presence is a valorising immaterialisation of all the socio-political considerations Bloom has taken up to this point in the text. What is precious is thereby redeemed from punk, pinnace and bawdy pop pulp, and elevated by a fantastically proud Bloom. All that the real father might have been in this episode is manifest in the imagined, silent son got up in a motley costume of comic opera authority which communicates all-round success: educational prowess, religious devotion, social standing. Rudy regards his father in a manner similar to that encountered by Reade's John Hayward as, desolate, he looks at the photograph of his father whose 'great, grave eyes were speaking to him from the picture ... implacable, resolute, stern' (p. 125). The boy seems, like the stolen child of W.B. Yeats' poem, to have been spirited away by the faeries: he is perfectly set, kept out of the imprevidible future's harmful way. This sight is an éclat of Eagleton's tragic modernism in which 'the present is suspended between an unbreachable past and an unattainable future'.[58] Tellingly, Eagleton's phrase juxtaposes another version of 'the irreparable past' and 'the imprevidible future'. Performance philosopher Alan Read would have it that, in looking through the fantastic image of the child, we discover the imperative to perform; acts mark presences in preparation for our final disappearance. In his lecture 'The Manual Labour of Performance' (2012), Read argued that performance confirms our ability to feel as it combats 'the palpable sense of not having lived'.[59] At the end of the script of 'Circe', the circus is overtaken by this projection in which all the maddening poignancy of lost promise can be seen.

CHAPTER 2

Imagined Communities at the Irish Circus

John Hinde's name is synonymous with postcards. It was in 1956 that the photographer's images of Ireland first went on sale to global travellers at the newly opened Shannon Airport in County Clare. Since then, millions of John Hinde postcards have been sent worldwide. Luke Gibbons derives from these images 'an uneasy feeling that we are getting a last glimpse of a world that is lost'.[1] Hinde's earlier career as a showman and his enthusiasm for the circus are, perhaps, less well known. Nevertheless, the saturated colours of his postcards might be reminiscent of the performance space, and a sense of belatedness might also be derived from his writing about that world.

Hinde moved to Ireland in 1949 with his trapeze-artist wife and briefly ran his own cinema and circus show, Circorama. Before then, he had travelled Britain and Ireland with English troupe Reco's Circus in 1944, 1947 and 1948.[2] He recorded the 1944 winter season and the journey from Belfast to Dublin in a travel journal subsequently published by Eleanor Smith in *British Circus Life* (1948). Hinde was careful to capture a detailed picture of these cities, as well as the circus he saw being built and performed within them. 'The Journey to Belfast' covers preparations for Reco's five-night appearance at the Hippodrome Cinema on Great Victoria Street. Hinde explains that rather than shipping acts and apparatus from England, Reco's co-ordinated with Ireland's Duffy's Circus to supplement their programme and hired circus machinery locally. Watching the business of preparing the cinema space for circus play, Hinde focused on the laying of the ring mat. The mat was unusual in its design, with a circular centre that was divided into quarters and fixed to the floor. Hinde remarks that: 'Of its kind it was an exceptionally fine one, and we learnt that it had been made by convicts in Belfast gaol.'[3] The surrounding city appeared as drab as the cinema screen had been before the circus came to town. Its streets and cobbled roadways were considered 'dingy and depressing'.[4] Performers' lodgings on Joy

Street and Hamilton Street to the east of the city centre, just south of Music
Hall Lane, were found to be reasonably comfortable, but lacking in the kind of
modern sanitary accommodation available in England.

As Reco's journeyed south to the Irish Free State, the troupe witnessed an
even sharper decline in communal welfare standards. The immediate context of
this visit must be acknowledged. Hinde and Reco's Circus were travelling north
to south in the late stages of the Second World War. Belfast, as a British city,
was actively involved in the conflict. Dublin, as the capital of neutral Ireland,
was subject not to a state of total war, but to a state of emergency. Therefore,
it is not only the differences in producing and delivering circus performance
in British Ulster or independent Ireland that are seen in Hinde's account: the
legacies of partition and the impact of international (dis)engagement upon
societies either side of the border also become apparent through his subjective
record. In 'A Visit to Dublin', Hinde explains that the purpose of visiting
Ireland during wartime was, in part, to purchase animals raised for sale by
Dublin Zoo at Phoenix Park. The circus was apparently especially anxious to
acquire black-mane lion cubs, since the zoo was at that time famed for raising
the species. Hinde was impressed en route to Phoenix Park by the 'appalling
poverty' and deprivation he witnessed immediately on leaving the city centre.[5]
He notes carefully the effects of the continuing and critical fuel situation. One
incident seems especially illustrative of Hinde's concerns: 'the taxi was drawn
up behind an open peat-cart at some traffic lights. Immediately children dashed
from the neighbouring doorways and gathered into their arms as many peats
from the back of the cart as they could carry – before the lights changed and
it moved on.'[6] What little peat there was arrived in lorries from rural areas to
dumps on the outskirts of Phoenix Park. This picture of an impoverished city,
its 'snow white' streets and its people freezing in the January cold is juxtaposed
with Hinde's account of meeting zoo superintendent Mr Flood to inspect wild
animals available for purchase on the edge of town: lions, monkeys, elephants
and reptiles.[7]

Hinde was not the first writer to provide such a comprehensive view of Irish
social and political life through circus narrative, and this chapter looks back to
two earlier examples: *Deoraíocht* (1910), by Pádraic Ó Conaire and translated as
Exile by Gearailt Mac Eoin in 1994, and *Sons of Sawdust, with Paddy O'Flynn's
Circus in Western Ireland* (1934), by the English artist Edward Seago. In the
years which separate these texts, the whole island of Ireland underwent seismic
shifts in political and social terms: a world war, violent revolution, war with
England, partition, and civil war. Ó Conaire and Seago manage these changes
in their writing about or from within circus communities; *Exile* and *Sons of*

Sawdust are bound by related cultural tensions. These events both hastened and hindered the delayed process of modernisation in the country, particularly its industrial development. While Hinde briefly became a part of circus life in urban Ireland, Ó Conaire and Seago situate their troupes in the rural west: the object of Revivalist myth-making. Yet neither of these works offers a picture-postcard image of Ireland; instead, these fragile stories reverberate with Gibbons' 'uneasy feeling' that originates in the possibly last look.[8]

The texts by Ó Conaire and Seago are relatable in three ways: in their simultaneous representation of circus life, political history and current affairs; in their focus on the dynamics of (circus) family life, which often centres on food, or its lack; and in their apparent reliance upon nineteenth-century literature, with sources including fiction, non-fiction and social commentary. Critics have hitherto received *Exile* as a psychological novel, remarkable and political, since it is supposedly the first work of its kind written in the Irish language. John T. Koch identifies *Exile* as 'a strange and brooding psychological novel, the first of the genre in Irish', while Pádraigín Riggs and Norman Vance discuss Michael Mullen's sense of 'psychological alienation'.[9] But in stating that *Exile* takes place in London and in failing to specify that certain episodes take place in the west of Ireland, critics ignore an essential aspect of Michael's story: the damage that is wrought by palpable feelings of internal exile. The precise political project of Ó Conaire's novel is, then, unclear – all the more so when we hear Michael's story in translation. Concepts of the autonomous citizen and a collective Irish identity are frustrated by obvious allusions to Victorian English literature and revisions of typical accounts of the Irish in nineteenth-century English journalism. These allusions are made prominent in Mac Eoin's translation, but the ways in which these sources now frame Ó Conaire's plot and characters have not yet been acknowledged. It is crucial to note that Mac Eoin's greatest and most suggestive liberty is in taking the word *taispeántas* to mean 'circus', rather than rendering it, in more precise terms, as 'show' or 'exhibition' (Ó Dónaill, 1977). The effect of this transformative characterisation of the performing world in which Michael finds himself is to admit the expressive relevance of English-language literature, and at times to prioritise the appeal of that tradition, over the original work. To translate *taispeántas* as circus can be seen, then, as an act of cultural colonisation.

Seago's travel journal *Sons of Sawdust* is similarly a fusion, or confusion, of literary and non-fiction genres; features and conventions proper to documentary narratives, biography and autobiography are all present, while chapters are headed with epigraphs taken from English poets. The Englishness of these epigraphs is crucial, and furthermore disjunctive, since the account of the artist's journey through the west of Ireland is littered with descriptions of the kinds of people, places and customs that might appear, for example, in W.B. Yeats' *The Celtic Twilight* (1893). Seago's assimilation of the ideas and the imagery of cultural nationalism may well have been unwitting, but his positioning of them within such a literary frame is nonetheless provocative.

Ó Conaire's protagonist in *Exile*, Michael, considers a destitute and menacing crowd of factory workers as contiguous, 'like one individual person'.[10] In his imagination and in this fictional depiction of community, it is the perceived homogeneity of the crowd as a single social unit that is taken by the external observer as the very cause of their destitution and their menace. Narrators Michael Mullen and Edward Seago are, in varying degrees, external observers: both chart circuses on the road to ruin from the perspective of an individual who does not naturally belong to the travelling community. Despite the precariousness of existence for these communities, these texts are chiefly concerned with endeavours to forge bonds of kinship and to substitute circus life for family life. It is remarkable that family and community were organising concepts for American sociologists Conrad Arensberg and Solon Kimball as they began in the late 1930s to sift the findings of the Harvard Irish Study. Arensberg and Kimball were members of a team of social and physical anthropologists and sociologists commissioned by the Rockefeller Foundation to travel to Ireland and to investigate at first hand how the country had – or had not – managed to balance tradition with modernity between 1931 and 1936. Initially, Arensberg developed the anthropological study *The Irish Countryman* (1937) independently. The title figure appeared, to him, to typify his experience of living in rural County Clare, and Arensberg placed his countryman in the context of work and leisure, viewing him in relation to other men and boys. At the centre of this anthropological portrait is 'The Family and the Land', an essay examining the ways in which the typical Irish countryman's family life was rooted in its natural environment. But when Arensberg and Kimball came to publish their research jointly in 1940, only one frame could contain everything they had discovered about Irish life – from practices at cattle markets to controls on sex and sexuality – and that frame became the title of the work: *Family and Community in Ireland* (1940). Their analysis led them to summate that: 'Everything one does or is can be referred to one's "blood".[11] Crucially, in their chapter 'Occupation and Status', Arensberg and Kimball felt confident enough in their research to state that their statistical findings for Clare 'repeats practically exactly the same story as that for Ireland as a whole'. (p. 239) They believed that families and communities on this island, as yet largely untouched by Éamon de Valera's programme of industrialisation, were unified by a set of common experiences. No matter how conclusive the social scientist's general sense may be statistically, it must and will be viewed within this argument with cautious hindsight.

The title of this chapter is, of course, borrowed from another text that has proved immensely influential within contemporary sociology. In *Imagined Communities: Reflections on the Origin and Spread of Nationalism* (1983; 1991), Benedict Anderson argues that a community exists through its perception in the minds of its constituents – those who believe themselves to be members of that group.[12] This idea is crucial to the present argument. Primarily, though at times unconsciously, both Ó Conaire and Seago compel us to ask: What is a nation, and how might it be constituted? In 'What is a Nation?' (1882), Ernest Renan considered that a people is a group who share both in the memory of having done 'great things together' and in the 'will to do the like again'.[13] These two conditions can be brought to bear on the distinct visions of Ó Conaire and Seago. The former arrests the development of his protagonist, the freak Michael Mullen, by symbolically limiting his ability to move away from both personal and shared past experience. Meanwhile, Seago – the English outsider looking in – trusts in the cohesive power of looking forward.

The Internal Exile: Pádraic Ó Conaire, English Literature, and Irish Culture

Ó Conaire's *Exile* was written while the author was living in London. It is the story of Michael Mullen, a young man from the west of Ireland who leaves home in search of work in the English capital. The novel opens shortly after Michael has been released from hospital following a motor accident that has left him without an arm and a leg, and terribly disfigured. For a time, he lives in a boarding house to such excess as his modest compensation can afford. Despite interventions on the part of Michael's maternal compatriot, the formidable Big Red-haired Woman, his inability to find work leaves him vulnerable to an invitation from Alfred Trott, the so-called Little Yellowman, to become, in Mac Eoin's translation, a circus freak and tour the British Isles. Michael travels with Trott's circus back to his native country, then escapes the hardships and humiliation of that life, only to return to London and abject poverty. Finally, he commits suicide under an oak tree in a public park.

Biographical similarities between Ó Conaire and his narrator Michael are remarkable. Born in Galway in 1882, Ó Conaire was orphaned at the age of twelve. He and his four siblings were raised by relatively affluent relatives from

Ros Muc, a village in the south Connemara Gaeltacht, and in County Clare. He moved to London in 1899 to take up a post within the British Civil Service and moved through the ranks of the Education Board from 'boy copyist' to the slightly more senior position of assistant clerk, remaining in that post until 1914 when he was asked to leave for unknown reasons. He returned to Ireland soon after he was dismissed, leaving his wife Molly Ní Mhanais and their four children behind him. He did not go back to the west but settled in Dublin. Ó Conaire was well known for drinking heavily and eating little; his translator Mac Eoin suggests that this way of life brought him to the paupers' ward of a Dublin hospital where he died in 1928: 'His sole possessions, apart from his clothing, consisted of a pipe, a piece of plug tobacco, an apple and a pocket knife.'[14]

Between 1901 and 1927, Ó Conaire wrote over 400 short stories and regularly published journalism in newspapers and journals including *New Ireland*, *The Freeman's Journal*, and the *Nation*.[15] His choice to write in Irish was politically motivated. Ó Conaire was an active member of the Gaelic League while living in London, later becoming more deeply involved with its organisation, and the form of *Exile* reveals much about its political potential. The work could be conceived as a string of short fictions sewn together, resulting in the kind of disjointed and interrupted journey narrative that characterises the twelve rural sketches collected as *Field and Fair* and translated into English in 1928 by Cormac Breathnach.[16] It is as though Ó Conaire has combined the writing styles with which he is best associated – the short story and the news article or feature – to create *Exile*, the first psychological novel in the Irish language.

Mac Eoin's readiness to indicate correspondences between the life of the writer Ó Conaire and the story of his character Michael is not unusual or particularly provocative. Brendan McGowan, in his introduction to Diarmuid de Faoite's bilingual translation of *Seacht mBua an Éirí Amach/Seven Virtues of the Rising* (1918–2016), includes Ó Conaire's morose reflections on the loneliness of life:

> 'No matter what you do', he cried, pointing finger solemnly at me, 'make a home somewhere and stick to it. Have somewhere you can call your own, even if it's only a mud-walled cabin. That is the important thing. Look at me and take warning. Don't smile. Don't think because you are young and healthy that you can play fast and loose for another few years and then settle down. To think that will only bring you to the position I'm in'.[17]

These warnings were given by Ó Conaire to his contemporary Liam O'Flaherty. Both in tone and substance, they would not sound out of place if they were found in *Exile* and attributed to Michael Mullen. However, there are other features to Mac Eoin's translation that carry readers away from the original matter of the novel in ways that are certainly thought-provoking, if not provocative.

Ó Conaire provides readers with a vivid account of the Irish migrant experience of nineteenth- and early twentieth-century London. Specific descriptions of London and Little Ireland (as the St Giles slum in which Michael lives from time to time was known) are reminiscent of the writings of Victorian social commentators in their regard for other cultures represented in the city – specifically, Thomas Carlyle's grotesque renditions of Irish itinerant workers in the essay 'Chartism' (1839), and Charles Booth's repulsive descriptions of Shelton Street, WC2, and areas surrounding Little Ireland in *Life and Labour of the People of London* (1891). In forging these connections, it is essential to recognise that the novelty of *Exile* is that these social issues are imagined, perhaps for the first time, in Irish. Ó Conaire apparently translates decades-old journalism and social commentary in English for his native audience in order to represent literally the impoverished migrant's experience. The novel is, then, a defiant moment of cultural exchange in terms of language, form and content which gives its readers a new and sensational experience of what it means to be in exile. These resonances are amplified in Mac Eoin's translation. A scene on the Embankment is exemplary; it could be lifted from Salvation Army founder General William Booth's *In Darkest England* (1890):

> I told every wretch I met to follow me and drink a cup of coffee with me. I had forty followers by the time we reached the coffee stall. They were thin and ragged. Some of them, when they saw the food, had a look in their eyes like the look in the eyes of a tiger. They were famished with the cold and the hunger. They wolfed the food whilst the sweat poured off them from the heat of the coffee and from the effort they had put into drinking it. Some of them had not eaten for so long that they were unable to keep down the food ...
>
> (pp 31–2)

In this passage, the confusing moment of cultural transmission is condensed in the telling catachresis that cannot decide whether Michael's charity cases are tigers or wolves. And it is at such moments of animalisation that *Exile* approaches another literary genre: the fable.

Ó Conaire and his translator Mac Eoin are sensitive to the slippage between language and sense, sound and nonsense on Michael's behalf. The meeting with the impresario Little Yellowman which precedes the scene on the Embankment takes place in a public house in the presence of a young sailor. Curious grammatical features in this episode include swift shifts in tense: presently, Michael and the young sailor 'are drinking hard', but in the next paragraph Michael provides entertainment in the past tense: 'I told my tales in English' (p. 24). These shifts are quite sensible in the original Irish syntax; their rendering in English is not quite insensible, and rather more suggestive, as they heighten the atmosphere of disorientation and dislocation that is at the heart of Michael's story, confirming that *Exile* might reasonably be read as a modern novel.

When considering the 'adulteration' of nationalist street ballads over time, David Lloyd writes with more general implications for the products of cultural nationalism that '"hybridization" is necessarily grasped by nationalists as the paradoxically simultaneous process of multiplication or disintegration and homogenization'.[18] That paradox is very much in evidence at this moment in *Exile*. Michael's physical half-ness is matched by his actual bilingualism or perceived multilingualism. In this scene, he begins to speak in English, 'but before long I changed over to Irish, without realising it' (p. 24). Mac Eoin works to subtly heighten the sinister and foreboding atmosphere of the scene by avoiding a literal translation of Ó Conaire's 'tháinig ionadh orthu uile chlós na teanga nua dóibh' – literally, 'wonder came upon them all on hearing the new language'.[19] What is 'new' to Ó Conaire becomes ominously 'strange' to Mac Eoin: Irish is described as a 'strange language' (p. 24), which is classified by Alf Trott as German. It is, like the scars on his face left by the motor accident, a mark of difference that might be interpreted along the lines of any kind of otherness. His unconscious ability to transition between two languages is no more to be celebrated than is his physical disability; rather, it further signifies the instability of Michael's identity as migrant. The coherence of this flow between Irish and English is upset in translation, as a reader of the English text pointedly realises that the foregoing has all occurred inside the subject's head, save for a very few lines of dialogue. At this moment of linguistic confusion, the sailor and Trott conspire to seize upon Michael's obvious and audible dissimilarity to cast him as an insane German murderer, just returned from a lion-killing spree in East Africa. Their malevolence thereby recalls the so-called 'African parallel' drawn contemporarily by William Booth. In that parallel, Booth considered that the incivility of the animal kingdom in 'darkest Africa' was comparable to the poverty of the 'pygmies' in 'darkest England'.[20] In *Exile*,

the symbolic resonance of the sailor imagining othered-Irishman Michael in the heart of British colonial Africa plunging a sword 'to the hilt in the heart of a lion' (p. 25) is unmissable. The young man becomes both a source of panic and a source of entertainment retrieved from some far-flung place; a living caricature, perfect for the circus, which makes Alf Trott 'as pleased as Punch' (p. 26).

Circus-owner Trott is consigned from first impressions to the othering pseudonym 'Little Yellowman'. Small in stature, funny in colour, and with a 'big, long, hooked nose' and 'long, pointed, little chin' that might belong to Dickens' wicked Fagin, this character produces, at first glance, an amalgam of pejoratively exotic, orientalised beings: the 'Chinaman' and the 'Jew'. These similarities are engendered within Mac Eoin's translation, as he turns Ó Conaire's almost playful 'a dhá shúil shoilseacha imithe isteach ina chloigeann' ('his two bright eyes gone into his noggin') into the more haunting image of 'two bright eyes sunk deep in his head' (p. 24).[21] Riggs initiated the suggestion that Ó Conaire also makes a more local reference in the Little Yellowman. She recognises in Michael's master '"Seán Buí" (literally "yellow John", the Irish version of John Bull)', and she connects this assertion to Robert Lynd's 1907 cartoon 'John Bull's Famous Circus' (Fig. 2.1).[22] Drawn in support of emerging Sinn Féin, Lynd's cartoon depicts republicanism's explicit critique of post-Parnell Home Rulers and their negotiations with the British Liberal

Party. Both parties are overshadowed by the supreme and singular authority of fantastic John Bull, characterised by Lynd as the ringmaster. The questionable exercise of ruling power is suggested in the cartoonist's use of the circus trope, within which a single charismatic ruler is positioned to beat the drum on a ramp descending towards the mob. Meanwhile, the Liberals' Chief Secretary for Ireland, Augustine Birrell, and Permanent Under-Secretary to the Lord Lieutenant of Ireland, Sir Antony MacDonnell, join Irish Parliamentary Party leader John Redmond. These politicians represent a parliament of fools dismissed by Lynd in the shorthand of circus bills as little more than sideshow distractions to England's main event.

Mac Eoin's translation also references another cartoonish figure who is instantly recognisable in the popular imagination: Punch, the vicious puppet who lent his name to the English satirical periodical which was famously harsh in its cartoon depictions of the Irish. John Tenniel's 'Two Forces' (Fig. 2.2) was published in *Punch* on 29 October 1881. The cartoon features a typically simian Irishman, whose hatband reads 'ANARCHY':

2.2 John Tenniel, 'Two Forces', *Punch*, 29 October 1881

In this way, an explicit association is made between the showman villain of Ó Conaire's novel and the infamous images of the Irish that circulated periodically throughout nineteenth-century England. Apparently, the Little Yellowman appreciates the value that the persona of a monster Irishman would add to his circus company, since it is a persona that would have been recognisable to contemporary leisure- and pleasure-seeking readers of such popular magazines.

The effect of this characterisation is to further exile Michael from himself, from the reality of his mental illness and physical disability and, most significantly, from his national heritage through the denial of his natural language in its conscious misapprehension. The elision between Ireland, Germany and Africa in the damnably exciting reclassification of Michael's nationality is reminiscent of earlier writings by the likes of social commentator Flora Tristan. When Tristan walked the streets of London in the 1830s, she found men, women and children in the Irish quarter of St Giles 'leaning', 'squatting' or 'lying about in the mud like pigs', 'their hair so filthy and dishevelled that they look like woolly-headed Negroes'.[23] Tristan concluded that: 'The ravings of a demented imagination could not equal the dreadful reality of such horrors!'[24]

In *Exile*, London looms horribly as the place in which the modern machine – the motor car – cripples Michael. The city is demonised as a kind of Leviathan or Frankenstein's monster, stitched together and barely enlivened by the bodies of those wandering souls it centrifugally sucks in. However, Ó Conaire's novel is decidedly complicated in its lack of contrast: the portrayal of his native place is scarcely more flattering than that of London. In 1908, Ó Conaire published the critical essay 'Seanlitríocht na hÉireann agus Nualitríocht na hEorpa', or 'Old Irish Literature and the Modern Literature of Europe'. The title suggests a will to position Irish culture within a European context – an ambition shared, of course, by Ó Conaire's better-known contemporaries including George Moore. And in representing the misery of Michael's existence as unremitting upon the migrant's return to home, Ó Conaire certainly matches, if not exceeds, the damning critiques of Irish family and community life for which *The Untilled Field* (1903) are celebrated.

In Michael's mind, Ireland in general and Galway specifically are locations of anxiety. After selling himself into the Little Yellowman's circus, he agonises over a question as 'many a poor exile had done before [...] far away from his home town': 'What would they say of me in Galway?' (p. 30). His neurosis extends to the memory of his dead mother and father, who are absent from the text save for their imagined shame and disbelief in the fate of their son. Arensberg and

Kimball explain the extreme difficulties of re-assimilation prosperous migrants faced on returning home: '[I]f he has been long away, [he] is declassed and to an extent deracinated. This is true of all his behavior, through all his relations with those from whom he went' (p. 262). Declassification and deracination are, of course, ongoing preoccupations for Irish artists, explored most notably in contemporary theatre by Brian Friel: these states of non-being are central to his play *Crystal and Fox*, which is considered at length in the next chapter. But in the historical moment of *Exile*, when even the able-bodied, wage-earning male is, to an extent, orphaned and ostracised until he has undergone Arensberg and Kimball's 'slow and painful' process of reabsorption, there is little hope for a figure like Michael (p. 262). He is convinced that return for a man of his surname, in such a state, to his native place is impossible under anything but a shameful mantle.

The reception Michael receives as disguised circus freak might be read as a metaphoric exaggeration of every exile's self-conscious sense of transformation at the point of return:

> And they were coming and going until a good part of the night was over. Every word that came out of their mouths I took as an insult. But, of course, they did not think I understood their speech. Even so, they made me hate them. In any other place, their talk would not have bothered me. But here in Galway, where I was born! Imagine if they knew who I was! If they knew that it was one of their own people who was being exhibited to them as a terrifying freak!
>
> Anger took hold of me. Madness and rage and hatred took hold of me. What could I do to really strike terror into them? I could not think of anything I could do. Why should they be coming to look at me anyway? Was I not a man? Had I not feeling and intelligence and understanding like every man? Are they Christians?
>
> (p. 46)

The west is critiqued through its people by revealing the customs and social codes which reinforce bonds of kinship. Michael vilifies and condemns his own community, as its population – no longer his people – jeer and leer at him as a circus spectacle. Any romantic images of the comforting home-place are dashed when the young man finds the place and the people changed, and that he is unrecognisable within this brutal community. The brutality of the circus – screeching steam engines, peals of laughter and threatening shouts – immobilises Michael from proving himself as 'one of their own' through language. He accepts the fact that they believe him to be Other because they believe he cannot understand their speech. Frequently in the novel, Michael is bereft of verbal language and left to express himself through roars, laughter, tears or silence. The cause of such primal, physical release is always misunderstood by his audience; it is taken by them as a source of entertainment.

While noise pollution generates a disorientating atmosphere for Ó Conaire's protagonist and his readers alike, the circus is generally devoid of colour – apart from the yellow which symbolically saturates its owner. Otherwise, fantastic hues (reminiscent of Hinde's postcards, perhaps) belong to Michael's mind. A kaleidoscopic shift in mental focus overlays the crowd when his first cousin, Mary Lee, appears at the booth. Her image is nearly iconic: she is at the centre of Michael's idealised 'many-coloured pictures' of the family life that might have been, which are set within a domesticated Eden of woodland flowers, chestnuts, pines and whitethorns, all growing beside a meandering stream (p. 50). These delusions are not dissimilar in their poignancy to the projection Bloom apprehends of his son Rudy at the close of 'Circe' in *Ulysses*. But in the present-time reality of *Exile*, Ó Conaire's Mary Lee is joined by her husband in the circus tent, and as the pair look upon Michael, the freak is rendered impotent, even in his madness and murderous rage towards the Little Yellowman. The shock of recognition is not mutual, for Mary cannot see the man who loved her under the madman's guise. Michael instantly recalls how her strict adherence to social custom robbed him of all good fortune:

> But for you, I should never have left home in the first instance. But for you I should not be in the shameful condition that I am in today. It is you who are responsible for every misfortune that came in my direction, Mary, if you only knew it. Neither myself nor my family had much wealth. My mother and five brothers had only one small holding between us, and, of course, Mary, you would not have been willing to marry me until I had first earned some money in England.
>
> (p. 48)

Arensberg and Kimball include near-identical narratives in their sociological study of small farmers in County Clare. In the absence of any rules of primogeniture, they found that the decision as to which son should inherit the farm had massive repercussions for the social, sexual and family life of those children who were apparent heirs. Though their survey was conducted twenty years and more after *Exile* was written, these findings proved to the leaders of the Harvard Irish Study that the traditional custom of life in Ireland had persistently continued 'to wield its power in essentially similar fashion decade after decade and generation after generation' (p. 300). In some ways anticipating the subject matter of Patrick Kavanagh's 'The Great Hunger' (1942), Arensberg and Kimball continue to reflect that: 'A social system centering so strongly round the institution of the family condemns a large proportion of its members to celibacy and long-preserved virginity' (p. 213). Others, like Michael, were forced into migrant exile.

Lloyd has called for a critical examination of 'both the specificity of Irish cultural and social forms and the active function of the novel in their transformation, not of its value as autonomous artefact but of the values which, as such, it represents and seeks to promote'.[25] *Exile* offers an excellent case study for such an analysis. Ó Conaire's decision to demonstrate Michael's sense of betrayal before an inhumane family and native community at the circus is not, perhaps, entirely original. It has already been suggested that worthwhile comparisons might be made between the returnee's experience as detailed in *Exile* and the short stories of George Moore. But the debt Mac Eoin suggests, as translator, that Ó Conaire simultaneously owes in this regard to English novelists of the nineteenth century has not yet been acknowledged. Aspects of the plot of *Exile* turn attentions to mid-nineteenth-century fiction, most obviously to Charles Dickens' *Bleak House* (1853) and *Hard Times* (1854). *Bleak House* is shrouded in that most evocative element, fog.[26] It seems that Ó Conaire's sense of the element is equally pervasive and invasive, and that Mac Eoin's translation is inflected through the recognisable images of this literary precedent. Michael sees fabulous London 'hiding under its marvellous cloak of fog' (p. 23). London gains from the fog a polluting power that is active in its occupation of its inhabitants: 'There is a fog. Heavy fog that would go into your mouth and down your throat; fog that would bring tears to your eyes; fog that would come in the door, and in through the windows, no matter how tightly closed' (p. 22). But the fog seen here is not, as in *Bleak House*, indiscriminate towards a list of fictional individuals observed by an omniscient narrator. Here, 'you' are directly implicated within this pathetic fallacy through anaphora, synecdoche and merismus. 'You' are the one choked and tearful with the inescapable atmosphere of Michael's psyche.

Dickens inscribed *Hard Times* to his friend Thomas Carlyle. Notably, Carlyle had characterised the Irish immigrant in his essay 'Chartism' as 'the ready-made nucleus of degradation and disorder'; and 'Chartism' is one of those social commentaries that echoes throughout *Exile*.[27] The circus is a subplot in *Hard Times*. It is represented as a lively, human counterpoint to the desiccated scientific facts of the schoolroom and gruelling physical labour of the mill: Sleary's circus is managed by sympathetic characters who constitute an alternative community model situated temporarily within the industrial society of Coketown. But Dickens' circus does not offer itself as a location of liberty and wonder on uncomplicated terms. The memory of the circus, which is seen briefly as the Gradgrind children defy their father, haunts the novel while Louisa and Tom prove the impossibility of sustaining the wonderful in their hometown. This allegorical function is partly due to the author's apparent discomfort in handling the physical, substantial elements of circus life. Helen Stoddart rightly considers the Dickensian performance space as 'something either already beyond his text or as an unstable or excessive metaphor, a gap, an absence or a ghostly presence within it'.[28] Dickens has little trouble in mastering a diffuse, abstract sense of circus, but it is as though he looks at the real thing in *Hard Times* along with the Gradgrind children through a chink in the tent fabric, before his imagination snatches him away from solidity. Ó Conaire, meanwhile, grapples with the physical aspects of showground living and its personalities. Here, it is essential to note again that Michael is not originally seen in a '*sorcas*'; Mac Eoin liberally translates '*taispeántas*' as circus, thereby loading the word with specific historical, cultural and literary significance. A crucial distinction in *Exile* is that the circus in which Michael is exhibited, or exhibits himself, is characterised as an industry in itself, controlled by the rules of capital and as exploitative of its workers as any other. References to wages, rises, and late payments due in recompense for the labour of circus performance create much of the tension in the novel, while legally resonant terms such as 'satisfaction' and 'damage' recur in Mac Eoin's translation (p. 136). Traditional cultural forms are thereby exposed as equally subject to the processes of modernisation.

Similarly, Michael's apprehension of family failure is crucial in Mac Eoin's translation to disillusioning preconceptions about the wonder of circus. The circus family unit is most often an object of Michael's scorn, derision and disgust, and the version of paternity available to Michael on the showground is particularly revolting. Michael regards tyrannical Alf Trott's concern for his circus acts as phony – moreover, nauseating and maddening – since it is based on a fabricated belief in the cohesive power of patrilineality. The 'devil of mischief' overtakes the young Irishman after Trott explains the origins of his family business, which concludes with a version of his promise to his dying father:

> [...] I have kept up the reputation of my family. I have never acted as master over my people, especially over the women, but have always been, as it were, *in loco parentis*, and if my father is in Heaven tonight, looking down on his beloved son, he will bear witness ...
>
> (p. 58)

Michael is bent regressively towards adolescent anarchy and rebellion by these words. He imagines killing the Little Yellowman, but settles instead on destroying his business. This destruction is effected by a performance of love for the circus act Trott fosters above all others, the Fat Lady. The Fat Lady is already sweet on Michael, and when she unwittingly accepts a sham marriage proposal, Trott anticipates great wealth in this grotesque union of freaks. There are brief moments when Michael's conscience complicates his plot and he is forced to check his behaviour towards the Fat Lady: he fears becoming genuinely attracted to the only woman in the world who would not find his condition 'obnoxious' (p. 56). Consequently, an ellipsis in the text suggests that she must be despatched along with her father to avoid this horrible possibility.

But Michael's greatest torments are those visions in which he conceives of himself as a father in vivid delusions. A particularly painful episode follows his encounter with Mary in George Coff's booth. He places himself, Mary as mother, and their three children in a simple Arcadia: a cosy house; a branchy wood; flowers; trees; nightfall. The children are ideally Irish: Pat, little Brigid and infant Colm are named for Catholic saints. Then a vision approaches:

> – any wonder that it is Mary I see, with Colm on her shoulder? But it is hard to please him. He has been expecting apples. Didn't I promise them to him this morning?
>
> … But time passed. The new year came. Colm was now able to walk by himself. Wearing little knee-breeches. Curly black hair falling down around his shoulders; He follows me through the wood, his voice making music for me …
>
> (p. 50)

This waking dream is one example from among the numerous Christian parables or allusions to the legends of the Catholic faith within *Exile*. Colm is seen like an Irish messiah: as an infant, he is borne upon the shoulders of his parents like Jesus upon the shoulders of Saint Christopher; as a child, his personal pronoun 'He' is capitalised like that of Christ himself. But this Edenic fantasy carries with it another version of *Exile*. Michael is forced to rouse himself from this 'false vision', which he has already spoiled in some senses by bringing home to his child nothing but disappointment (p. 50). Subsequently, Michael debases himself as he is forced to identify with a wild beast of the circus: 'moving to and fro in his prison. To and fro, to and fro without relief, as if he were remembering all that he had left behind him in his native country' (p. 51). Referring the reader back to the dehumanised poor that the young man led to the coffee stall on London's Embankment, the personification of the animal in whose movements Michael sees a reflection of himself is further realised by the grounding of the beast in visceral terms. It might be that the creature's upset is not a by-product of memory but – like Scrooge's ghost Marley – just a symptom of bad digestion.

Looking back on their study of County Clare in the 1930s, Arensberg and Kimball opined that rural youths drew from the family 'that strength which gave them entrance and ensured their survival as they encountered the new values of the urban world and its social class divisions' (p. xi). Ó Conaire's fiction reverses the sentiment of that positive perspective. One of the novel's most bizarre episodes betrays the fantasy of family life in the most graphic terms. During his second stint in London after his escape from the Little Yellowman's circus, Michael stays at Hammer's lodging house in Little Ireland. He sits and watches from his window the man who bids goodbye to his wife and children as he leaves for work at a laborious occupation which requires him to carry a sledge-hammer. In that family, Michael sees the realisation of the vibrant and multi-coloured pictures he has constructed for himself of his ideal family. But the heavy-handed and ominous repetition of the Hammer as house and the hammer as tool signals that these images are extremely fragile, and that Michael and his neighbours live entirely within the threat of being beaten. In one of his final city wanderings, Michael happens upon a scene just outside Hammer's which drains all colour from his revered projections:

> But what's this? A grimy back-street. Snow churned into mud under people's feet. Everything a grey colour. A gathering of men, women and children. They are very excited. Terrified. Disturbed.
>
> A young woman is lying on the dirty grey slush. She doesn't stir. There is a man standing by her, a huge sledge-hammer on the ground beside him. He is half-drunk; five men are holding him; some of them want to kill him straight away. The woman on the snow is his wife. The sledge-hammer on the ground is his (was he not seen carrying it this morning?), and if the woman isn't dead, the new-born baby is …
>
> (p. 142)

The father's angst, disappointment and misery are released in violence upon those who are vulnerable, voiceless, and without an advocate to plead on their behalf. This attack gives the appearance of street theatre to the crowd of witnesses. In their excitement, terror and disturbance, they mirror those assembled in Michael's circus booth when images of his own family swim before his eyes, blocking out his duplicitous first cousin Mary Lee and her second-cousin husband, Michael, who is so pointedly the narrator's doppelgänger that he even shares his name. In this repetition, the man with the sledge-hammer is another emanation of Michael, performing in actual terms that which he has only managed in his mind.

Unlike the hammer-wielding, homicidal father, Michael most often assumes a passive position in relation to women. Bizarrely, quasi-family structures in *Exile*, both within and without the circus setting, are marked out by kissing: Michael recounts experiences with both the Big Red-haired Woman and the Fat Lady. The kisses are depicted from Michael's perspective as at turns surprising, grotesque and parasitical embraces, in which he yields to the women who overbear him. This character of kissing is reminiscent of that described by Sigmund Freud in 'Three Essays on the Theory of Sexuality' (1905), and specifically of the psychoanalyst's exploration of infantile sexuality. Freud insists upon the relationship between breastfeeding, kissing and sucking another part of one's own body in early infancy. The pity contained within the onanistic experience of sucking one's self forces the child, and later the man, to seek out the lips of another – to exile himself from his own sexual experience. According to Freud, those habitual thumb-suckers who go on to habitual kissing as adults 'will be inclined to perverse kissing, or, if males, will have a powerful motive for drinking and smoking'.[29] The Freudian notion of infantile sexuality can be brought to bear on the kisses Michael does not so much share, as receive from the Big Red-haired Woman. Symbolically, she is, of course, Mother Ireland. Her public displays of affection towards her compatriot are maternal and reveal her natural need for both the homely and the uncannily familiar; through them, another kind of complex Freudian sexual impulse is represented. As the Big Red-haired Woman carts Michael back to her rooms through the London fog in his wheelchair, he reflects upon how: 'You would think I was a child, and she my mother.' Once back in her home, 'she takes hold of my hand, and begins to fondle it with kindness and affection, as my mother used to do long ago, when I was a small child' (p. 32). In their relationship is contained the fantasy of returning to an earlier version of the dependent self and, in the Mac Eoin translation, to un-circused Ireland.

Michael's unromantic relationship with the Fat Lady is also symbolically incestuous. As members of Alf Trott's circus, the two are, primarily, figurative siblings under his supervision *in loco parentis*. The Fat Lady repeats and supplements this relationship in her letter to Michael addressed to 'Dear little brother, dear little son of my heart' (p. 78). Michael receives this correspondence, which alerts him to Trott's own murderous intent and his own grave danger, while hiding out in a London lodging house. Despite its serious contents, the letter is at once girlish, saccharin and subject to ridicule by the other male boarders. The flavour of the Fat Lady's affection for Michael is important. Her kisses mimic her lips and her mouth, which smack and slobber around her masses of food, and Michael figures himself as yet another thing that she consumes. When it is revealed that the Fat Lady is not only the Little Yellowman's figurative daughter as one of his acts, but, in fact, his biological child, the relationship between the excessive woman and the wasted man becomes an even more significant allegory. The Fat Lady, as Alf Trott's child, is an Englishwoman. Michael is an Irishman ultimately forced into her arms by the symbolic Mother Ireland: in their final encounter, the Big Red-haired Woman stands stoic, enforcing social codes and fulfilling legal promises on behalf of the Fat Lady. Throughout the novel, the Woman's appearance has been compared to that of a Roman emperor, and at last she is seen in a manner reminiscent of Tenniel's Britannia.

Ó Conaire reviewed social codes governing women's sexual role in his later short story 'Little Marcus's Nora' (1921). Again, it is an ambivalent morality tale of emigration and return, but differs from *Exile* in its rendition of the female experience. Nonetheless, comparisons can be drawn between novel and story in the repeated exploration of the migrant body pushed to sustain itself through exploitation: where Michael becomes a circus freak, Nora slides into alcoholism and falls into prostitution. She lives in this way for nine years, supporting her family in Ireland with the money she makes, until she is forced to encounter her first love and his wife in a London restaurant. The couple's respectability is revelatory, as Nora sees her own course towards a 'normal' life in the Catholic Church. A parish priest writes to his equivalent in her local parish in Ireland, and she is sent home to her father Marcus for restoration by 'her native air and home atmosphere'.[30] Her life in London is concealed from her family and her local community by the priest, but Nora herself is unable to contain her seemingly natural waywardness. Her drunken misbehaviour causes her father public shame and he banishes his child to England once more. The community remains unaware of her past as prostitute, but the story concludes with Marcus painting out his daughter's name on the boat that he has bought with the money Nora sent home. Again, Ó Conaire pushes the migrant body to physical extremes in Nora's story, and records the impossibility of returning unchanged to the native community.

While Michael's circus act is tremendous, it is not particularly physical. He is confined to the circus booth – roaring from time to time and rattling his wooden cage – because of the exaggerated disability that fakes the amputation of his one remaining leg. The limits of Michael's human body are more harrowingly encountered outside the persona of George Coff: in the sensational descriptions of how his crutches feel, in the exhausted examination of his tired muscles and, crucially, in the painful recreation and pathetic management of his hunger. Franz Kafka's 'A Hunger Artist' (1922) impossibly echoes *Exile*; a reader senses that Mac Eoin must have had the short story in mind as he translated Ó Conaire. Kafka's title character, the unnamed sideshow attraction, is worn down by dissatisfaction with himself and with the world's contempt for compassion and understanding. The deeply depressed human artist dies after refusing to break his fast; in doing so, he is misperceived as becoming increasingly inhuman until his display cage is pushed in among those of other performing animals. Finally, he is contrasted with an animal actor who replaces him after death: a panther moves restlessly about its cage like the circus beast with which Michael identifies in *Exile*. In Edwin Muir's translation of Kafka's story, the crowd's attraction to that animal is described in similar terms to that of the people who stand around and gawp at the mother and child hammered to death, or near-death, by the father: 'it was not easy to stand the shock of it. But they braced themselves, crowded the cage, and did not want ever to move away.'[31]

Although Kafka reveals what Maud Ellmann has termed the 'complicity between the themes of hunger, writing, and imprisonment', he also represents hunger as a choice.[32] Accordingly, as Ellmann would have it, the hunger he conveys becomes a release mechanism that attempts to spring the artist out of history, society and gender. Michael's hunger is different: it leaves him with no choice other than to sift through the collection of rubbish in his pocket – 'pebbles, buttons, crumbs, nails and the rest' – to find a bone button: '[I] popped it into my mouth. I began to swallow the saliva that gathered around it. I had discovered that it relieved the severe pain' (p. 96). Again, in this desperate moment, Ó Conaire's translator Mac Eoin selects the verb 'to suck' and, in doing so, alludes to another literary figure who has chosen to go hungry. Samuel Beckett's *Molloy* (1951; 1955) was published in French and, later, English forty years before Mac Eoin produced the first English translation of *Exile*. It is difficult not to think of Michael Mullen as Molloy recalls a moment of his own dereliction:

> A confused shadow was cast. It was I and my bicycle. I began to play, gesticulating, waving my hat, moving my bicycle to and fro before me, blowing the horn, watching the wall. They were watching me through the bars, I felt their eyes upon me. The policeman on guard at the door

told me to go away. He needn't have, I was calm again. The shadow in the end is no better than the substance. I asked the man to help me, to have pity on me. He didn't understand. I thought of the food I had refused. I took a pebble from my pocket and sucked it. It was smooth, from having been sucked so long, by me, and beaten by the storm. A little pebble in your mouth, round and smooth, appeases, soothes, makes you forget your hunger, forget your thirst.[33]

There is none of the tenderness of Joyce's scene between Rudy and Bloom in Beckett's lonely Platonic projection of Molloy and his bicycle ornamented with a clown-like horn. For both Molloy and Michael, the practice of sucking on something inedible is pathetically infantilising. But while Molloy has wilfully refused food, Michael's hunger is an imposed and unjust punishment: a recognisable symptom of his destitution in the historical and social contexts of Edwardian London. Having left the west for a second time and escaped the furious circus family and blood relatives who have followed him to London, Michael describes a scene in a city park:

> I stopped at the park where the poor wretches lying on the grass had seemed like a diseased giant.
> They are still there. But this time I do not see them as black spots on the flesh of the giant. No, they are more like jelly-fish left on a beach by the tide. As if they had been waiting for a very long time for the tide to come in again and float them away. But are they really waiting for a tide? Hardly. They are, if truth be told, waiting for the coming of spring, the season of renewal and hope for the future. Waiting for the sun to restore warmth to their bones and for the coming of the season when they can again move freely around the country as independent as kings.
>
> (p. 145)

Mac Eoin negates the sprightliness of Ó Conaire's original sentence 'Is leis an earrach nuair a thiocfaidh brí agus spreacadh i ngach ní atá beo, atáid ag feitheamh', as he writes of the anticipated spring.[34] The result is a somewhat more factual account of the scene, which has its own correspondences with contemporary texts. As Mac Eoin renders it, Michael's temporary sympathy with this beached mass of the beastly poor recalls reports published as independent studies by journalists and philanthropists between the 1840s and 1930s such as *Starving London* (1886) by the German anatomist A.S. Krause, and press articles such as the *Daily Telegraph*'s 1904 series 'The Land of Starvation'. James Vernon considers Krause's work and the *Telegraph's* series as exemplary of what he terms the 'humanitarian discovery of hunger' over this period.[35] Within this phrase, there is certainly the suggestion that such a 'discovery' has something in common with those representations of otherness made by magazines such as *Punch*: what the eyewitness account saw in London's poor was at least fascinating and compelling, if not entertaining. Certainly, it sold newspapers.

As these accounts raised awareness of the social issues crippling England, Vernon argues that the country was increasingly well-prepared to watch with interest the 1905 and 1908 hunger marches during which thousands of men converged on London to speed the passage of more civilised and compassionate welfare legislation through the Parliament of Great Britain. Connecting the pageant-like spectacle of the hunger march with the political statements made later by hunger-striking Irish nationalists such as the Lord Mayor of Cork, Terence MacSwiney, Vernon contrasts 'the brutal inhumanity of a state prepared to allow its subjects to die' during the first decade of the supposedly 'modern' twentieth century with 'the willingness of the strikers to risk their own lives to further their claims of citizenship and independence'.[36] Michael is found to have lost the final vestiges of his independence in the postscript to *Exile*, which takes place in the same city park populated by the beastly poor. In the end, 'This poor man' is seen by a now-omniscient narrator as just another spot on the giant's flesh, having committed suicide beneath an English oak (p. 150).

Ellmann writes: 'Hunger is the traditional example Marxists use to show that human needs are shaped by human history rather than physiology alone.'[37] Ó Conaire's social awareness is clearly influenced by comparable ideologies. The trouble for his character Michael is that he is, perhaps, ahead of his time, and so struggles to elicit not just the curiosity, but the sympathy of his horrified audience. Vernon remarks that:

> it was not until after the Great War that the figure of the unemployed man moved to the center of ethnographic reports on hungry England; no longer needing a racialised other to prove their virtue as victims, at that point they became the regular human face of hunger in a way unimaginable in the 1880s.[38]

But hungry Michael is more problematic still. He signifies one of Carlyle's Milesians or the provincial hunger marcher: an Other who constitutes a physical manifestation of social, political and colonial discontent on the streets of London, within the centre of power. He is not the distant cause of humanitarian sympathy that Vernon describes in his analysis of news reports of the Irish Famine in 1840s England; his hunger is somehow a belated, immediate and premonitory confrontation of the continued failure of the state to sustain its not-always-willing subjects. Furthermore, the meaning of starvation varies as his character shuttles between geographic locations of modernity (London) and tradition (the west of Ireland). Other interpretations of Terence MacSwiney's hunger strike might help to assess the symbolic resonance of Michael's hunger. Paige Reynolds considers MacSwiney's experience as a playwright as preparatory for his role as political martyr as she explores what she describes as the 'revisionist depiction of the hunger strike' constructed by MacSwiney and his supporters.[39] Unlike previous acts of starvation in the Irish tradition that had been played out privately as devotions to a higher divine power, MacSwiney's widely publicised hunger strike was intended to cause political disturbance – but, Reynolds argues, it was not designed to attract the attention of the English government. Instead, MacSwiney was exploiting the spectacular potential of starvation to impress 'two audiences of his peers: the national public, who in modern times articulates its opinions through the press and shapes policy through the electorate, and an international public, who helped to fund and publicize the Irish quest for freedom'.[40] Ó Conaire stages Michael's hunger in *Exile* for similar reasons. The effect of his suffering is directed towards the national public in order to make them look critically at their own behaviour.

Through Michael's hunger, Ó Conaire once again returns his reader to nineteenth-century customs – not, this time, in a translation of a British literary classic, but instead to the folk memory of the Irish Famine. In the undated manuscript drafts of *Love of the Circus*, American circus enthusiast Townsend Walsh (1872–1935) details the Irish clown Johnny Patterson's travels with Coffey, 'the Skeleton Dude'. There is some confusion over Coffey's nationality, but his contemporary (and fan) Walsh is convinced that he was, like Patterson, a 'native of Erin'. Walsh records how lucrative Coffey's act was both within and without the ring:

> Patterson would walk him into the bar and introduce him to all assembled, 'Gentlemen, you see before you the thinnest mortal that walks in shoe leather. What'll ye have, ye spalpeen?' Then, after this informal 'opening', the place was theirs and they never had to pay for a drop of what they imbibed.[41]

Stewart Parker seems averse to this macabre idea in *Heavenly Bodies* (1986). His rendition of Johnny Patterson mentions his friend 'The Living Skeleton', and the playwright is alert to the symbolic possibilities realised in such a character. Parker makes a laboured pun on Coffey's name, transforming him into Mickey Coffin of County Clare, born not long before the Great Famine. Parker's Coffin, 'a vegetarian drinker' who will take anything liquid provided it is not nutritious milk or beef tea, turned to the art of hunger at the age of nine. By that time, Parker's Patterson states, 'all the other boys were dead of hunger'.[42] Mickey's exploitation of his critical position is almost Darwinian: he adapts to conditions and triumphs where the rest of his generation fail.

Hunger is not a source of entertainment for Michael, it is the source of bitter regret. It seems crass and profoundly distasteful to suggest that the continuing popularity of living skeletons resulted from a sense of wilful choice or ownership of starvation, or something like the damning idea that Kafka's circus audience has tired of the appearance of famished bodies 'in times like these'.[43] Perhaps the difference lies in the permissibility of the act of looking: the circus hunger artist might be observed for a fee, while compassion and common decency should prevent the gaze from settling on those who starve involuntarily. However, it has already been suggested that there is something compelling and popularising about mediated accounts of famine in the late nineteenth and early twentieth centuries. A similar transformation occurs in academic writing investigating the Irish Famine, the fulcrum about which Irish history turns in such enduringly influential studies as F.S.L. Lyons' *Ireland Since the Famine* (1971). Cormac Ó Gráda accounts for the impact of the Great Hunger upon social relations and family structures in his analysis of 'Amhrán an Ghorta' ('The Famine Song'), which was still popular in the Kerry town of Dingle in 1937, when de Valera's government officials travelled the country collecting family folk memories from children for national posterity. Ó Gráda explains how such songs 'suggest both resignation and resentment': there were no marriages or matches made; dowries were used instead to pay for migrant passage out of Ireland; young men 'lost their vigor', while female beauty went to waste; the country became one of 'old folk tending livestock in dewy fields'; ultimately, 'people hardly recognized one another anymore'.[44]

Certainly, there is something uncomfortably close to a lament for the Famine in Mac Eoin's translation of the one direct reference to that period in *Exile*. Michael studies his compatriots in the immigrant population of London:

> When I arrived among them, there were only about forty people among them still alive of those who had come from Ireland after the Great

Famine. Some of them had retained a knowledge of the Irish language, its stories and sagas, and there were good musicians among them. But they belonged to the past, and their children and grandchildren were little credit to them.

(p. 105)

The final sentence of this extract is, in the original, two sentences, reading: 'Ach bhí a ré beagnach thart. Bhí clann na scéalaithe agus na seanchaithe ann, bhí agus clann a gclainne, ach nár mhór an chreidiúint iad.' The first would, in its literal translation, sound somewhat kinder and gentler – 'But their era was almost passed' – anticipating the second sentence that subsequently reads more like free indirect discourse as we enter the minds of those who survived the Famine.[45] But Mac Eoin chooses to attribute these harsh sentiments to Michael, and from his translation it would seem that Ó Conaire participates in a cultural tradition that grieves for the fantasy of this disintegrated community. At once, Michael is brought closer to that generation of 'old folk' in his state of exile in London where he repeats the collective trauma of the 1840s. His chosen descriptors of Famine migrants' children and grandchildren reverberate with the most radical writings in defence of Irish heritage, but carry the idea of cultural nationalism into a disquieting racial commentary. These later generations are ignorant and negligent, allowing for the dissolution of their language and culture. Irishness is polluted through intermarriage, with the resultant exhibition of 'only the worst of their racial characteristics' (p. 105). This is the problem with cross-breeding 'animals', Michael explains, before adding disquietingly, 'Others, however, take the opposite view' (p. 105). Here, a family's encounters with hunger as history are not viewed as they are in 'A Hunger Artist', when the father lifts his children up to the performer's cage to illustrate the story of 'earlier years', thereby comforting them with the natural yet naïve promise 'that new and better times might be coming'.[46] Michael refutes the will to hope in his regard for subsequent generations. Such desolation might belong to Kafka, but the repulsive expression of the young man's nationalism is certainly not proper to that author. At once, it looks back and forward: to the nineteenth-century ethnographer and to the dominant, totalising political movements of the 1930s. Perhaps inadvertently, it was Ireland's ambiguous interaction with those movements that resulted in the quasi-Dickensian state of appalling, grasping poverty John Hinde witnessed in Dublin while on tour with Reco's Circus in 1944.

Wandering Sociologists and Political Rovers in 1930s Ireland

Arensberg and Kimball were sensitive to intergenerational dynamics when they observed an 'intermediate clique' of men gathered at the home of Joseph McMahon on the outskirts of the village of Rynamona, County Clare (p. 193). Nicknamed Oscair after the hero of Irish myth for his proven strength, McMahon occupied a peculiar position in Rynamona society: a rural carpenter of just over forty years of age, he lived, worked and socialised on a very small plot of land at a distance from the centre of the community; as Arensberg and Kimball instruct, a plot that would have been termed an 'interstitial area' (p. 191) in urban sociology. A group of seven men aged between thirty-five and sixty collected around him, apparently drawn to Oscair's house by his reputation as a good singer, a jokester, and a repository of folk tales. However, the sociologists surmised that these men in fact came to Oscair because of their social status. They observed that they were all landless and could not, therefore, attain the full status of the 'small farmer'. Arensberg and Kimball realised through their interviews that Oscair's house was 'a sort of catchall for those whose position in Rynamona was not clearly defined [...] a halfway stage in their advance from the status of young men to that of old' (p. 193). For that reason, the attitude of the old men of the group towards its younger members was obviously irritable, if not hostile: they were regarded as 'transitory', 'impermanent' and 'unimportant' (p. 193). Moreover, the younger generations seemed subject constantly to 'codology' or codding, a colloquialism for hoaxing or humbugging (p. 193). While some members of this group came and went, sloughing off past habits of behaviour as they moved up the social ranks through the acquisition of land by marriage or inheritance, others remained with Oscair, the permanent centre of that shanty community. For Oscair was a 'playboy', and could never expect to advance beyond this social position (p. 194). His mythic identity thereby assumes another order of significance. Oscair, son of Oisín and Tir na nÓg's Queen Niamh, issues from the Land of Eternal Youth. Less fantastically, this twentieth-century man seems to be stuck at a point of arrested social development.

Arensberg and Kimball explain exactly the situation of men like Oscair:

> In the identifications of Irish familism, they were condemned to celibacy. Neither could feel comfortable in the old men's *cuaird*. There was no place for them except, as Oscair's behaviour showed, as playboys and entertainers. So they too must occupy an interstice in the structural alignments of rural social life.
>
> (p. 194)

Comparably, circus entertainers in Ireland found themselves pushed to the margins during the 1920s and 1930s, especially those performers who continued to travel over from England as per the norm of earlier decades. In the 1870s, Thomas Frost recorded the difficulty of managing Dublin audiences bent on rioting where 'grounds for manifestations of national antipathies between English and Irish' were identified in the circus acts performed.[47] In the 1920s, it seems that it was almost impossible to manage political tensions revealed by an English troupe's arrival on the Irish scene. Madame Clara Paulo – a pioneer, as one of only a few women owners in English circus history – recalled the violent reaction to her family's show. She and her husband Frank Paulo joined Buff Bill's Menagerie and first visited Ireland during the Great War. 'Frisco Frank', master of a fortune-telling pony, and Clara, a wire-walker, founded their own circus while still in the country.[48] Their early experiences were characterised by financial hardship and open hostility towards them as English performers. They began showing their limited acts at the interstices of crossroads, supplementing their acrobatics with amusements more commonly found at country fairs: a hoop-la and a gun stall. On Sundays, they benefited from the popularity of donkey and pony races. These crossroads cannot be compared to those romantic and lively meeting places that de Valera was (incorrectly) supposed to have imagined for political purposes in 'On Language and the Irish Nation, or, The Ireland That We Dreamed Of' (1943).[49] Instead, these circus exiles strove for community assimilation through hard physical graft. The couple made enough from their performances to buy a small tent which was erected in more central locations in and around County Cork. However, circus historians Rupert Croft-Cooke and Peter Cotes describe vividly – and partially – how this attempt to settle more permanently angered the local community:

> The southern Irish hated the English and although they usually had a soft heart for the circus folk, after one performance bricks were thrown at the tent and at Cork a gang broke in and wrecked everything. The tent was beyond repair, it had to be abandoned and the old life of performing at crossroads resumed.[50]

The poverty resulting from the family's dislocation from Irish society in the early 1920s led Madame Paulo to the Blarney Castle in the days after her daughter was born. Mother, with baby strapped to her, hung over the castle parapets to kiss the famous stone and wish her child should never join a circus.[51]

Political cartoons and posters of the 1920s and 1930s perpetuated this demoralising impression of the circus and other popular entertainments. These forms became a means of belittlement for major parties seeking to lead Ireland after the Anglo-Irish and civil wars. Resultant images and texts look back to Lynd's 1907 postcard of John Bull at his famous circus, but rather than pitching Ireland against England, these satires instead illustrate tensions internal to the Irish Free State. This renewed exchange perhaps began in 1922 when nationalist revolutionary and Fianna Fáil MP Constance Markievicz produced an etching of Cumann na nGaedheal's accidental leader, W.T. Cosgrave:

2.3 Constance Markievicz, 'Comic Cosgrave', 1922, Etching, National Library of Ireland

The simplicity of the original etching's reproduction (see Fig. 2.3) suggests a limited circulation. Cosgrave is diminished in miniature, sitting in an impish cross-legged pose on an ornate, throne-like chair. He holds up a card printed on the backside with a Union Jack in a gesture that suggests an oath is being sworn. This pose is reminiscent of how Johnny Patterson's final performance of 'Do Your Best for One Another' in May 1889 might have been staged: the clown supposedly waving an Irish flag in one hand and an English flag in the other. A pathetically decent collar and tie peak from beneath the foolish garments of: 'Comic Cosgrave. Jester in Chief to the Freak State. As Seen in the Empire'. Markievicz's drawing returns us to the tension central to the idea of Michael's freakishness in *Exile*: that to be a freak is to be half the man you once were physically, but to be double in the sense of duplicity. As the Irish jester brandishing the Union Jack, Cosgrave appears to be a kind of double agent. Dwarfed by the symbol on which he sits, his exaggerated features render the diminutive figure idiotic and recollect centuries of English political cartoon Irishmen – witness Tenniel's anarchic monster. The artist's typewritten caption reads: 'Comic Cosgrave tells us that it is a short step from the bar to a Judge's chair. We ask him was it a big jump from behind the bar to the President's chair?' The inference of image and text is roundly an ugly one, bringing to bear social as well as political tensions in its implicit comments on pedigrees of colony, race and class. The dominant metaphor – politician as jester or clown – slots it into a developing tradition of satiric propaganda that spoke to a wider audience as it looked beyond the solo performer to the world of the fool.

Ten years later, Cumann na nGaedheal artists parodied the 'Fianna Fallacy Puppet Show' (Fig. 2.4). The show's protagonist, de Valera, was seen to cause Machiavellian strife between two political forces by then subordinate to the republican movement. The discord between the beleaguered Labour movement and the defunct National League is figured as ridiculous, as their leaders take on the roles of pugilist Punch and shrewish Judy in order to personify the dangers posed to Irish peace and prosperity by a Fianna Fáil victory.

This poster was one of a series of designs by artists working for Cumann na nGaedheal that were intended to capture the popular imagination, and the popular vote, during the 1932 General Election. Another prime example is 'Devvy's Circus' (Fig. 2.5).

Structurally, this mock-up circus poster has much in common with Robert Lynd's 1907 cartoon. It declares sarcastically that Devvy's Circus is 'absolutely the greatest road show in Ireland to-day!' Fianna Fáil candidates are cast as slippery and inconstant in their political performances. De Valera is introduced as the Spanish Senor, a 'world-famous illusionist, oath swallower and escapologist', while his apprentice Seán Lemass is reimagined as a French acrobat who nightly performs a daring tight-rope walk, crossing 'from the Treaty to the Republic'. Other leading figures in the party are billed as fire-eaters who make faces at the circus' British lion, quick-change artists who switch social class at the drop of a top hat, and fortune tellers who tell only of misfortunes. In the end, the election itself is seen to be as predictable as a lucky dip – 'if it comes off, that is', the poster artist quips.

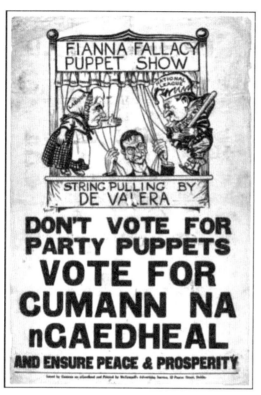

2.4 Artist unknown, 'Fianna Fallacy Puppet Show', 1932, Poster, National Library of Ireland

2.5 Artist unknown, 'Devvy's Circus', 1932, Poster, National Library of Ireland

Despite the imaginative ingenuity of Cumann na nGaedheal's poster designers and artists, Fianna Fáil secured their first electoral victory in the 1932 general election. De Valera thus became President of the Executive Council of the Irish Free State, an office he held until the Republic of Ireland was constituted in 1937 and his role metamorphosed into that of Taoiseach. It was, then, through the western counties of de Valera's Ireland that the English artist Edward Seago travelled with Paddy O'Flynn. Elements of Irish social life and Irish circus life glimpsed in the accounts of Arensberg, Kimball and Clara Paulo are identifiable in Seago's memoir of this journey, which began as Ireland geared up for the 1932 election campaign.

The External Observer: Edward Seago, English Literature, and Irish Culture

Edward Seago was captivated by the circus as a young artist. In the late 1920s and early 1930s, he travelled Britain, Ireland and the continent with a number of troupes, producing records of these journeys in sketches, paintings and prose. Critic Horace Shipp suggests that, in this way, Seago was (unusually for him) very much *à la mode*: painters including Steven Spurrier, Augustus John and Laura Knight were all drawn to the circus as subject. Writing in 1952, Shipp insists on associating Seago with other artists in order to position him as 'the expression in our time of the great fundamental English tradition'.[52] For Shipp, this tradition had been passed down from Nicholas Hilliard to William Hogarth to Joshua Reynolds to John Constable and on to Edward Seago; and tradition, in relation to Seago's individual talent, is defined by the critic as a 'belief that the basis of painting is visual – a recording of what the eye sees'.[53] This may well be true of Seago's canvases: the landscapes and seascapes that won, and continue to win, him Royal patronage.[54] However, there is arguably far less objective accuracy in his style as an illustrator as it is in evidence in his circus travel journals, *Circus Company* (1933) and *Sons of Sawdust* (1934). Most often, Seago's pencil sketches are placid and sentimental illustrations such as that of Paddy O'Flynn reproduced at Fig. 2.6. These illustrations have more in common with, for instance, those made by the forgotten commercial artist Nemo for *The Circus: a delightful day with the circus folk* (196–?) in the familiar style of 1960s children's picture books.[55] By way of contrast, there is nothing of the personality or intensity that characterises the frankly executed showman's portraits made by Jack Yeats early in his career as a painter: *The Circus Dwarf* (1912) might be considered exemplary of his style during a transitional period

2.6 Edward Seago, 'Paddy O'Flynn', 1934, Reproduction of pencil sketch, in *Sons of Sawdust*. The caption reads: 'Smile at us, pay us, pass us. But do not quite forget.'

between illustrating and painting.[56] In an odd way, Seago's circus art might have more in common with that of later Yeats, whose increasingly abstract circus images experiment with form and colour, and assume allegorical and symbolic resonance through allusive titles, or those that are personally expressive, such as *Alone* (1948): a canvas painted after the death of his wife Cottie, in which a solitary figure is seen in the midst of a collapsed circus tent. Similarly, one might say of Seago's circus illustrations that they are not so much visual, but instead particular visions of that world refracted through a romantic sensibility.

Seago wrote *Circus Company* after touring England with Sanger's Circus. John Masefield suggests in his introduction to the work that this is *the* definitive account of circus life, since it demystifies and de-romanticises that way of life. If we accept Masefield's celebration of the 'reality' of Seago's prose as well-founded, then the artist's writing about the circus performs a rather different function to his paintings and drawings of the circus. But his descriptions of Irish characters work to challenge the basis of Masefield's appreciation for *Circus Company*. In the course of the book, Seago becomes especially close to the Dales, a family of horsemen from Sligo, and it might be supposed that it is from the Dales that

Seago learns that '[a] famous clown of former days was Johnny Patterson'.[57] The artist records, as best he can remember, two of Patterson's songs that he has been taught, both of which demonstrate that 'Patterson was evidently a patriot, for most of his songs were of his Motherland and full of pride of Irish hearts'.[58] In such passages, we see Seago's visionary, rather than visual, sense creep into his prose. His rather clumsily expressed fascination with – at times, fetishisation of – Irish culture and Irish politics, which centres in *Circus Company* on the Dale family and figures like Johnny Patterson, is carried forward into his next work, *Sons of Sawdust*. Views of circuses pitched in pastoral England are replaced with images of a troupe camped beside 'wild open bogs ooz[ing] with romance, and fairy lights twink[ling] in the hills'.[59] And that troupe just so happens to belong to an ailing clown who – apparently unbeknownst to Seago – shares his name with W.B. Yeats' Teller of Tales in *The Celtic Twilight* (1893; 1902), little bright-eyed Paddy Flynn.

Like *Circus Company*, the mode of *Sons of Sawdust* appears initially to be simultaneously biographic and ethnographic; the aim is to create a faithful rendition of the circus' route through the west of Ireland. Seago is careful to record the ways in which life on the road is regulated and expressed. He includes a glossary of the key circus terms that pepper the text, and phonetic spellings of how words are pronounced in Irish accents – for instance, the name of his close friend, circus clown and trick rider Sean O'Leary is rendered as 'Sarn' (p. 9). Seago explains the acts that take place, and the order of shows that always end with the Irish national anthem. He details how failing circus programmes are necessarily supplemented with other entertainments, in much the same way as Paulo's resorted to hoop-las and pony races. Boxing matches contested by local youths turn circus proprietor and principal clown Paddy O'Flynn into another kind of ringmaster, while O'Flynn's relatives manage a circus-cum-travelling cinema. This forerunner to John Hinde's Circorama screens cowboy films in canvas sheds, 'rather like that of a lion show on a fairground', to musical accompaniment ranging from 'Land of Hope and Glory' to a modern ragtime (pp. 140–1). It is possible to see in this instance the failure of the live circus to capture and maintain the audience imagination in an age of newly technical media. In this way, there are comparisons to be drawn with 'A Hunger Artist'. The panther overtook the human performer in Kafka's story; in *Sons of Sawdust*, the human story told through the film projector is captivating when seen in the lion's shed. Looking ahead in British modernist literature, Seago's anachronistically jukebox-like circus gramophone might be interpreted as a prototype of Miss La Trobe's chuffing sound system in Virginia Woolf's *Between the Acts* (1941).

Seago also reveals how circus performers are sought and engaged by troupes on the road as he records the placing of an advertisement for a ground act in the showman's journal, the *World's Fair*. A young man turns up in answer to the advert, dressed and behaving in a manner that further proves that the American West was then in vogue in western Ireland. The aspiring ground act claims to be fresh out of Buffalo Bill's Stateside circus, 'an it's no more genuine son of Mexico ever walked into the ring!' (p. 166). Seago's response to this young man continues to develop confused ideas of racial difference: 'I nearly laughed, for never could one wish to see a more pukka true-born Irishman, whose tongue rolled round the country' (p. 166). There are, then, three nationalities implicated in the ground act's interview with Paddy O'Flynn and the troupe's reception of that performance. The phony Mexican and the true Irishman are immediately obvious; the colonial Indian is also seen in the term 'pukka': with its origins in Hindi and Panjabi, the word has been a colloquialism in English for the real and the genuine since the eighteenth century, increasing in popularity in the early twentieth century. Given this linguistic mix, there is something almost tautological to Seago's insistence upon the young man's homogenous nationality. The artist seeks to expose the artifice of the exoticised circus persona in order to reinforce his own typical notions of such foolish Irishmen with nonetheless poetic brogues spoken by tongues that alliteratively 'roll round the country' and who are presumably, like Patterson, 'full of the pride of Irish hearts'.[60]

Colonial India is suggested earlier in *Sons of Sawdust* – a text in which the English–Irish dynamic is but one example of international interplay. The work deals casually with racial difference at many levels, and often unconsciously. At times, the well-meaning English observer comes out with some reflections on circus life and circus characters that would cause discomfort in readers today. His story begins in Liverpool before his passage on a steam packet to Ireland with Sean. The men lodge with mutual friend Black Alfred, who is described as 'woolly-headed', 'as black as coal' and 'with the whitest eyes and teeth' Seago has ever seen (p. 16). Meanwhile, his home furnishings are considered independently of any racial difference and viewed as typical of his class: there are the 'usual yellow lace curtains, and in between them the eternal aspidistra' (p. 17). Seago and Sean spend a contented evening with Alfred, who puts Sophie Tucker on the gramophone, makes Indian curry for supper, and boasts that he once served a cup of coffee to the Prince of Wales. These are less fraught renditions of the kind of racial confusion which afflicts Michael in *Exile* when, in the public house scene, he becomes George Coff, the fantastic German killer of East African lions who, in fact, speaks Irish in a London public house. Jumbles of nationalities exhibited through characters such as the Mexican-Irish-American ground act and Black Alfred are comparable to the garbled gramophone's assorted accompaniments for the *Sons of Sawdust* talking picture show, but the author seems to be unaware of assembling his own Great Exhibition in such a telling catalogue of colonialism.

Post-colonial Ireland is Seago's main subject and he demonstrates that a circus would need to be careful when and where it played such tunes as 'Land of Hope and Glory'. The English artist sees Ireland from the outset as 'a land of mysteries (and certain solid facts where politics were concerned!)' (p. 13). Seago is keen to prove and maintain his ignorance of these parenthetical 'facts' when speaking to a village shopkeeper in County Kerry. The puzzle is an important metaphor for Seago in this episode. When pressed by the shopkeeper for an explanation of why he might be in that part of the country – 'maybe it's politics, or the like of which, that is occupyin' of your mind?' – Seago's anxious response casts the Irish question as 'rather a puzzle', and certainly one which he is not keen to solve (p. 62). Arensberg and Kimball flattered their own personification of Ireland in saying that the country 'really has no need of people to represent her' (p. xxv). Seago, meanwhile, wishes to avoid any impression that he might speak on behalf of those better placed to understand 'her'.

Seago's awareness of the 'solidity' and 'factuality' of Irish politics derives, in part, from certain testing experiences on the road with Paddy O'Flynn. One night in Connemara, clods of turf and stones are hurled at the circus wagons by incensed locals who believe from the red, white and blue circus bills innocently posted around the village that an English circus has come to town; the barrage takes on 'the character of machine-gun fire' (p. 151). The notion of audible difference and the role of sound-sense in creating one's identity or moments of identification are important here, though ultimately ineffective. Paddy O'Flynn and Sean O'Leary attempt to calm the crowd down with calls out of the wagon, in their Irish accents, protesting that: 'It's a show what's proud to belong to the old county, and sure it's Ireland herself what should be proud to have it on her roads' (p. 147). Regardless, the Irish show looked 'English' to the crowd. This body of locals maintains the sense that the circus is different whatever the accent of its defenders might indicate about national identity. They refuse to disperse until the simile of machine-gun fire is outperformed by the single blast of Paddy's shotgun.

Seago's Ireland is not characterised as culturally diverse. Nor, intriguingly, is the landscape differentiated to mark out one village, town or strip of road from another. As in *Exile*, these descriptions are refracted through earlier versions of similar stories. Explicitly, epigraphs for each chapter are taken from the work of poets including William Blake, William Cowper and George Meredith. Lines from 'Songs of Innocence: A Dream' (1789), 'A Review of Schools' (1822) (incorrectly attributed by Seago to Percy Shelley) and 'Dirge in the Woods' (1887) which depict an interrupted, perturbed pastoral co-ordinate to produce a sense of reckless travellers moving through, and at the mercy of, a sublime Irish landscape. Taken together, these epigraphs read like a polite anthology of nineteenth-century English verse. There is, though, a conspicuous lack of Irish writing. It seems, then, that Seago is full of the pride of English hearts and lends his country's culture in support of the Irish circus stories he tells.

As a young man, the painter knew no greater pleasure than to imagine himself into a community by watching, following and painting a meet of hounds; as an established artist, he was favoured by King George VI.[61] However, it is essential to note that a reader's apprehension of Seago's expression of his own 'Englishness' is founded on conscious fictions. He records in *Circus Company*:

> Nothing gave me more pleasure than to go to a meet of hounds. These were often within a few miles, and whenever possible I followed them in a car. In the evening I would go for a long tramp round the dark narrow lanes, and my imagination would carry me again through the day's hunting, when I myself was taking part on a bold young thoroughbred to finish well up at the front at the end of a glorious gallop. In such runs I frequently put my horse at colossal fences, and even on occasion would actually collar the stag. But at the end of the nightly ramble I would return with a bump to solid facts, and realise that my only way to master bold blood-horses and fearsome objects was on canvas.[62]

Again, Seago introduces the notion of solidity into his project as an artist. It is instructive to reconceive this realisation in relation to *Sons of Sawdust*, which is not a work on canvas but a written work with literary aspirations that imaginatively situates the genial Englishman among full-hearted Irish subjects.

In addition to the poetic epigraphs, Seago appears to draw upon another literary genre to create his sensational images of Ireland. Travel writings by Englishmen visiting the country in the nineteenth century are not directly referenced, but are nonetheless echoed in Seago's prose. As he paints in the attitude of his time the Irish people he observes, there is a certain amount of Anthony Trollope's patronising benevolence towards the native population. At these moments, tone and matter jar. Trollope's 'very jolly life' in Ireland and his very English relief that '[t]he Irish people did not murder me, nor did they even break my head' are accounted for in *An Autobiography* (1853), and these phrases might belong to Seago.[63] Author-artist William Makepeace Thackeray's illustrated refutation of twee and fruity tourist guidebooks, *The Irish Sketch Book 1842* (1843), is perhaps another influence. Thackeray's critical observations are recalled in the twentieth-century artist's description of the same desolate, bone-shaking roads between western towns. This is a locale that both men find, at times, supremely depressing. Thackeray describes the rural environs of the Kerry towns:

> As far as the country went, there was here, to be sure, not much to be said. You pass through a sad-looking, bare, undulating country, with few trees, and poor stone hedges, and poorer crops; nor have I yet taken in Ireland so dull a ride. About half way between Tralee and Killarney is a wretched town, where houses are changed, and where I saw more hideous beggary than anywhere else, I think. And I was glad to get over this gloomy tract of country, and enter the capital of Kerry.[64]

Similarly, Seago considers the road from Kenmare to Tralee as uncommonly rough. Arensberg and Kimball explain that, in Clare, 'roads determine the intercourse of the communities with one another' (p. 278). By this logic, the state of the roads that Seago travels would suggest that there has been some breakdown in communication between communities. This sense is reinforced by the landmarks picked out by the artist: headstones in the chapel graveyard are 'scarcely distinguishable among the rocks', while the curlew cries mournfully overhead (p. 81). A glaring mother and her brood of screaming children regard Paddy O'Flynn's Circus with intense hostility from the doorway of the family dwelling: she stands in this barren place like a desexualised and uninviting relative of Davin's lonely cottage woman in Joyce's *A Portrait of the Artist as a Young Man* (1916). At the end of the road, Tralee itself is a real let-down for Seago: 'a low-lying, semi-industrial place, with very little poetic glamour' (p. 134).

But although Seago might be seen to participate in a tradition to which Thackeray's sketchbook belongs, he certainly diverges from its tone in his careful and attentive descriptions of the people the troupe pass on the road. Thackeray indiscriminately subjects the inhabitants of Tralee to cruel caricature. Comparatively moderate portrayals of Catholic worshippers on Assumption Day, 1842, have them 'moaning' and 'tossing' in an unforgettably 'strange, wild scene, so entirely different [...] from the decent comfortable observances of our own church'.[65] More grotesquely, the nineteenth-century observer lists a cast of freakish, beastly characters encountered in the next town over, Listowel:

the epileptic idiot, the old man with no eyelids, the woman with a child at her 'hideous, wrinkled breast' and the children without number belong in Joyce's Nighttown and not at Paddy's Circus.[66] The difference in Seago's observational prose style is clearly illustrated in his treatment of the Catholic pilgrims he sees on mountainsides around the Galway village of Kilcolgan. The group includes women in standard red petticoats and black shawls, who are accompanied by bushy-eyebrowed men with the lower flaps of their jackets unbuttoned to show their belt buckles. The men's rough-skinned hands have broken fingernails, and their leather-laced boots are well-worn. Courting couples climb the hill together with fingers 'tightly locked' (p. 142).

These simply composed sketches of Seago's fellow travellers have more in common with the pen-and-ink written and drawn studies made by J.M. Synge and Jack Yeats as they travelled Wicklow, west Kerry and Connemara in 1905. Some of Seago's passing wayfarers belong to towns and villages to which, apparently, circuses had not ventured for years. One of those towns is Dingle, where Synge records how even a shabby circus brought in the punters on the stormy night that he and Jack Yeats spent in that same town. People from across the surrounding countryside press into the precariously constructed circus tent, and by the time the performance begins, Synge remembered that: 'The crowd was now so thick I could see little more than the heads of the performers, who had at last come into the ring, and many of the shorter women who were near me must have seen nothing the whole evening, yet they showed no sign of impatience.'[67] He continues to describe the acts: 'gymnasts', the 'gaudy horse-woman' and 'the usual dirty white horse', and the clown who came out 'to the great delight of the people'.[68] When Paddy's troupe arrives in Dingle, where 'Ireland seemed to come to an end' for Seago (p. 105), the clown believes that 'they'll not be expecting much in this part of the world' and so his small and fading show will do well there, since it was 'a better show than Dingle had seen for a good many years' (p. 109). But it would seem that the poor show put on by the sons of sawdust could not even measure up to the muddy, gaudy, grubby and rowdy performance which Synge and Yeats had attended two decades earlier. Paddy fails to delight Dingle and his indifferent audience deters those bystanders loitering outside the tent, who look on with the same disappointed attitude as their donkeys (p. 110). People and animals alike seem, to Seago at least, paralysed by poverty and isolation. In his mind, the country around him shares his perspective: watchful hills do not stare blankly – worse still, menacingly – in the manner of the eye-like windows in Ó Conaire's beastly London. Instead, they emulate his inquisitive concern as he looks upon a pathetic group of internal migrant workers:

> I had grown to love Ireland more and more. Yet it was a sad country, and the stark little tragedy which I could see going on before me made it sadder still. Those great rugged hills were sad … the winds which of a night-time whistled over the bog were sad. And they were sad-eyed little donkeys which loitered by the road. Once in a while we passed a jaunting car, with a load of huddled figures, their backs to each other, and their legs covered in a long black rug. When they came to a hill, most of the passengers would dismount and ease the burden of the raw-boned leggy horse.
>
> (p. 91)

In this passage, the Milesian poverty which so panicked Carlyle on the roads of England in 1843 is seen in its original setting. There is no meaningful confrontation between the observer and his individuated subjects; what Seago sees are faceless forms. As in *Hard Times*, sympathy goes to the personified animal that betrays the suffering of the human subject: the knackered 'raw-boned leggy horse' duly, and dully, remembers the Jupes' performing dog Merrylegs as it is commanded to work for the impersonal 'figures' or 'passengers'. Broadly, the English artist's assumption of a critical position in relation to this group of huddled figures is problematic. When he gives his eyes to the Irish landscape so that it might see the 'little tragedy' going on before him, the scene takes on the atmosphere of performance. The migrant workers are showmen on the road appealing to the interest of audiences against the backdrop of Romantic scenery, just like the circus within which this external observer has situated himself.

Meanwhile, Ireland's internal exiles – Paddy O'Flynn and his performers – see things quite differently. From their perspective, the peasant Irish are grotesque. The limited expectations of entertainment-starved Dingle are temperate examples of how Paddy and Sean sometimes cast their audiences. Paddy considers the Kerry people as generally mean, attempting to gain admission to the circus with old eggs rather than money. Under pressure, their views of the peasantry are far more extreme. When barefooted women and unkempt men shake their fists and stone Paddy's wagons, Sean returns a clod of earth forcibly, crying: 'Keep yer bloody country to yourselves […] I'm thinkin' that it's youse guys what makes me wish I didn't belong to it' (p. 89). When the crowd in Connemara first pipe up and the civic guard refuses to defend the circus, Paddy exclaims: 'So they won't give an honest Irishman protection against a pack of ignorant, turf-cuttin' tadpoles!' (p. 144). There are, then, degrees of Irishness, which depend on honesty, integrity and verifiability. It is therefore fitting that Paddy's sentiments should resonate with the tone of Old

Mahon's final lines in Synge's *The Playboy of the Western World* (1907) as he says to his story-telling son: 'we'll have great times from this out telling stories of the villainy of Mayo and the fools is here'.[69] In this way, the record of perspectives in Seago's journal works to invert the perspective of the Cumann na nGaedheal election poster 'Devvy's Circus'. The rural shopkeeper and the peasant farmer who Arensberg and Kimball took as representative of all Ireland are regarded contradistinctively by this Irish circus: they are underdeveloped, uncivilised and 'primitive' (p. 271).

Seago explains that, in the eyes of the rural population, the circus folk are no-good mountebanks and vagabonds. It is not just himself as Englishman, but the whole troupe that is considered a race apart – indeed, his title has it that they are mythically born of the showground sawdust. Arensberg and Kimball reinforce the notion that a wanderer's ties with the town force him down to the position of an 'outcast lowest class' (p. 272). Significantly, Arensberg and Kimball reserve their individuated character sketches for Oscair's partially outcast crew of transitory playboys. Seago gives the same attention to his travelling players, and the group portrait of Paddy O'Flynn's Circus offers a family construction of sorts. Though his main character is the road, Seago – like Ó Conaire, but on less extreme terms – organises his plot around family stories that branch off that narrative through-line, and in consequence, the sense of structure Anne Byrne has given Arensberg and Kimball's family study might be applied to *Sons of Sawdust*. Like the sociologists, Seago reveals 'a story, chapter by chapter, of the importance and centrality of the family [...] which produced and reproduced a self-sufficient, traditional rural community'.[70]

There are two kinds of family for the members of Paddy O'Flynn's Circus: their circus kin and their blood relations. David Herlihy defined the family as a group of people who eat together; Seago's circus life-writing might be offered in support of that definition.[71] In *Circus Company*, the final notice of Seago's long-awaited assimilation into the Sanger's community is served when the Dales of Sligo welcome him into their wagon for afternoon tea. In *Sons of Sawdust*, journeying, hard work and show times are broken up by frequent communal meals – always, it would seem, of cheese and onions – prepared by the troupe's substitute mother, the 'knock-about, good-hearted slut' Amy (p. 36). The family lives of the members of Paddy O'Flynn's crew are used to celebrate the alternative structures provided by the travelling show. So too are their love lives and romances. Cheese-and-onions Amy, for instance, has less escaped than disposed of a violent husband to join the company. Although their ways of living are notably unconventional, Seago realises that they are ordered by a strong moral sense that is seen to surpass social codes governing normal life. Sean has a particularly pronounced sense of decency, despite indulging his young man's prerogative to fool around with 'ordinary tart(s)' until he finds himself a good wife (p. 52). This is revealed in his attitude towards Paddy's nephew, Frankie Mulligan, who has ridden a bicycle for eighty miles from his mother's circus to escape his young wife and child. Sean considers his actions unmanly and 'hathen', and longs to correct Frankie's behaviour through violence (p. 68). The suggested act reorganises the gruesome tableau that Ó Conaire's Michael sees polluting the snow of a London street. In *Exile*, it is the father who dashes out the brains of his wife and child; in *Sons of Sawdust* the father himself is the object of violence in Sean's grotesque fantasy of graphic punishment which further binds food and family life: 'I'd like to get that bleeder on the ground, and fake his blasted head till I'd got enough of his brains to make a sauce for me dinner' (p. 68). Sean's social sense motivates his violence towards Frankie, the transgressor of communally defined decency. He can afford to go to extremes in this imaginary act and prove himself victorious by eating out the brains of his opponent like some mythic hero. There is, after all, 'a great gap between a gallous story and a dirty deed'.[72]

Seago's family stories of blood relatives frequently tell of lost loves and frustrated or troubled relationships. At times, they reveal a painful sense of dislocation, not only from the circus company, but also from the wider community. The First World War has unexpected resonance at these sad moments. Paddy O'Flynn, illiterate and 'illegitimate son of an "Irish gent"' and a 'true-born show-woman', lives a bachelor life in the wagon in which he was born and runs the circus he inherited from his adoptive father (p. 55). Single now, he was once attached to a circus girl who made him a mock-military jacket to perform in as proof of her fondness; but, like Ó Conaire's Mary Lee, she went on to marry another. When the circus pulls into Dingle on Armistice Day, Paddy remembers not only his own four years of service in the trenches, but also the mother of that young woman who lost two sons in the conflict. The death of her boys sent her to the asylum, and Paddy recalls how one day she raved at the injustice of it all to a country policeman:

'Everyone was talkin' of "remembrance", and "honour the glorious dead". What have I got to remember?' she said. 'Our men … nice bloody men some of 'em was. They took me sons an' left me, an old woman tearin' her hair out, with seventeen entire horses on her hands. Aye, and they said they'd take me wagons an' all … an' I got an extra shot in, an' if they'd come any more I'd have shot every God damn one of the bastards.'

(p. 104)

The impact of the First World War is emphasised in many accounts of British circus life. Violet Sandow describes how the circus cheated the army in her interview for Barbara Gibson's *Oral History of the Circus* (2001):

> 'they', the government people, just took men to sign up. They took the horses too. V[iolet] recalls how the Dick Turpin horse was taught to go lame. When they came to look at the horses they insisted on looking at this horse, and after 'cue' it became lame. Of course they did not want this horse. Meant V[iolet]'s (maternal) grandfather had a horse left.[73]

This process of requisitioning is accounted for in Seago's record of an Irishwoman's experience. The mother turns violently on the state as it intervenes in the management of her own estate as she manages her grief. Her concern is not with debunking those old myths of 'glory' and 'honour'. Instead, her anxieties are far more local and personal, as the dissolution of her family occurs in a shocking instant. She becomes like one of Arensberg and Kimball's 'incomplete farm families', who are 'felt to be departures from the normal; they are subjects for commiseration' (p. 67). Despite the massive responsibility for circus livestock she is forced to take on, her instinct is to rail against any social definition of victimhood and preserve what remains – the wagons in which they live and work – to constitute the memory of lost family.

Under the leadership of de Valera, the Irish government enacted the Constitution of the Republic of Ireland in 1937. At Article 41, the Constitution recognises the family as the fundamental unit of Irish society, the basis for social order, and superior to positive law as a moral institution. De Valera's government was, therefore, the first to guarantee the protection of that social and moral institution. In Seago's pen portrait, circus performer Sean is ahead of his time in his conviction that the boundaries of the near-sacred family structure must be diligently policed. However, Sean also appears to be acutely aware of moments at which the state itself might damage the distinctive ways of his family life. The O'Learys were divided and dispersed over the British Isles when their own circus broke up: Sean and his brother Derry shuttle between England and Ireland; his sister Molly performs as a revue girl in the north of England; his parents have settled in south London. According to Seago, Sean dreams of bringing his family back together in his own small show; he would paint his name on the side of the wagons to prove that the circus belonged to him. Sean becomes inextricable from the show, and the show from his native land, as he imagines a means of perpetuating the family line in some sort of social centrifuge: 'A tiny speck, on a scrap of land, in a vast world of conflict, and that speck would settle, and grow, and gather other specks around it' (p. 53). However, Sean is reportedly convinced that the family cannot be reunited or thrive in Ireland at that moment because of the puzzling political situation. Awkwardly, Englishman Seago adopts Irishisms as he ventriloquises Sean's concerns:

> He knew that his country was in a queer state, to say the least of it, and had vivid memories of the days when it had been even more disturbed. He knew the plight of the travelling showman at such a time, and he wondered if that time might come shortly again. He remembered, too, seeing his cousin brought from a wagon and made to walk along a wall while a body of men took shots at him. Surprisingly enough, that cousin was still alive ... but he was a crippled man, and had never walked again.
>
> (p. 27)

This recollection of brutality – perhaps at the hands of the infamous Black and Tans; perhaps at the hands of guerrilla fighters during Ireland's civil war – speaks plainly of the impact of Anglo-Irish relations on the circus performer's body, and is therefore distinct from the symbolic creation of Ó Conaire's crippled circus freak, Michael, out of a motor car accident in London. Sean's concern for the preservation of his family is at the root of this memory, and it is the foreboding sense of the family unit's temporariness and vulnerability that overarches *Sons of Sawdust*.

Arensberg and Kimball recognise that 'Irish behaviour is deeply influenced by beliefs in the inevitability of supernatural rewards and punishments' (p. 391). It was also evident to the Irish that transgression against religious sanctions was thought to bring 'disaster' (p. 393). Seago records the close intertwining of Catholic religion and folk superstition in the imagination of his subjects. These social orders are most closely bound in Sean's mind: he is convinced that they travel the road only thanks to the gracious permission of Ireland's original indigenous race, the Little People. An early sketch of Sean's moral and philosophical self progresses through stages of established religion, secular faith and pre-Christian beliefs: the sketch unravels a sense of universal communal practice, only to be wound up again through Seago's reconstruction of his national identity. The portrait moves from the young man's great respect for Catholicism and curiosity in all world religions, to his idea of an agnostic after-life as real and physical as the travelling show (white-robed angels throng with a gathering of dogs, horses and other circus companions), before mention is made of one of his greatest fears: the cry of the banshee.

Seago deals rambunctiously with Sean's other side: his 'wild charm' and
'Irish temper' that prove '[t]he blood of his country flowed through his veins,
and the speech that came from his tongue' (p. 54). Again, the voice is signal of
an individual's membership of a national community. In the end, however, an
outsider's voice – that rather embarrassing banshee cry – breaks in. Tradition
is interfered with by modernity, as the creature's altered voice comes through
the wireless in the form of an SOS to pull Sean off the road, thereby breaking
down the temporary social unit of Paddy O'Flynn's Circus and carrying Sean
away from the west. Seago accompanies him from Dublin to London via
Liverpool on the journey home, which depends on bus, ferry and motorcar to
bring Sean to Mitcham, where his father is dying. This is the return journey
from pre-Christian to established religion, since Seago records that 'religion is
most evident in the life of a showman at his death, for the funeral is a big thing
to circus people' (p. 53). But it is also a course that is followed throughout the
text from locations of the romantic to locations of the real; from the fabulous
sounds of legend, to those actual experiences of the world that legendary
sounds signify.

John Hinde's journal of Reco's 1944 tour is included in Eleanor Smith's social
study of *British Circus Life* (1948). Smith's own attention to Ireland focuses
on the presence of superstition within the circus. She retells 'a strange legend'
of Fossett's Circus, which exemplifies the troupe's distrust of conventional
settlement and 'the fixed'.[74] At some point in the past, the Fossett family had
enjoyed great prosperity and chose to invest their fortunes in a country estate.
They purchased a house and parkland that stood, like Michael's imaginary
family home, jewel-like among trees and lakes. After a summer's work, they
arrived in gaily painted wagons to spend the winter in their richness. One of
the Fossetts, however, had an uncanny sense about the place and the move into
this fixed abode was postponed. The family preferred their familiar wagons
that night, but their rest was interrupted:

> A ghost-coach, of course, had disturbed them; there could be no other,
> no more comforting, explanation. They had, indeed, saddled themselves
> with a haunted house. They left, but they no longer prospered. A hundred
> unlucky incidents occurred. It was all the fault of the house. One night,
> months later, they returned, and burnt it down to the ground ....[75]

Reminiscent of the fated atmosphere of Big House novels, it appears from this
perhaps allegorical anecdote that punishment will be meted out upon those
who leave off their own traditions and reimagine themselves as members

of a new community by entering spaces and structures to which they do not properly belong or which they do not legitimately possess. In the Fossett story, the family house, which is symbolic of social order impressed upon the natural landscape, is necessarily erased; its conceived architectural permanence is destroyed in favour of the temporary and the mobile. But the trouble is, the first departure proves the impossibility of returning unchanged to the point of origin, or of that point of origin remaining unchanged as it awaits a homecoming. Seago the author-ethnographer is always keenly aware of Ireland pushing its singular influence back upon him. He ends his account of Irish circus life, in England, longing for the community of the Little People to which he might never belong, only further observe. Ó Conaire, meanwhile, refuses to make any distinction between urban poverty in industrial England and the inhumane cruelty of rural Ireland. His cultural export, the haunted exile, is imprisoned by his ideally Irish family life and trapped within the limits of his nation's shared history. In Michael's end, we are shown the futility of burning those unlucky effigies down to the ground.

CHAPTER 3

Irish Circus History and Ireland's Theatrical Heritage

Mid-way through Act One of Samuel Beckett's *Waiting for Godot* (1956), Vladimir and Estragon pause to assess the quality, and formal qualities, of their performance:

VLADIMIR:	Charming evening we're having.
ESTRAGON:	Unforgettable.
VLADIMIR:	And it's not over.
ESTRAGON:	Apparently not.
VLADIMIR:	It's only beginning.
ESTRAGON:	It's awful.
VLADIMIR:	Worse than the pantomime.
ESTRAGON:	The circus.
VLADIMIR:	The music-hall.
ESTRAGON:	The circus.[1]

For the past sixty years, these two stage characters have appeared to converse with theatre audiences as they place *Waiting for Godot* within the frame of popular performance. In ten lines of dialogue, consisting of just twenty-six words, Beckett elides theatre with pantomime, music hall and – ultimately and insistently – the circus. The predominant focus of this chapter is upon that final equation, where theatre is seen in relation to circus. In the 2004 Rough Magic production of Stewart Parker's *Heavenly Bodies*, Owen Roe took on the role of circus clown Johnny Patterson. Directed by the playwright's niece, Lynne Parker, it was staged in the Abbey's studio theatre, the Peacock. Roe, who defines himself not as an actor but as a performer, commented that one of his favourite lines as Patterson was the quick quip 'Paddy the Clown', since it signified for him a comic tradition 'turning on itself almost'.[2] In some senses

94

acutely aware of the performance history that feeds into *Heavenly Bodies*, Roe nevertheless denied Patterson's circus heritage in developing his persona, deriving this Paddy's sarcastic and corrosive force of personality from other sources. He said: 'I always thought of Johnny as more rooted in the music hall than the circus – I saw him as a music hall clown.'[3] From this statement, it seems that the conventional boundaries separating theatre from circus from music hall are at once strictly policed and liberally flexible in our present moment. The intention of this chapter is to dismantle these artificial boundaries and to give purpose to the historically co-dependent and continuing relationship between these forms. In this way, it approaches the central philosophical argument of this book, as it considers the function and purpose of representing the circus in other media.

The following argument centres on mid- to late twentieth-century works by the poet W.B. Yeats, his painter brother Jack B. Yeats, and the playwrights Brian Friel and Stewart Parker; much is revealed about these texts when they are read in relation to the history of the circus in Ireland. Principally, the motives that lay behind the introduction of the circus to eighteenth-century colonial Dublin are noted for their similarity to the motives that lay behind the establishment of an Irish national theatre as the country moved towards independence 150 years later. Tensions between the artistic, political and economic aims of both circus and theatre ventures are clear in the historical accounts reviewed in support of this understanding. But in addition to revealing ideologies fundamental to the cultural development of an independent Ireland, each of these primary texts is, to an extent, biographical or autobiographical, thereby paralleling national and personal histories. W.B. Yeats' *Last Poems* (1939) are exemplary in this regard, especially the reading of 'The Circus Animals' Desertion' given here. The title of Paul Muldoon's Clark Lecture Series, given at the University of Cambridge in January 2015, was 'Yeats and the Afterlife'.[4] Arguably, what is represented in 'The Circus Animals' Desertion' is a life without an afterlife, as the anxious poetic voice conveys the isolating impossibility of continuing creation. In effect, the reader is shown the self-deprecating and self-effacing Stephen Dedalus of 'Proteus', but denied the redemptive revision of the artist in the form of Leopold Bloom. Similarly, Friel diffuses the potentially transformative energy of performance in the nebulous ending of *Crystal and Fox*. Meanwhile, Parker distinguishes himself humorously in *Heavenly Bodies* by cranking his characterisation of the playwright Dion Boucicault heavenwards, then suspending the progress of his *deus ex machina* in reverse along Rabelaisian lines, before finally giving the last word to his circus clown, Patterson. Light is shed on the motivations for the mixture of popular media that is apparent in *Crystal and Fox* and *Heavenly Bodies* by reviewing the contrasting fortunes of Ireland's leading circus troupes – Duffy's and Fossett's – in the second half of the twentieth century. These histories demonstrate how the two circuses interacted with recorded media in distinct ways, and detail the dissolution of the traditional family structures that supported their practice. Comparatively, the destruction or disintegration of family life is a major concern for both Friel and Parker.

Beckett plays a supporting role throughout the chapter. His friendship with Jack Yeats is widely noted.[5] In 'Republics of Difference: Yeats, MacGreevy, Beckett' (2005), David Lloyd reassesses the memory of Jack Yeats as an Irish cultural institution by contrasting Beckett's reviews of his work with those which transformed the painter into a political radical expressing the spirit of the Irish nation on canvas.[6] Lloyd's argument is analysed here by reflecting upon the similarities in the painterly and playwriting styles of Jack Yeats' circus works; it is furthered through an appreciation of the manic desolation in the voices speaking W.B. Yeats' 'High Talk' (1938) and 'The Circus Animals' Desertion' (1939), poems conveying a mood of belated defiance that might fruitfully be compared to the atmosphere of Beckett's writing. Critics have lately suggested the lasting influence of W.B. Yeats' poetry on Beckett: in his lecture 'Hearing Things: Samuel Beckett's William Butler Yeats' (2014), Gerald Dawe gave an extensive account of how *Last Poems* became especially and increasingly significant and expressive for Beckett towards the end of his life.[7] That 'Ireland's greatest poet' should turn to popular entertainment tropes in this final volume to represent his own career is a provocative move, and one which this chapter seeks to understand more fully.[8] In their turn, Friel and Parker experiment with Beckettian themes and styles in *Crystal and Fox* and *Heavenly Bodies*, plays that use circus characters and conventions as part of broader efforts to explore the roots of Irish theatre. Essentially, Friel and Parker mimic what is certainly the most famous and provocative question in Ireland's theatre history. Like the first stage Irishman, Shakespeare's Captain Macmorris, they ask: what is my nation?

The Circus in Ireland and an Irish National Theatre

Philip Astley has been regarded as 'the father of the modern circus' since the mid-nineteenth century.[9] The retired cavalry instructor first conceived of a circular playing place for his own-brand entertainment in the 1760s. Daring feats of horsemanship were displayed at Astley's Amphitheatre on London's

Westminster Bridge Road alongside animal trainers, vaulters, tumblers, jugglers, and other kinds of physical performance reminiscent of ages past. In 1782, the composer Charles Dibdin opened a rival venue, the Royal Circus, further east along the Thames near Blackfriars: his avowed mission was to combine 'the business of the stage and the ring'.[10] This union of theatre and circus was lucrative and Astley was quick to imitate the enterprise. His desire for the legitimacy enjoyed by patented theatre owners was betrayed in the structural development of the London amphitheatre: the ring was flanked by smaller stages, and the kinds of acts that would occur in each zone were strictly separated. But his early ventures were hindered by the snobberies and restrictions of a theatrical elite. This elite's lobbying efforts, motivated by anxieties about the instant popularity of the circus, resulted in the Theatre Licensing Act of 1776, which placed restrictions on Astley's shows. Crucially, prose dramas were prohibited at the circus. It was not until the Theatres Act was passed in 1843 that circuses were permitted to include such performances in their programme. But the right to feature prose drama was a secondary concern for Astley: the showman was in pursuit of an honorific royal patent.

Helen Burke records that when the Dublin Amphitheatre Royal opened on Peter Street in 1789, Ireland had its first circus.[11] Astley, meanwhile, enjoyed his first patent. The Irish Stage Act was passed in 1786, closing all theatres save for the patented Theatre Royal. Following negotiations with Sir Capel Molyneux of the Irish Privy Council, Astley was granted a patent in 1788: his establishment became the Dublin Amphitheatre Royal and he thus became the only patented theatre owner in the Irish capital. Burke suggests that this English circus was positioned in Dublin as a substitute for Irish theatre, claiming that the cavalry instructor's ventures had been given the 'official stamp from the Irish colonial state precisely because of its reactionary potential'.[12] As England worried that violent democratic revolution might spread from France across the Channel and take hold most effectively in colonial Ireland, authorities felt that they could depend on Astley and his circus acts to promote loyalty to the Crown. Helen Stoddart has described Astley's 'peaks of near hysterical patriotism' in dramatic scenarios such as the pantomime *All For Their Country, or, the Loyal Volunteers*, which obviously glorified the foiling of French attempts to land at Bantry Bay.[13] Burke details how the impresario's productions proved incendiary in Ireland on the eve of rebellion: articles published in December 1797 in United Irishman paper the *Press* reflect upon Astley's attempts 'to render as subservient to his word of command' his Irish audiences, with one columnist concluding that Astley was the 'principal savage' of his own circus.[14]

A century later, W.B. Yeats would write of how the performance of a stage Irishman reduced him to pantomimic inarticulacy in his autobiographical essay 'Dramatis Personae' (1896–1902). He quotes from a letter he sent to his uncle George Pollexfen which describes a Masonic concert: 'Somebody sang a stage Irishman's song – the usual whiskey, shillelagh kind of thing – and I hissed him, and lest my hiss might be lost in the general applause, waited until the applause had died down and hissed again. That gave somebody also courage, and we both hissed.'[15] Such provocative performances were inspiring. In 1897, the Manifesto for the Irish Literary Theatre described the project thus: 'We will show that Ireland is not the home of buffoonery and of easy sentiment, as it has been represented, but the home of an ancient idealism.'[16] When Lady Gregory quoted this description in *Our Irish Theatre: a chapter in autobiography* (1913), she prefaced the statement with the derisive clause, 'it seems now a little pompous'.[17] But in the moment, there was an urgent need to correct the speech impediment of Shakespeare's Macmorris and ask outright: 'What is a National Theatre?' This question was at the heart of Yeats' 1903 essay 'An Irish National Theatre'.[18] His treatise in *Samhain* came six years after he had composed the 'Manifesto for the Irish Literary Theatre' (ILT) with Lady Gregory and Edward Martyn, and a year before the Abbey Theatre opened. Yeats chronicled this definitive period in Irish cultural history in 'Dramatis Personae' where he recalled the statutory legal challenges faced by the founders of the ILT: 'Dublin had two theatres, the Royal and the Gaiety, that had been granted patents, a system obsolete everywhere else. No performance, except for charity, could be given but at these two theatres; they were booked for the best months of the year by English travelling companies and in the worst months were expensive.'[19] The theatrical project of Yeats, Lady Gregory and Martyn was, therefore, obstructed in ways comparable to Astley's circus venture. Conversely, there are relevant moments of contrast in the motivations of the pioneers of the modern circus and the progenitors of Ireland's national theatre. In 1903, Yeats vowed: 'I would sooner our theatre failed through the indifference or hostility of our audience than gained an immense popularity by any loss of freedom.'[20] This cri de cœur is heard in direct opposition to the enterprise of eighteenth-century circus innovator Charles Dibdin to unite the business of the theatre and the ring. It was the financial success of Dibdin's circus-theatre that sent Philip Astley across the Irish Sea in search of a lucrative theatre patent that would result in the replacement of Irish theatre with English circus: a consolidation in low cultural form of the colonial project against which Yeats and his contemporaries were still fighting with the power of the 'higher arts' over 100 years later.

An Irish Institution: The Circus for Jack Yeats as Playwright and Painter

Jack Yeats did not hold Ireland's national theatre or Dublin's intellectual elite in uniformly high regard. In them, he saw another kind of staged Irishness. A letter to Thomas MacGreevy in March 1927 begins with an unflattering review of a lecture the artist had attended, which concludes dismissively: 'Farewell the not very original and amiable Irish. Those that come will in every sense of the word be very original and with the teeth skinned. So let the parboiled footed, spongey minded "stand clear of the gates".' The letter continues to offer a round-up of recent cultural events in Dublin. Yeats refers to a performance of 'John Fletcher's Don Juan' describing how: 'All the drippings of Dublin were in the theatre.'[21] In later years, Yeats appealed to MacGreevy's sense as theatre critic as he sent him scripts for his own plays, which were rejected by the Abbey. Yeats wrote warmly and gratefully in September 1933:

> I'm flattered, in the heart, when anyone gets any kind of squeeze out of one of the plays. Though what will hold the stage, for an audience, is a thing that I don't believe any one knows with certainty enough to have a side on it but I have respect for producers who slap down their own money. They are in the ring and fighting.[22]

The Abbey did not produce one of Jack Yeats' plays until after the death of his brother, W.B., in January 1939: six months later, *Harlequin's Positions* (1938) was performed by the Abbey Experimental Theatre Company on the Peacock stage. Like other works that Yeats described as his plays for 'Larger Theatre', *Harlequin's Positions* had grown from his 'Miniature Theatre': a stage for brief fantastic stories whose plots were pastiches of popular sources and whose players were crafted out of pasteboard and paint. These miniatures were delightful and enchanting to the audiences for whom they were intended: the children of the Devon village of Strete, for instance, who were invited to Christmas showings of *Onct More's Circus* in 1901 and 1902. However, the subsequent transformation of Yeats' small-scale visual sense to the Larger Theatre was far less successful, and the Abbey's decision not to produce them seems a fair one. Ian Walsh has argued that '[t]he primacy of the word in Irish theatre can be traced to the origins of the Abbey Theatre in the Irish Literary Theatre', and it would appear that in attempting to cater to Abbey producers, Yeats lost something of his original sense of theatre art.[23] John Purser proposes that Yeats as dramatist allowed himself to be influenced by Dion Boucicault's melodrama because 'he was picking on a playwright who broke through the melodramatic mould with heroes who were anything but conventional.'[24] Boucicault's *The Shaughraun* (1874) was the first play that Jack Yeats ever saw, and the experience led to an important change in his perspective on and receptiveness to different forms of art. He would comment that: 'Boucicault's light-toed peasants were more supernatural than Shakespeare's sugar-filled holiday tarts.'[25] But Yeats' expression of admiration for the 'light-toed' wit and apparent unconventionality of Boucicault as it is communicated in his own plays is converted into dense dialogue that is, at best, cryptic; at worst, confusing. More broadly, the plots of Yeats' longer plays are unreasonable, purposeless, and lack the punch that his metaphorically pugilistic producers might promise.

Bruce Arnold has attempted to redeem the general aimlessness of the entire body of Jack Yeats' drama by proffering certain generic confines: the stories of the miniature plays, at least, he writes, 'are slight, yet revealing. They engage our attention at the level of fable or quest.'[26] In considering the two *Onct More's Circus* entertainments, Arnold isolates the 'difficulty of circus': 'that action could not be contained in the dialogue, except perhaps in the exchanges between clowns.'[27] It would be a shame to accept Arnold's redemptive, productive reading of Jack Yeats' plays, whatever their scale, and the pejorative terms he uses in relation to his near-wordless circuses, since their potential to impress exists solely in how they *appear*, as the sequence of images and scenarios are presented, rather flatly, to the audience. Further, Jack Yeats' plays depend upon the theatre as a communal space in which actors and audience co-ordinate to produce the *experience* of action. Crucially, the artist derived his fundamental dramatic principles from his experience of circus. Yeats expressed beliefs in novel form that endowed audiences with the power and the responsibility to break through the fourth wall and give the play text a third dimension. 'But let the Beginning be in a circular confined place, a circus tent,' he wrote with biblical emphasis in *Sligo* (1930).[28] The novel's first-person narrator harbours a certain disdain for the authority of the modern dramatist working beneath the proscenium arch who ignores the theatre of everyday life as they entreat exasperatedly: 'When is the drama in a Circus ring going to take hold of the drama that can be seen all around and at which the audience seem to have a part?'[29]

Such a breakthrough makes Jack Yeats an exemplary Irish dramatist, if the terms of Anthony Roche are to be accepted. Roche clearly alludes to the performance philosophy of W.B. Yeats, as articulated in essays such as 'The Tragic Theatre' (1910), in defining the most notable features of Irish theatre. He begins with the 'ever-present tension between the written and the spoken' and continues:

Secondly, it redefines the spatial relationship between actors and an action up there on the stage, and an audience separate and down here. In terms of plot in Irish plays, we know that very little happens by way of formally distinct events galloping before our fixed gaze in dizzying succession. The movement of the plot is more like the expansion or creation of a circle; the painful situation in which on-stage characters are placed is deconstructed and made tolerable as audiences come to participate and share in it, as it extends to and is extended by them.[30]

In Roche's animated terms, the generalised notion of the plot of Irish plays appears before audiences like one of Philip Astley's dramatic feats of horsemanship – his so-called 'hippodramas' – as inconsequential events are made to 'gallop' across the stage. Applying this definition to the plays of Jack Yeats, the dizziness of deconstruction within these works results from the playwright's magpie-like collection of attractive words and phrases from diverse leisure, pleasure and entertainment pursuits: to Yeats' mind, it was not only theatre producers who were 'in the ring and fighting'. As Purser traces influences on the language of his later, longer plays, the critic lists patter and conventions borrowed from the boxing ring, the salesman, the séance, the melodrama and, parenthetically, 'its cousin the cinema'.[31] According to Purser, it was the potential for confrontation between performer and public that recommended these forms of discourse and entertainment to Jack Yeats the dramatist. But in *Sligo*, the narrator specifically desires a return to a style of performance that is – at the very least – circused, or circus-like.

The essence of this discussion of the playwright Jack Yeats is comparable to the re-examination of the painter Jack Yeats conducted by David Lloyd in 'Republics of Difference'. In his essay, Lloyd returns to oft-quoted reviews of Yeats' paintings by Beckett and their mutual friend MacGreevy to evaluate how it is that Beckett's preference for the formal, visual qualities of Yeats' painting – a preference overwhelming any symbolic or allegorical meaning they might convey – has been neglected critically in favour of grandly interpretative readings that have enabled the institution of Jack Yeats as Ireland's national painter. Lloyd effectively demonstrates how disjunctive images committed to canvas by Yeats anticipate the dramatisations of personal disturbance that would occur in Beckett's plays, especially the monologues of the 1960s and 1970s. Lloyd argues that, through Beckett's vision of the Yeatsian image, we see 'rupture and discontinuity and the radically unreconciled relation of subject and object, and [Beckett] appropriates the painter no less forcefully to his apprehension of the "issueless predicament of existence"'.[32]

Lloyd's sensitive analysis of Jack Yeats' broad style and specific technique as it changed over time serves to reinforce this perspective. His reading of the painting *The Double Jockey Act* (1916) (Fig. 3.1) highlights the free brushwork that deprives the individual figures of circus clown and horse, trick riders and ringside audience of the certain definition in form that is characteristic of Yeats' early illustrations:

3.1 Jack B. Yeats, *The Double Jockey Act*, 1916, Oil on canvas, National Gallery of Ireland

To revise Lloyd's terms: certainly, there is no reconciliation or intercoursing between the human figures in this painting. Each body appears entirely isolated in its own physical response to the situation; each expression differs, and each communicates internal contemplation. However, there is an apparent correspondence between human and other forms: the vertical stripes of the clown's costume complement the horizontal stripes of the circus tent. All three performers are coloured in the same palette of reds and blues that distinguish them (the clown especially, in his make-up and motley) from the black-coated, flat-capped men in the crowd. Helen Stoddart finds Henri Bergson's theories of laughter instructional as she endeavours to define the comic atmosphere of the circus space.[33] Following Stoddart's lead, the present reading of *The Double Jockey Act* is advanced by incorporating elements of *Laughter: an essay on the meaning of the comic* (1900). Bergson believed that people laugh when 'something mechanical is encrusted on the living'.[34] In the case of Yeats' painted clown, that something *material* should be encrusted on the living performer indicates the comic spirit, as the performer's costume appears to have been cut crossways from the same cloth as the performance structure, the circus tent. Clown and venue are thereby one and the same entity. Here, too, we see that playing place described in *Sligo*, where the role of the audience, as they slide into the players, is not vocal but actual and physical – their heads are given body by the back and croup of the piebald horse, the circus animal. The clown, meanwhile, seems propelled and uplifted by some invisible vehicle that is beyond our apprehension. In its elision of human, animal, material and mechanical forms, this image might then be taken as an approximation of the plays of Jack B. Yeats: plays that represent a confusion of registers and discourses not to develop a satisfying plot according to fundamental dramatic principles, but instead to illustrate a series of perhaps discontinuous moments. Jack Yeats the dramatist shows his audience players on a painted stage.

Acting Out the Circus: The Mock-heroics of W.B. Yeats' Memory

Jack Yeats' conversion to a freer style of painting occurred around 1915. The artist also suffered a nervous breakdown at that time. Hilary Pyle describes the lasting effects on his work: 'Something collapsed inside the artist. At this time, and from now the sketches in his few notebooks are interspersed with subjective scribbled concepts in "dream", or "half memory", grim faces reminiscent of Kirchner, and even some whirling geometrical abstracts which had never before come from his pencil.'[35] The concept of memory is also crucial to Lloyd's appreciation of the artist. For him, Jack Yeats' later painting is:

painting as anamnesis rather than mimesis. Memory here is neither the retrieval of time past nor the repossession of a lost object, but the performance of that occultating light in which the figure merges and dissolves. [...] In these paintings, memory is presented, not as the past regained, but as an enigma for the present. And that enigma is only reinforced by the teasing, highly literary titles affixed to the paintings, titles that seem to allude to an explanatory framework outside the canvases, to a tale in which they might become clear, but which yet eludes the viewer. They transform what might have been symbols into allegories that cannot be reduced to conceptual clarity, to interpretative mapping. This is a figuration without a possible turn to the literal.[36]

This definition of represented memory in Jack Yeats' paintings has certain resonance for how memory should be understood in W.B. Yeats' *Last Poems*, particularly the two 'show poems' 'High Talk' and 'The Circus Animals' Desertion'. The term 'show poem' is used here in two senses: primarily, and most simply, it refers to works in which there are references to various kinds of performance; secondarily, and perhaps rather heretically, Yeats' 'show poems' are understood as conditioned, like show dogs, to display the finest and most refined qualities and characteristics of an entire poetic career in one form or being. Malachi Stilt-Jack is an exemplary specimen, standing in 'High Talk' as that figuration without a possible turn to the literal; as anamnesis and not mimesis. He is, after all, 'all metaphor':

> Processions that lack high stilts have nothing that catches
> the eye.
> What if my great-granddad had a pair that were twenty foot
> high,
> And mine were but fifteen foot, no modern stalks upon
> higher,
> Some rogue of the world stole them to patch up a fence or
> a fire.
>
> Because piebald ponies, led bears, caged lions, make but
> poor shows,
> Because children demand Daddy-long-legs upon his timber
> toes,
> Because women in the upper stories demand a face at the
> pane

That patching old heels they may shriek, I take to chisel and
>   plane.

Malachi Stilt-Jack am I, whatever I learned has run wild,
From collar to collar, from stilt to stilt, from father to child.

All metaphor, Malachi, stilts and all. A barnacle goose
Far up in the stretches of night; night splits and the dawn
>   breaks loose;
I, through the terrible novelty of light, stalk on, stalk on;
Those great sea-horses bare their teeth and laugh at the
>   dawn.[37]

Bergson's concept of the mechanical encrusted upon the living is instructive when reading the poem. Those living beasts – the ponies, the bears and the lions – might well be contained by control mechanisms – leads and cages – but Malachi surpasses them all by fashioning and grafting on prosthetic limbs that make him loftier. By the same stroke, *Last Poems*' 'Long-legged Fly' (1939) is also suggested: '*Like a long-legged fly upon the stream / His mind moves upon silence*.'[38] But in 'High Talk', the vehicle for the simile that was the eponymous insect has matured into a total metaphor, signalling that metaphoric Malachi is at once an object of concentrated meditation.

Yeats' indirect allusion to his own writing continues. The words upon the windowpane that so excited the company in the 1930 play of that title are overwritten in the poem with a face turned towards women who appear caught somewhere between real and imagined worlds in a confusion of person and created fiction that is similar to Jack Yeats' circus clown and circus tent: they are 'women in the upper stories'. In his attempt to satisfy their needs, Malachi is at once diminished by his own eye-catching instruments of 'High Talk' in the eyes of his children: his techniques transform and debase him as he metamorphoses into the figure-of-fun Daddy-long-legs. By the final verse paragraph, all-metaphor Malachi – that persona without a known, and therefore nameable, point of origin – stalks on in the unforgiving spotlight as though anticipating the final words of Beckett's *The Unnamable* (1953): 'I can't go on, I'll go on.'[39] That 'novelty of light' is a near synonym for the term used by Lloyd to illumine Jack Yeats' paintings, and to deploy 'that occultating light' here returns us to the séance setting of *The Words Upon the Window Pane*, where voices instead of figures merge and dissolve in uncanny transmissions.

W.B. Yeats wrote to his father on 14 March 1916:

we know that poetry is rhythm, but in music-hall verses we find an abstract cadence, which is vulgar because it is apart from imitation. This cadence is a mechanism, it never suggests a voice shaken with joy or sorrow as poetical rhythm does. It is but the noise of a machine and not the coming and going of the breath.

The force of Yeats' opposition of the abstract with the rhythmical is derived specifically from the poet's sense of timing. Criticism is aimed at mechanical poetry of synthetic emotion that is delivered in the popular performance venue where moments of joy and sorrow are predictable and expected, thereby abstracting the original and authentic causes of joy or sorrow. This is antithetical to those spontaneous overflows of feeling that are the stock in trade of the inspired poet: music hall verses are contemptible as predictable spews of hackneyed sentiment. This opposition is staged again in 'The Circus Animals' Desertion', where Yeats' plays are recovered in a disenchanted parade of dwindling imaginative and attractive power. In this respect, the poem might be understood as comically contrapuntal: the circus animals are possible poets as their breath comes and goes, embodying the abstract cadences of the synthetic popular performance venue. But these are remembered beasts, and the original structuring rhythms of their breath have died out:

I

I sought a theme and sought for it in vain,
I sought it daily for six weeks or so.
Maybe at last being but a broken man
I might be satisfied with my heart, although
Winter and summer till old age began
My circus animals were all on show,
Those stilted boys, that burnished chariot,
Lion and woman and the Lord knows what.

II

What can I but enumerate old themes,
First that sea-rider Oisin led by the nose
Through tree enchanted islands, allegorical dreams,
Vain gaiety, vain battle, vain repose,
Themes of the embittered heart, or so it seems,
That might adorn old songs or courtly shows;

But what cared I that set him on to ride,
I, starved for the bosom of his fairy bride.

And then a counter-truth filled out its play,
The Countess Cathleen was the name I gave it,
She, pity-crazed, had given her soul away
But masterful Heaven had intervened to save it.
I thought my dear must her own soul destroy
So did fanaticism and hate enslave it,
And this brought forth a dream and soon enough
This dream itself had all my thought and love.

And when the Fool and Blind Man stole the bread
Cuchulain fought the ungovernable sea;
Heart mysteries there, and yet when all is said
It was the dream itself enchanted me:
Character isolated by a deed
To engross the present and dominate memory.
Players and painted stage took all my love
And not those things that they were emblems of.

III

Those masterful images because complete
Grew in pure mind but out of what began?
A mound of refuse or the sweepings of a street,
Old kettles, old bottles, and a broken can,
Old iron, old bones, old rags, that raving slut
Who keeps the till. Now that my ladder's gone
I must lie down where all the ladders start
In the foul rag and bone shop of the heart.[40]

There are comparisons to be drawn between the figures in 'The Circus Animals' Desertion' and those in Jack Yeats' *The Double Jockey Act*. By Part III, the 'I' that is old age personified – emphatically so, given the repetition of 'began' from Part I – looks very much like the painted clown who Yeats prevents from fading into the background by running the stripes of his costume counter to the stripes of the circus tent wall. The older brother's poem gets closer to Bergson's original suggestion that we laugh when something mechanical is encrusted upon the living: old kettles, bottles and tin cans are more comic still since their age suggests malfunction and they are thereby rendered useless. The concept of 'imperformance' is advanced by Jack Yeats in his play *The Wonderful Traveller* (*c.*1906), which he described as 'An Old Fashioned Harliquinade'.[41] In the play, a comic policeman in pursuit of two fugitives mispronounces the word 'inform' as 'imperform' in a kind of onomatopoeic expression that is apt within this discussion. 'I' is a tinker borrowed from Synge and lent to Beckett, as the poet's mock blazon transforms the speaker into an imperforming down-and-out, peddling wares on Clown Alley, thereby uniting the business of the stage and the ring in ways that Charles Dibdin would never have wished to imagine.

Lloyd's satisfaction with the enigmatic 'highly literary titles' of Jack Yeats' paintings can be revised in relation to W.B. Yeats' poem to no less pleasing effect. The circus as 'low' cultural reference point operates similarly, seeming to allude to an explanatory framework outside the verses. The jest is that the framework is not elsewhere but, in fact, ever-present. Where all was metaphor for Malachi in 'High Talk', in 'The Circus Animals' Desertion' 'I' can only exist within frames of images stolen from circus and theatre. In *Yeats and Modern Poetry* (2013), Edna Longley writes that:

> Yeats's self-image as poet spans actor, character in a play (sometimes Shakespearean tragedy), theatre director, impresario. Two late backstage poems, 'High Talk' and 'The Circus Animals' Desertion', share the word 'show'. The former, where the poet speaks as bravura actor, proclaims and exemplifies the need for form to be performative: 'Processions that lack high stilts have nothing that catches the eye'. […] The latter, where he speaks as ringmaster, probes the prior psychic need driving 'Those stilted boys, that burnished chariot'.[42]

While Longley is quite correct in stating that the poet assumes roles of both performer and producer, her situation of the speaker 'backstage' is inadequate. It does not capture the complex of perspectives effected in both poems, especially in 'The Circus Animals' Desertion', which removes both poet and reader from the scene of the action, dislocating them from the representation of memory that the poem undertakes: Yeats is chained to his seat, like the speaker of Arthur Symons' 'Prologue' to *London Nights* (1895), as he watches himself upon the stage. More problematic still is Longley's conception of the speaker as 'ringmaster'. The possessive pronoun 'my' in line six surely invites a discussion of the ownership of these animals – these expressive circus images – but the speaker's relationship to them is not characterised as masterful or commanding as the 'ringmaster' epithet would suggest. Instead, the voice is overrun and embarrassed by the free-wheeling vulnerability of those talented creations that are 'on show', a maddening emotion underscored by the idiom 'and the Lord knows what'.

Rather than give the power of the ringmaster over to Yeats' 'I', as Longley does, it is better to implicate this active voice as a paradoxically passive spectator witnessing the circus animals' metaphoric desertion; to position 'him' within the crowds who received and sometimes misconstrued that which was presented to them – those players and painted stages which operated as national emblems beyond the control of their creator, Yeats. This complex perspective might be best aligned with the viewpoint of the poet-playwright's brother, the artist. In January 1942, an exhibition of paintings by Jack Yeats and Sir William Nicholson opened at the National Gallery in London as the follow-up to a show of the paintings of Walter Sickert. The kind of parallax that proved the genius of Sickert, and which Jack Yeats sought to emulate, is at play in W.B. Yeats' poem.[43] Patricia Goldstone considered this parallax view essential when she came to adapt 'The Circus Animals' Desertion' for the stage in 1974. Goldstone, as playwright and director, hoped to circumvent 'the temptation to present the play as a literary document rather than as a theatrical spectacle' by translating the central metaphor of Yeats' poem 'into the physical language of the Big Top itself'.[44] Goldstone's act of translation necessitated the incorporation of a variety of forms not present in the original text: the poet himself became The Magician who was undone by the slapstick escapades of other characters including 'Maudie' and Iseult Gonne and the parodic hybrid Niamh-Oisin.[45]

Goldstone's existentialist dissection of theatre and its reconstitution into alternative popular forms begins to resemble the kind of performance advocated by the narrator of Jack Yeats' *Sligo*: 'When is the drama in a Circus ring going to take hold of the drama that can be seen all round and at which the audience seem to have a part?'[46] Actor and audience are near doppelgängers in this vision of a circused drama: their shared or dual roles are indecipherable from one another and subject/object distinctions break down in performance. Crucially, the circus is refused in the instant in which it is invoked by W.B. Yeats: its captivating energy, conveyed in the past tense, is converted immediately into that which is proper to something like theatre. But the effect of this conversion is to reduce the theatre, through literary burlesque, to a form more closely akin to pantomime or music hall. Overwhelmingly, music hall, burlesque, circus and theatre are as awful as each other upon reflection, and Yeats' speaker thereby enters kinship with Didi and Gogo as they wait for Godot.

Bust and Boom: Variety Acts at Ireland's National Circuses

Paul Durcan's poem 'The Beckett at the Gate' (*Going Home to Russia*, 1987) takes place in part at the Gate Theatre during a performance of an unnamed Beckett play. The production features the actor Barry McGovern, who is renowned and respected for his interpretation of Beckett's characters, and not just those written for the stage. Supposedly, the unidentified play is all the rage among Dublin's intellectual elite, but the speaker's obligation to attend places him in a near-empty auditorium beside a young woman, Michelle. She is consumed entirely by her own amusement:

> She gave herself over to her own laughter
> To such an exuberant extent
> That she was entirely inside it – within the orbit
> Of her own transparent laughter,
> All rouge and polythene.[47]

Michelle, as an obviously desirable object (too straightforwardly objectified, perhaps, in the spiteful synthetics of 'rouge and polythene'), is simultaneously a figure to beware. She is compared to a string of biblical women including Eve, Judith and Mary Magdalen. The speaker, meanwhile, assumes implicitly the role of Holofernes. Ultimately, he finds himself unable to act upon his desire when he is later faced with the woman at a bus stop in Ringsend:

> She scrutinised me serenely
> As if she had never seen me before –
> As if she had never seen me before.[48]

Michelle's apparently, emphatically ignorant behaviour propels the speaker into what sounds like a Beckettian imagined space, but is more properly the metaphoric landscape of Malachi Stilt-Jack: 'I'll go on, I think, I'll go on.'[49]

The muse's lack of interest and the speaker's debilitating impotence recalls Durcan's earlier poem 'The Lion Tamer' (1983), which in turn recalls Mr Bloom's sadomasochistic circus fantasies.[50] The expressivity of the circus metaphor for men suffering from performance anxiety is also carried forward into the later poem. Mimicking and then faltering over the phoney and off-kilter English colloquialisms of avid Abbey Theatre-goer Joseph Holloway, the narrator of 'The Beckett at the Gate' explains why he, Michelle and their fellow audience were beside themselves:

Well, it was out of the top drawer,
As Joseph Holloway would have put it,
Or would not have put it.
Not since the Depression of the 1950s
And the clowns in Duffy's Circus
Have I laughed myself so sorry,
So sorry that I was ready to shout,
If anyone else had shouted:
'Stop Beckett! Stop McGovern!'[51]

This extract takes us back to the auditorium of 'Dramatis Personae', where a young W.B. Yeats found himself hissing at a stage Irishman's antics. Here, it seems that the problem is the pollution of the Irish theatre with the almost English voice. Crucially, the means of defining the comic experience within this national theatre is through reference to what was once Ireland's National Circus: Duffy's.

The 1950s was a depressing time for Duffy's. John Duffy and Sons' National Circus chose to skip Belfast and Dublin and concentrate on smaller towns during the truncated 1953 tour for financial reasons. Longer stands in big towns and cities had become the norm for the larger shows over the previous two decades, but Duffy's return to past ways – taking in 163 towns north and south of the border – was intended to maximise business in each location. The seven Duffy brothers were regularly released for tours with Buff Bill's Circus in England and cine-variety and pantomime performances in Dublin, Cork and Limerick. One of the brothers, Arthur, would develop an independent career as a trombonist, playing cabaret and private functions with his band The Jazz Freaks. The death of patriarch John Duffy three years later led to a family dispute that would cost the circus its prestigious and profitable national status: the feud split the company in two, with John's homonymous sons John James and James touring separately in 1959 and 1960. Amateur historian Richard McMinn reported dramatically in *Circus* magazine that, in these two years, 'the knives were out and the bemused Irish public was destined to witness a war to the death'.[52] James' initial venture, Duffy's National Circus, was the first to fail in 1960. Its reliance on street parades to generate interest was counter-productive, since the public felt that they could see the best of the show without having to buy a ticket. Meanwhile, John James chose to experiment with a circus-variety programme, but his only tour in 1961 was similarly fated.[53]

Fossett's, Duffy's major rival, were more successful over the same period. Ted Fossett's death in 1951 supposedly made sons Bobby, Teddy and Johnny the world's youngest circus proprietors. Their decision to maintain a Western theme throughout the decade was savvy, tying into the vogue for American cowboy series in comics, popular fiction and on television.[54] Teddy in particular made effective use of film and television throughout his management in various ways; in later years, his efforts would be rewarded by the national broadcaster, RTÉ, as Bibi Baskin hosted primetime Saturday night variety show *The Big Top* (1992–3) from the circus.[55] In the early days, the Fossett brothers were keen and quick to demonstrate their acumen more variously. Combining in their own way the business of the stage and the business of the ring, Fossett's derived revenue from lucrative tie-ins with other popular festivals. The profitability of the circus' first coincidence with the Kilkenny Beer Festival and the Rose of Tralee Festival in 1964 ensured these partnerships lasted into the future. Fossett's were also savvy in reviving traditions and staging grand memorial shows. In 1968, they marked the bicentenary of Philip Astley's first performances lavishly. Teddy had taken the lead from his brothers as both businessman and performer by this time, and as ringmaster of the Astley's celebration, he began proceedings with a welcome to the 200th year of world circus.[56] Contemporaneously, his efforts had claimed a coveted mantle from Duffy's: Fossett Bros Circus had become Ireland's National Circus – a title it retains.[57]

Fossett's continued to travel to Northern Ireland in the late 1960s and 1970s despite the return of prolonged sectarian conflict; this was, apparently, a proud boast of Teddy Fossett.[58] During the seventies, Teddy himself became increasingly active politically: at once, the bureaucracy of hostile local authorities deprived Irish circuses of traditional sites and the right to fly-post advance publicity, while Ireland's formal entry into the European Economic Community made it easier for foreign circuses to travel to the country. As a means of preserving the interests of his circus, Teddy returned to an ambition of his father's. Fossett's Circus began lobbying the Irish parliament for art form status in 1973.[59] But for all his opportunistic bravado, Teddy Fossett's obituary published in trade magazine *Circus* in the late 1990s tells a rather less triumphant story of this time. It concludes that the owner of Ireland's National Circus regretted many of the social changes that he had not only witnessed but exploited, and their effect on his family's way of life.

The Illusion of Coherence: Brian Friel's Crystal and Fox

This moment in Irish circus history is a moment of splits: the titanic contest between two of Ireland's oldest show families; the competition for audiences on both sides of the border; the near-biblical family division at Duffy's; the staging of Teddy Fossett's public persona that masked private anxieties. According to Fintan O'Toole, theatre in Ireland shared in this dichotic moment. In an article for *The Guardian* headed 'How Poetry Joins Dramatic Action', O'Toole wrote retrospectively in 1990: 'If there is a characteristic image of Irish theatre in the last three decades, it is the image of the split personality.'[60] Elmer Andrews' reading of Friel's *Crystal and Fox* would accord with this perspective. Andrews classifies the play as 'characteristically Beckettian' in its picture of 'unaccommodated man stripped to the bare essentials of life, confronting the basic questions of existence, situated in an unspecified, empty landscape'.[61] That 'unaccommodated man' is showman Fox Melarkey, whose persona evokes Beckett's tramps and clowns for Andrews – figures who are, for him, 'dichotomised creatures, split, like Friel's, into the essential Self and the apparent Self'.[62] The extent to which Friel himself would accept Andrews' potent and influential psychoanalytic reading of his plays must be limited, since the playwright voiced his dislike for what he perceived as 'the complete dehydration of humanity' and 'a complete abnegation of life' in the works of Beckett (and Harold Pinter) in a 1970 interview with Desmond Rushe for Catholic magazine *The Word*.[63] Nevertheless, Andrews' grasp of a familiarly Beckettian thrust to *Crystal and Fox* is certainly appreciable. In the play, Friel propels his characters towards points of origin only to ultimately emphasise the fact that there is difference in repetition: the impossibility of remaining intact and, thereby, of achieving a satisfactory return to that first place.

Crystal and Fox looks at the decline and fall of 'fit-up' outfit the Fox Melarkey Show as it travels the country surrounding Friel's fictional town Ballybeg, County Donegal. The fit-up – a form once popular across the rural British Isles – brought theatre, variety and circus acts to isolated audiences. Fittingly, Fox's show features the acrobatic husband-and-wife team El Cid and Tanya; the ageing clown, Paddy 'Pedro' Donnellan (who, in his confusion of national identities, might remind us of the Tex-Mex cowboy who turns up to play with Paddy O'Flynn's Circus in Seago's *Sons of Sawdust*); Pedro's performing dog, Gringo; and Crystal, Fox's wife and lead actress in the company's renditions of melodrama. As a story of a disintegrating business, Friel's play might be seen to draw accurately from life, reflecting in many ways the contemporary afflictions of real entertainers. Audiences of the Fox Melarkey Show appear disenchanted with live performance and are captured instead by recorded media. Early in the piece, the troupe discuss how, in the past, they could have depended upon 'tragedies' – a train crash or an explosion in a school – to pull in audiences, but no longer.[64] 'Television,' says Crystal, 'has spoiled them.'[65] Unlike the real impresario Teddy Fossett, Fox has no interest in exploiting the potential of recorded media in order to sustain his live show, and it is pertinent to note that, at the time of writing and producing *Crystal and Fox*, Friel could see himself having no truck with the cinema. In a broadcast interview with John Boyd for BBC Radio 4 Northern Ireland in 1970, the playwright criticised the medium for the ease with which it could sell mediocrity to an audience, adding sarcastically (if a little prematurely): 'I would be very interested in making a film if I can write it, direct it, shoot it, and play in it myself. And, since I'm not very competent at any of these things, the chances of making a film are remote then.'[66] A similarly sceptical attitude towards the cinema is conveyed in James Mateer's memoir *A Life on the Open Road* (1996): a personal history of family life in a fit-up show travelling Ulster in the Depression of the 1930s. Mateer explains how his father, Bob, brought melodramatic plays based on fictions such as the Victorian penny dreadful *The String of Pearls* (1846–7) and Dickens' novel *Hard Times* (1854) to rural audiences, but was compelled to disband his company – consisting of brother, wife, parents-in-law and two small children – and enter another kind of working world as a postmaster, while movie theatre proprietors moved into ever more isolated locations to exploit lucrative markets.[67] Where the circus seemed to overtake other live popular forms in the exchange between Beckett's Vladimir and Estragon, recorded media was evidently winning out in the competitions for audiences' attentions commented upon by Friel and Mateer.

It is dramatically ironic that destruction does bring the Fox Melarkey Show one final audience. That destruction is the disintegration of the family and performing community within the piece that is witnessed by the 'real' audience who watch *Crystal and Fox*. Friel's notes for the set and stage design establish that, in faithful productions, the acting area should be divided in two by a 'flimsy and transparent framework which runs at an angle upstage'.[68] The players in the Fox Melarkey Show therefore exist within what might be termed after Beckett an angle of perceivedness: the audience is given to understand that one-third of the stage is the space occupied by the fit-up marquee.[69] But the right-hand side of the stage is reserved for those scenes where the 'life' of Fox, Crystal and their company is played out. Increasingly, the scenes of 'real' life overtake those of the performing world, as the fluctuating boundary between performance and the personal is wilfully deconstructed. Given Friel's fractional descriptions of the stage, it is interesting that both Elmer Andrews and Geraldine Higgins should describe Fox as 'ringmaster' of his travelling show. Higgins uses the term concretely, describing Fox the fit-up manager as 'both mastermind and ringmaster'.[70] Andrews is far more abstract, and far

more confused, in stating that Fox is 'a truly mythic ringmaster'.[71] As in Edna
Longley's commentary on 'The Circus Animals' Desertion', the character of
the ringmaster is casually and imprecisely invoked to add the attractive energy
of the circus to critical responses in metaphoric terms. It is also used to gift
authority to individuals – Yeats' poetic voice and Friel's protagonist – who, in
fact, deliberately corrupt or imperform (to use Jack Yeats' term) their roles as
the directors of the action that is contained within the narrative of poem and
play. Fox is not, principally, the circus actor his critics have cast him as hitherto.
Instead, his experience in various styles of popular performance – as travelling
actor, accordionist, and wheel of fortune-spinning sideshow huckster – should
be seen in relation to the circus form.

The function of Fox's wheel of fortune is to signify, in primary colours
reminiscent of the hues that saturate Ó Conaire's *Exile* and in total black, the
risk inherent in a blind belief that it is possible to realise a peculiar dream.
The manner in which that dream is relayed in Episode Two of *Crystal and Fox*
reveals further unwitting correspondences between the plots of *Exile* and Friel's
play. Fox narrates the dream to his son Gabriel, an economic migrant returned
to depressed Ireland from depressing Salford, where he has been in search of
work: he has been on the railways; he has been a dish-washer; he has recorded
everyday life as street photographer. Gabriel is, then, a returnee, facilitating
a kind of cathartic release for his self-obsessed father with probing questions
which, it is sensed, only a son could ask:

> FOX (*Pleasantly; almost casually*)   Weary of all this … this making-
> do, of conning people that know they're being conned. Sick of it all.
> Not sick so much as desperate; desperate for something that … that has
> nothing to do with all this. Restless, Gabby boy, restless. And a man with
> a restlessness is a savage bugger.
>
> GABRIEL   What do you want?
>
> FOX   What do I want? I want … I want a dream I think I've had to
> come true. I want to live like a child. I want to die and wake up in heaven
> with Crystal. What do I want? Jaysus, man, if I knew the answer to that, I
> might be content with what I have. (*Without stopping*) I like your jacket.[72]

Gabriel is the figure who silently measures the variations in his father's personae,
and, as such, he must remain external to Fox's visions and longings. During their
confessional, the father refuses to admit the presence or existence of his son,
choosing instead to incorporate himself as a child into his own dream-being.

The continuum between the retelling of the dream, the articulation of an existential crisis, and the blasé, banal reference to the lived and physical real world impresses an audience with the fact that Gabriel's father is a man to be watched. Having been encouraged to release the valve on the bitterness of promise that is either lost or impossible to fulfil, Fox's unsettling desires result in the increasing malevolence with which he successively casts out his band of performers, and which is finally inflicted upon his family. His collusion with state authorities who act as menacing paternal substitutes for Gabriel ultimately severs him from Crystal, horrified as she is by her husband's selfish ability to turn on their own child. In this treacherous act, he does not simply remove his son from the scene, but also erases himself as father. Father, son, and belief in the satisfactoriness of one's self alone all fall on the same sword in the play's final soliloquy, which is appropriately appealing and introspective by turns. When Andrews compares the destructive will of Fox Melarkey with that of Frank Hardy in Friel's later play *Faith Healer* (1979), he concludes that, for both men, 'the desire to penetrate to the "private core" takes the form of a kind of negative capability which presses toward non-identity, non-being'.[73] A state of non-identity is simply and silently achieved at the close of *Crystal and Fox*: Fox is left with his head buried in his arms.

Critics follow Andrews' lead in finding the extensive similarities between *Crystal and Fox* and *Faith Healer*. Giovanna Tallone's 'Brian Friel's Fox Melarkey and Frank Hardy' (1999) is perhaps the most exhaustive of these comparative studies. Her understanding of the process of stylisation undertaken in both plays is pertinent, as she explains the stagecraft that transforms props and the playing place into the body of the protagonist – in much the same way, it might be argued, as Bloom becomes the body of Molly's book *Ruby: the Pride of the Ring* in *Ulysses*. For Tallone, Fox Melarkey and Frank Hardy are incorporated and substantiated before the audience since 'Fox Melarkey *is* his own show' (original emphasis) and the advertising banner in *Faith Healer* is 'the quintessential Frank Hardy'.[74] Tallone's conception of how the performed body of the popular performer is constituted in stage mechanics can be associated with the foregoing discussion of the comic occurrence that entails becoming other – be that the approximation of clown to circus tent in Jack Yeats' *The Double Jockey Act*, or Malachi to Stilt-Jack and ageing voice to old chattels in W.B. Yeats' 'High Talk' and 'The Circus Animals' Desertion' respectively. The comic effect of that absolute identification with the performance medium is as complicated in Friel's plays as it is in any of the other texts, perhaps in part because what is represented is a chimerical kind of mixed media – of theatre, circus, variety and 'fit-up' – that is more deftly composed than the heteroglossic plays of Jack Yeats.

In all cases, the melange of popular performance styles might be reconsidered alongside the concept of the 'attendant' that is defined by Gilles Deleuze in *The Logic of Sensation* (1981; 2012) through comparative analysis of characters in plays by Beckett and figures in paintings by Francis Bacon. Deleuze introduces the 'attendant', who is typical to both artists' work, once he has established that 'Beckett's Characters and Bacon's Figures share a common setting, the same Ireland: the round area, the isolator, the Depopulator'.[75] He describes this curious being:

> Even Beckett's characters require attendants that measure the intimate allotropic variations of their bodies, and that *look inside their heads* ('Can you hear me?' 'Can anyone see me?' 'Can anyone hear me?' 'Does anyone care about me at all?'). In both Bacon and Beckett, the attendant can be reduced to the circle of the circus ring, to a photographic apparatus or camera, to a photo-memory. But there must be an attendant-Figure for the variation-Figure. And doubtless the double variation, moving in two directions, can affect a single Figure, but obviously it can also be divided between two Figures. And the attendant, for its part, can be two attendants, or several attendants (but in any case the interpretation of the attendant as a voyeur or spectator is insufficient, merely figurative).[76]

In the concluding parenthesis, Deleuze expresses the same will to confuse figures within the playing place – whatever that might be, since canvas, theatre, photograph, circus ring and the so-called private theatre are all implicated or indicated here – in a manner reminiscent of Jack Yeats' narrator in *Sligo*. After all, it is 'the circle of the circus ring' that begins this translation of the theorist's list of potential attendants. The anxiety stemming from how one is perceived in the hereafter that is audible in the poetic voice of W.B. Yeats' *Last Poems* and in the lines of Friel's Fox – whether anyone will hear, see or care about what one has done, and what one has failed to do – is measured, at least in part, from that location.

The spatial and formal complexity of *Crystal and Fox* was not well received when the work was first produced. Hostile reviews published after the play opened in Dublin criticised its quick shifts and changes. It was felt that 'too many things happen too fast, and often in inexplicable ways, which compresses the full development of the play's motifs'.[77] It would seem, rather perversely, the television generation watching Friel's play were unable to keep pace with the rhythms and cadences borrowed by the dramatist from variety and the circus. Also contained within this criticism is a will towards predictable narrative and explication; a will towards realism. F.C. McGrath's post-colonial interpretation of Ireland's relationship to realism posits Friel as the latest inheritor of a 'distinguished tradition of Irish mendacity'.[78] Corresponding with arguments made in the previous chapter concerning the political project behind the choice of certain creative forms, McGrath furthers claims advanced by Declan Kiberd in *Inventing Ireland* by stating that: 'The Irish rejection of realism, however, is not merely voluntary but structurally compelling. Realism, objectivity, and a worship of facts are only possible within a homogenous, consensual community.'[79] The bind in which Fox Melarkey finds himself is that the rejection of realism is, in fact, no longer compelling and audiences are no longer willing to suspend disbelief to the extent required by these once-popular forms. Writing of the Fox Melarkey Show's fictional audience, Scott Boltwood broadens the implications of their disenchantment:

> the audience witnesses only Fox's incompatibility with a contemporary Irish culture which his troupe no longer satisfies. The same is true for the Irish Republic; in none of the early plays do we witness the diachronic decline of the state, only the present where it is portrayed as as hostile and uncultured as Melarkey's road show.[80]

Boltwood's unforgiving misperception of the culturelessness of the Fox Melarkey Show undoes the critic's own point by its snobbery and its false conviction in the idea that Fox Melarkey is his own show. In a more patient appreciation of the media – better still, the performance cultures – represented in *Crystal and Fox*, it becomes appreciable that Friel contains his critique of the culturelessness of the present Irish Republic within the traditional forms themselves: within circus, variety and the fit-up show. Critical responses to the play when it was first produced synchronise with its contents: like the voice behind 'The Circus Animals' Desertion', Fox and Friel are equally incompatible with their contemporary audience.

It was an unrealised ambition of W.B. Yeats to organise a travelling theatre company whose performances to rural audiences would run tangentially to the centre of Ireland's national theatre, the Abbey, in Dublin.[81] Sixty years later, in the lecture 'The Theatre of Hope and Despair' (1967), roving performers presented themselves to Friel as metaphors for the state of his art form in contemporary Ireland. The playwright described how he aligned himself as an artist with traditional forms and their responsiveness to at-times hostile conditions:

The arts grow and wither and expand and contract erratically and sporadically. Like beachcombers or Irish tinkers they live precariously, existing from idea to idea, from theory to theory, from experiment to experiment. They do owe something to the immediately previous generation; they owe something to the tradition in which they grow; and they bear some relationship to current economic and political trends. But they are what they are at any given time and in any given place because of the condition and climate of thought that prevail at that time and in that place. And if the condition and climate are not right, the arts lift their tents and drift off to a new place.

Flux is their only constant; the crossroads their only home; impermanence their only yardstick.[82]

Various levels of literary and pop cultural allusion at play in this extract reinforce Friel's major argument. Stephen Dedalus, the beachcomber of ideas, is brought into view; Synge and Beckett too step forward in the specifically Irish tinkers; an artist is as much a showman as he plays in his metaphoric tent at the crossroads. Above all, Malachi Stilt-Jack looms over the statement, while Friel talks impersonally of the need to stalk on through fluctuations of hope and despair. Fifteen years later, he surveyed the work of the Field Day Theatre Company and reinforced the itinerant foundations of that project on its second anniversary. Friel's symbiotically artistic and political enterprise, which aimed to redefine the concept of a national theatre, was rooted in a negative zone of dispossession:

Seamus Deane has written a number of essays on me, and that's one of his persistent points, that I'm some sort of displaced person, you know? If there are parallels in my own life I don't know. There is certainly a sense of rootlessness and impermanence. […] In some kind of a way I think Field Day has grown out of that sense of impermanence, of people who feel themselves native to a province or certainly to an island but in some way feel that a disinheritance is offered to them.[83]

The dramatist had insisted on the idea of disinheritance before. His recourse to metaphors derived from or associated with disestablished, traditional performance forms is perhaps explained through comments made in an interview with Eavan Boland in 1973. Friel said: 'All over the English-speaking world theatre is in a state of chaos. And in this country, where we don't have a theatrical tradition, we don't know whether we should attend theatre, or go and be entertained by it, or go as a kind of package tour to it.'[84] Friel's implication is that the theatre experience in Ireland is alternately considered as an adoptive descendant of the Mass or in contrast to lighter, more frivolous entertainments. His trio of descriptors for passive states of witness is almost Yeatsian, recollecting as it does 'The Theatre, The Pulpit, and The Newspapers' (1903), an essay in which W.B. Yeats outlines his own revisionist project as he sets out what Warner Berthoff has described as 'his wearying fight for an "Irish Literary Theatre" free of parochialism'.[85] Seven decades on, it would seem that the visionary's tiresome project was, as yet, incomplete.

In his earlier short story 'The Illusionists' (1963), Friel wrote of a similarly disorientating moment at which the lever swung from hope to despair and when Irish theatre's two parent forms competed for attention.[86] The story's narrator places his remembered self on the threshold between childhood and adolescence. Two scenes are described: the last visit of illusionist M. L'Estrange to his village primary school, where the boy's father is the school's principal and entire staff, and a disastrous dinnertime with L'Estrange at the narrator's family home. The most obvious reason for the plural title intervenes parenthetically on the recollection of the end of M. L'Estrange's show: '(I was always embarrassed at Father bowing, as if he had been part of the entertainment.).'[87] At home that evening, a drunken M. L'Estrange gives voice to the kind of disrespectful thoughts the narrator believes he had as a boy about his father, who is finally sent to bed by his wife, blind-drunk and emasculated. Far more disturbing is his father's defacement and desecration of the illusion itself: the English-accented Monsieur Illusionist L'Estrange, famed for his brilliance in cities across Europe, is exposed as Barney O'Reilly, the country boyo from County Galway. When the boy is forced to follow L'Estrange into the dark and return his forgotten hat, he is faced with a monstrous conversion: the all-powerful performer now prostrate with drink, corpse-like, and occultishly effeminate with hands like the witch in *Hansel and Gretel*. To see this powerful symbol so degraded compels the boy to return to his mother, who comforts and dissolves his distress with the memory of past joys, and the promise of their repetition, God willing. The indication that she herself is an illusionist is far subtler. Ultimately, 'The Illusionists' enacts a conversion of one artificial system of belief into another – or, more precisely, a reversion to a system in which the subject of truth is polluted by the matter of belief. Anticipatorily, this is a moment of faith healing in Brian Friel's fiction, which is obviously flawed and problematic, but nonetheless conclusive within the given narrative.

That the diabolic figure from whom the boy retreats in a return to his mother's simpler, pastoral vision of pleasure and plenty should be called M.

L'Estrange enables an important, if somewhat surprising, connection. In Flann O'Brien's obscure play *Faustus Kelly* (1943), the green-clawed Devil himself appears briefly in the prologue: a silent tableau in which urban council chair and would-be TD Mr Kelly signs away his soul. Thereafter, the Prince of Darkness is represented on stage by a stranger wearing a bowler hat and striped trousers who is named by a desperate Kelly as 'Mr Strange'. But it is not just Kelly's soul that is up for sale in the play; the corruption of the soul of the nation is also a matter of comic concern. Act One takes place in the council chamber and during the urban council meeting, and ex-TD Shawn Kilshaughraun makes a submission in favour of continuing support for the tourist association:

> We must do everything in our power to bring the beauties of this town that is so full of grand ... historical ... rich ... archaeological and scenic wonders to the notice of the world at large – and to the notice of our own grand flesh and blood beyond the seas, the sea-divided Gael in America. Not three guineas I'd give them but four.[88]

A weary response to this performance comes from fellow council member Reilly: 'I never seen an American in this town in me life bar lads that come with Duffy's Circus.'[89] Reilly's quip and the Duffy's reference reveal that enchantment is an American import and not an Irish export, thereby undercutting Kilshaughraun's determination to stage the nation through the medium of the tourist association in the presumed hope of attracting wealthy returnees. And in naming the former politician after Boucicault's most famous protagonist – a mock-heroic character written into existence by a dramatist who played the American market – O'Brien signals his own intention to defy and to revise dramatic conventions established, according to Purser, in the wake of Boucicault's supposed originality.

Essentially, these sentiments are managed in George Moore's bitterly allegorical short story 'A Play-House in the Waste', which was published in *The Untilled Field* (1903), a collection that is coincident with the founding of the Abbey Theatre. Reversing the advance publicity process advocated by Councilman Kilshaughraun (which he falsely believes will make Ireland obvious and attractive to the sea-divided Gael), Moore's authorities pity the disappearance of the 'poor Celt' awash in America.[90] The community the story represents is no longer enchanted with the idea of emigration, but neither are they rooted contentedly at home. Their sense of dislocation is similar to that experienced by the boy in 'The Illusionists', as Moore's narrator regrets: 'Even the well-to-do want to go away. The people are weary of the country, they have suffered too much. I think that they wish to lose themselves.'[91] The parish priest Father McTurnan's project – to provide fantastic relief by building a play-house and staging the miracle plays he witnessed during his time in Germany – is intended to capture the imagination with a proto-Brechtian, anti-naturalistic theatre where home industries and the Catholic Church have failed. The focus of communal disappointment is therefore similar to that offered by Yeats in 'The Theatre, The Pulpit and The Newspapers' and to Friel's denunciation of the state of Irish theatre in his interview with Eavan Boland. Inevitably, however, the play-house becomes a site surrounded by repulsive superstition, as it commemorates for the community an abuse of life in its most vulnerable state. An infant child born to the girl cast by the priest in the part of Good Deeds in his miracle play is supposedly murdered by its grandmother, the suggestively named Mrs Sheridan, and is seen as a ghost clutching at the play-house thatch.

The burial of a bastard child born to a performing parent, the child's haunting memory, and the community's subsequent rejection of faith in performance powerfully suggest 'A Play-House in the Waste' as a source for *Faith Healer*. Moreover, the hostile sentiments expressed regarding America in Moore's story prefigure Friel's own anxieties for Irish culture in the mid- to late twentieth century, as they are expressed in 'The Theatre of Hope and Despair'. Friel lamented the perceived negative influence of the American theatre on dramatic arts worldwide. Borrowing an image from Seán Ó Faoláin, he derided the insufficiency of 'American dramatic ants' who he considered too weak to constitute a species of their own. W.B. Yeats, writing in 'An Irish National Theatre', echoes throughout Friel's continuing attack, especially his distaste for the 'shrewd business managements' who pack out Broadway theatres because they satisfy audiences by then addicted to 'rudimentary and thoughtless entertainment': '"serious" theatre will soon find that it can't get a foothold on Broadway at all'.[92] His interview with Desmond Rushe in 1970 is littered with similar opinions, comparable to Reilly's jibe about Duffy's Circus in *Faustus Kelly*, but far less obscure and far more vehement. It is no longer the theatre alone but the very nation itself that is vulnerable to Americanisation. Even the desirability of a reunited Ireland is less clear than it used to be, because 'the turn the Republic has taken over the past nine or ten years has been distressing, very disquieting. We have become a tenth-rate image of America – a disaster for any country.'[93]

Friel dramatised, sometimes controversially, his anxieties over the Americanisation of Irish culture in his breakthrough piece *Philadelphia, Here I Come!* (1964) and in *The Mundy Scheme* (1971), a play that in some ways extends the more desolate themes of *Crystal and Fox*. *The Mundy Scheme* centres on the fantastic and macabre transformation of the west of Ireland into either an overflow cemetery for international urban centres or a US naval base by Irish-American returnee, the Texan Homer Mundy. Friel was not the only theatre-maker ready to deploy such grotesque visions of Ireland in relation to America. In 1982, community theatre company Wet Paint were commissioned to produce a work that would raise the profile of a campaign to grant performers in Dublin street act licences. The company devised *Jem Casey's Historical Tour of Ireland*, which was mischievously marketed as an alternative to those tourist attractions which turned theatre into the kind of 'package tour' that Friel so despised. Played on Dublin's Grafton Street, principal actor Owen Roe describes the piece as 'a hokey version of Irish history that was also a satire on the *Rambo* culture that was popular at the time [...] the whole thing was clowny and grotesque'.[94] Roe recalls that the comedian Hal Roach was unintentionally present for one of Wet Paint's performances. Roach, known as the King of Blarney, had begun his career on the stage as an illusionist and magician. His later move to comedy proved successful and lucrative: he broke a world record by performing for twenty-six years at the Irish Cabaret hosted by Jury's Hotel, Ballsbridge. Roach produced his crude and derogatory humour on an industrial scale, and one can only imagine what might have been W.B. Yeats' opinion of his mechanical repetition of Irish stereotypes made audible in the blunt rhythms of such monosyllabic lines as: 'We laugh at ourselves here in the Emerald Isle. Yes, we do. We laugh at wakes, funerals, death, marriage. You name it, we laugh at it.'[95] But the comedian's depreciation of the nation was apparently favoured by a contingent of returning Irish-American tourists. Stand-up show *An Audience with Hal Roach* (1988) was filmed at Jury's for television broadcast on the night when American Ambassador Margaret Heckler was in attendance. Heckler commented to introducer Mike Murphy that when Roach went on his American tours, it was as though 'one of the treasures of Ireland is missing'.[96] His bit about the Widow Quinn is exemplary of his style of humour:

> My dear people, let me try in my own inadequate way to describe to all of you the Widow Quinn: a wild woman from the hills of County Carey [*sic*] with a figure like six miles of bad road. Long red hair all down her back, none on her head. An ugly woman, God bless her. When she went to the zoo she had to have two tickets: one to get in and one to get out.[97]

In his so-called jokes, Roach doubles up the Irish in order to cast them as both spectacle and spectator: his collectively self-reflexive jest supposedly absolves him of any accusations of political incorrectness. But out of the specific context of a given performance, Hal Roach was subject to this same corrective process that day on Grafton Street when faced with a grotesque reflection of his own life's work in the form of Jem Casey, Ireland's historical tour guide, and his attendant company of fat-bottomed Americans. In Roe's memory, it was as though the King of Blarney experienced something of the anguish of perceivedness: 'he stood watching *Jem Casey* and he was disgusted. Because we were making fun of his bread and butter. Paddy the Clown …'.[98]

The persona of Jem Casey was borrowed, of course, from O'Brien's *At Swim-Two-Birds* (1939). Roe developed Casey's physical presence from two quite distinct traditions. His movements were informed by his work with the Oscar Mime Company, Ireland's first mime company that worked in the style of the Commedia dell'Arte. More provocatively, the actor's facial expressions imitated Irish caricatures familiar to nineteenth-century English audiences through *Punch* – caricatures which were brought to life on the nineteenth-century stage by rollicking Irish clowns such as Tom Barry, Barney Brallaghan and O'Donnel at venues including Astley's London Amphitheatre. As *Jem Casey* developed, Roe amalgamated and embodied images of the Irish included in the impassioned illustrated treatise *Nothing But the Same Old Story* published by Information on Ireland in 1984, which told the story of anti-Irish racism in England through pictures.[99] The book's title is borrowed from Paul Brady's furious song of the same name; its lyrics are printed on one of a number of frontispieces and face an endorsement by the then Greater London Council leader, Ken Livingstone.[100] Given the situation of this reference in the present argument, it is relevant to note that Brady contributed a performance of an extended version of 'Nothing But the Same Old Story' for Hummingbird Productions' landmark series *Bringing It All Back Home* (1991): a brother in Boston absent from the published lyrics gets a mention on the television. But the brother's invitation to join him in America is not accepted, since the voice has made plans with a 'girl from his home place' to 'move back and give it a try'.[101] Problematically, the prevailing sense is that they never get around to going back, or going anywhere, and that Brady's 'dressed up monkey in a cage' is stuck playing his accordion for the entertainment of a culpable crowd.[102] The verses transmit similarly overwhelming levels of disenchantment with the idea of emigration as 'A Play-House in the Waste' and *Crystal and Fox*. Brady's persona is akin to Gabriel Melarkey who loses his way as migrant in Friel's amorality play, constricted as he is by the same double-bind that afflicts Michael in *Exile*. In novel, play and song, the naive belief in the mythic possibility of bringing it all back home, or of going back to the home place, is consistently undermined.

Giving Voice to Irish Theatre: Stewart Parker's Heavenly Bodies (1986)

Roe returned to *Nothing But the Same Old Story* twenty years later when he played Johnny Patterson in the 2004 Rough Magic production of Stewart Parker's *Heavenly Bodies*. The actor considered his time as Jem Casey as preparatory for the role: 'I took my look from *Punch*: I wore a flying helmet and was made up with simian features. The whole thing was clowny, grotesque – borrowed from the Irish caricatures of Victorian England; William Carleton, that kind of thing. So when it came to doing Johnny Patterson, I was ready!'[103] It is possible to trace the wider influence of Flann O'Brien, and especially of *Faustus Kelly*, in Parker's last plays, *Northern Star* (1984) and *Heavenly Bodies*, which investigate ventriloquially Ireland's theatrical heritage. Where O'Brien follows Moore's lead in representing Boucicault and Bernard Shaw in the names of his characters Shawn Kilshaughraun and the English-accented Irishman Mr Shaw, Parker is perhaps more ambitious in an endeavour that is revisionary in the sense of both rehearsing Irish theatrical conventions and thereby questioning their authority. In *Northern Star*, Parker adopts the technique used by virtuoso mimic Joyce in 'Oxen of the Sun', assuming the styles of major Irish writers for the theatre from Farquhar to Beckett and sustaining those styles throughout episodes in the life and death of the founder of the United Irishmen, Henry Joy McCracken. Audiences to the rebel's staged failure are left with an image that is familiar, perhaps, from Moore's 'A Play-House in the Waste' and from Friel's *Faith Healer*, but that is conveyed by Parker in an effort towards Beckettian syntax: 'We never made a nation. Our brainchild. Stillborn. Our own fault. We botched the birth.'[104] Distinctly, in *Heavenly Bodies*, it is no longer individual writers who are imitated in order to interrogate Irish cultural and political history. Instead, Parker unwittingly confirms that the circus is an exemplary version of the Deleuzian attendant: it is the clown Johnny Patterson who, as the medium's envoy, is invested with the critical power to look inside the head of Dion Boucicault and tease out the broad implications of the playwright's existential anxiety.

Parker suggested how performance forms might be compellingly combined as he surveyed Ireland's cultural foundations in his John Malone Memorial Lecture, resonantly entitled *Dramatis Personae* (1986). In this lecture, Parker was prepared to radically reconstruct the cultural institutions of the whole island of Ireland. By way of introduction, Parker identified the 'dramatis personae' who had a hand in forming his own outlook as an artist: the author of the miracle play *Everyman*, Bertolt Brecht, Samuel Beckett, and John Malone joined the proud owner of a conjuring set: Parker's child self one Christmas. In representing these figures, Parker posed his audience some challenging questions. Speaking out of the context of Troubles Belfast, he asked what role drama might play in his society at that time. His sustained conviction in the power of the miracle to enchant communities distinguishes his perspective from Moore's bleak outlook as he answered rhetorically:

> I find myself thrown back on *Everyman* and the Christmas conjuring set by these questions. Since those days, I have been endeavouring somehow to discover or develop a form of drama for myself which can accommodate both these poles: the poetry and the trickery, the spiritual journey and the glitterball, the message and the sight-gag, the ludic and the ludicrous.[105]

It might be surmised from this mission that Parker would have been far less concerned than Brian Friel was by Irish audiences' perceived inability to deploy the correct verb when describing the action of going to the theatre.

Lynne Parker relates her uncle to Beckett in saying that, '[l]ike Beckett, Stewart was interested in the metaphysics of vaudevillian and circus motifs'.[106] *Heavenly Bodies* represents an effort to intersect metaphysical concerns with physical performance, as Parker resurrects the clown Patterson to inquire into the legitimacy, in both personal and professional terms, of the playwright Dion Boucicault. The inquiry is undertaken through the performance of vignettes drawn from the life of Boucicault that operate in a similar fashion to those relayed in 'The Circus Animals' Desertion', in that they recycle and revise episodes in personal history that have assumed considerable significance and exercised widespread influence in national cultural development. But unlike Yeats' 'I', Parker's Boucicault is yet to enter into a state of self-awareness in actual, spiritual or metaphorical terms. This Boucicault's will is not to self-denigrate or interrogate, but to secure his own history and immortality: delusions of grandeur convince him of his more noble origins and his right to a place in the canon of literary theatre.

Legitimacy is the central concern of *Heavenly Bodies*. The kind of charitable reading of Boucicault's heroes Purser offers (in an attempt to reason out Jack Yeats' preference for the melodramatist over Shakespeare) is disputed by Patterson's attitude and by Parker himself, who gives his caricature of Queen Victoria a line that sounds rather like a rewrite of one of Hal Roach's self-reflexive jokes: 'You show us our Irish subjects in the manner that renders them the most beloved to us.'[107] Nonetheless, the perhaps illegitimate appeal of Boucicault's plays to the popular sensibility of later generations of those Irish subjects was also recognised by circus troupes travelling the country in the depressed 1950s. John Banville remembered the enchanting source for the fictional company Prospero's Magic Circus that is central to his novel *Birchwood* (1973):

> I should explain that the circus is a circus I knew as a child when my family spent the summers by the seaside in Rosslare. It was a travelling circus that pitched its tent for a week in the centre of a field of chalets where we stayed. As I say in the novel, it was more a theatre than a circus: interspersed among the acrobatics and the clowning they played scenes from melodramas, by Boucicault and the like. There was an act in which a chicken was hypnotised – the hypnotist later came and sat in front of the stage and played the accordion. I went to every performance that week, seven performances at a shilling each – seven performances and possibly a matinee also. I was entranced.[108]

Significantly, Banville resists the idea of the circus in much the same way as does Owen Roe in his characterisation of Parker's Patterson as a music-hall clown and not a circus clown, despite the playwright's clear and careful indication of the facts of Patterson's performing life in dialogue and stage directions. In interview, the actor reconsidered the role: 'I always thought of Johnny as more rooted in the music hall than the circus – I saw him as a music hall clown.'[109] In resisting that specific term, Banville and Roe unconsciously relate themselves to Parker's Boucicault, who far more emphatically denies any association between his art, which defies definition, and the allegedly less fraught and less self-reflexive performance concept of circus.

Heavenly Bodies opens metatheatrically with an acting class led by Boucicault in which students perform extracts of Wilhelm Meyer Lutz's opera *Faust and Marguerite* (1855). As Parker's play continues, and Patterson assumes a Mephistophelean role, he is complemented by the figure of the Phantom Fiddler who wanders onto the stage in silence at pivotal moments: Boucicault is convinced that this is his father, but his entreaties to the Fiddler are as futile as Bloom's to his son Rudy in 'Circe'.[110] Boucicault's claim to a place among the stars of Irish theatre are frustrated, chiefly by Patterson's revival of the playwright's supposed sell-out of Irish stereotypes to English and American producers and audiences. The clown attacks:

> You flattered the daylights out of them, with your silver-tongued charming peasant rascals, and all their winning, wheedling, conniving

ways … your colonial soul discovered its strength in fraudulence and deceit, Dizzy had you right, you were in the conjuring business, you conjured up a never-never Emerald Isle, fake heroics and mettlesome beauties and villains made of pasteboard, outwitted through eternity by the bogus grinning peasant rogue as only you could play him – with the blather and codology and the gaslight moonshine.[111]

When he played the provocative but apparently virtuous Johnny Patterson, Owen Roe seemed aware that the clown was similarly vulnerable. Relating Parker's character to one of the models for his own performance of him, Roe appreciated that 'he knew his roots. But there's also something of Tony Hancock about him: the more he builds himself up, there's farther for him to fall.'[112] The real Patterson's own transactions with not only American circus promoters but also those in Ireland and England resulted in him conveying his national origins in stereotypical costume and content which have been detailed in the first chapter of this book. The idea of buying in and selling out personae is implicit in a review published in Canada during his North American years. On 18 August 1877, the *Toronto Daily Leader* ran enthusiastically with: 'This great wit, a new importation, not only a clown but a Celtic clown, is not one of the least of the attractions belonging to the Great London Show.'[113] Patterson is represented as object and possession, and the depersonalised Celtic clown becomes a profitable commodity of England's capital show. Parker's reliance upon a character who, in reality, cultivated the persona of the stage Irishman for financial gain as a means of revealing Boucicault's own acquisitive hypocrisies is, then, problematic – and self-consciously so. Cultural history is revised in order that the clown might exist within an angle of perception that does not strike the subject down in anguish, but rather elevates him to the status of witty and ironic hero. To quote Roe, his 'Paddywhackery' becomes that much more complex: 'comic, but dark'. It is fascinating that the actor should have worked to achieve that compound mood by co-ordinating Patterson's 'Paddywhackery' with comic performance styles he perceived as 'British' in a quote that is worth repeating:

I always thought of Johnny as more rooted in the music hall than the circus – I saw him as a music hall clown. I suppose I know more about British music hall than Irish music hall, but do you know Billy Bennett? 'Almost a gentleman'? I thought of Patterson as that kind of comedian.[114]

In this way, Patterson becomes a peculiar hybrid of stage Irish and Englishmen whose roots are, in fact, far from fixed.

Arguably, Parker redeems Patterson from the pathetic end that finished off his career as a circus Irishman, and transforms him into a powerful political symbol. This act of non-standard revisionism advances the dramatist's inquisition of what an 'Irish' artist was, is, or might be, which began in earnest in *Northern Star*. After all, he firmly believed that 'we learn nothing of consequence other than through Play'.[115] The raison d'être for the Field Day Theatre Company advanced by founder Brian Friel is brought back to mind in Marilynn Richtarik's sensitivity to the pathos of Parker's Boucicault, who suffers from a 'potent sense of dispossession'.[116] But for some critics, Parker's own central importance to the development of Irish theatre has been somewhat dispossessed. Gerald Dawe noted, and lamented, the playwright's absence from Kiberd's *Inventing Ireland*, since he could not 'think offhand of another playwright who, in the space of roughly a decade between the mid-1970s to the late 1980s, offered more light *specifically* on the various historical Irelands which inhabit the country called Ireland' (original emphasis).[117] Lynne Parker picked up on both Parker's undoubted sensitivity to those various historical Irelands and his sense of play as she produced *Heavenly Bodies* for the Abbey in 2004, enhancing those questionable histories which are stably constructed within the play text through music and stagecraft. Roe remembered in interview how the original music for this production, composed by Helen Montague and Ellen Cranitch, functioned to this end. Parker's revision of Patterson's ballad 'Do Your Best For One Another' was 'set to one of those nasally, Irish tenor-type tunes – really typical, like your uncle at a wedding'. Contrastingly, Roe described how the clown's account of the Famine:

> was played with this long low moan from a violin; it mirrored what was said. The horror of what was said was reflected. My delivery was definitely *not* an angry delivery – it was more as though Johnny Patterson was a journalist in a war zone. And it was beautifully underscored.[118]

While revealing Stewart Parker's so-called 'strategies of mischief', Lynne Parker described her own comic devices that played with sound in other, less harrowing ways:

> When we did *Heavenly Bodies* in the Peacock theatre, it coincided with the Abbey's production of *The Shaughraun*, and we tried a little theatrical mischief of our own. We rigged a tannoy, such as you would find backstage at any theatre, and created the illusion that as Boucicault described the scene, the real thing was being filtered down from upstairs, complete with

live audience reaction. It was a spooky effect, and strongly reinforced the point that whatever Boucicault's concerns about his literary immortality, his real and undisputed connection with the audience was alive and kicking in 2004.[119]

The Abbey's production of *The Shaughraun* was directed by John McColgan, most famous for his involvement in the phenomenally successful *Riverdance* enterprise. Recalling Lynne Parker's employment of the Tannoy as mischievous medium, Roe delighted in the fact that '*That* was what we were satirising' and continued: 'I don't know, I didn't see it but I've heard that it was a very broad production. Someone described it to me as "Bingo night at the Abbey"...'.[120] With this received opinion in mind, it is worth reflecting finally on a lost landmark of Irish entertainment history.

Circus historian George Speaight accounts for the decline in popularity of urban circuses across the nineteenth century.[121] By the early twentieth century, that decline hastened as the appeal of the cinema became widespread. While some former circus venues closed and were entirely repurposed, others adapted and survived by responding to the changing tastes of audiences. Belfast's Hippodrome, where Reco's Circus had performed in the 1940s, was necessarily reconfigured from season to season as a venue for all sorts of entertainment and leisure pursuits. The original performance space – a variety theatre with a thirty-six-foot by forty-six-foot proscenium arch stage – was built in 1907 beside Belfast's Opera House. By 1931, it had been reconditioned, becoming the Hippodrome Cinema. Annually, a live and vivid circus temporarily coloured the Hippodrome, replacing what John Hinde thought of as the drabness of the cinema screen and the bray of loudspeakers.[122] In later years, the Belfast Hippodrome would see IRA bomb damage, house a bingo hall, and finally be razed in 1998 to make way for a multi-storey car park.[123] The building was, then, a kind of attendant to Irish history for over ninety years. As Lynne Parker and her company made *Heavenly Bodies* and *The Shaughraun* coincide, the Abbey Theatre complex brought together circus, theatre, dance, song, live and recorded music, and – for some, at least – bingo, all under the one roof. And so it would seem that, in another life, the Belfast Hippodrome might have become Ireland's national theatre.

CHAPTER 4

Revisioning the Circus

The true image of the past flits by. The past can be seized only as an image that flashes up at the moment of its recognizability, and is never seen again.

Walter Benjamin, 'On the Concept of History' (1940)[1]

American photographer Bruce Davidson was honeymooning in Ireland in 1967. This celebrated member of the Magnum Photos Co-operative had been preoccupied with the circus as a photographic subject from the outset of his career, and during his stay in Ireland he took a series of photographs at James Duffy and Sons Circus for *Holiday* magazine. It was while on another *Holiday* assignment in Wales two years earlier that the photographer had realised how to harness what he thought of in his youth as the 'magic' of the photographic process.[2] In Wales, he says, 'I started to stage-direct the picture.'[3] Davidson brought to an unspecified location in semirural Ireland his characteristically acute sensitivity to local, social customs and his startling ability to reveal, if not criticise, in a single shot all the complexities of impersonal social orders surrounding the people he photographed. These traits are in clear evidence in his work at Duffy's: dynamic compositions featuring artists and audiences inside the big top are complemented by 'stagey' group and family portraits taken on the showground. Jennifer Watts considers 'the stylized placement and framing of his subjects, the use of artificial light, the direct gaze of the participants, the staging and drama of it all' as the consolidation of 'years of working, looking, and being in the field'.[4] Davidson's photographs of circus family units are particularly gripping in this regard.

The performers in Fig. 4.1 do not offer themselves freely to the camera; instead they present themselves on bold, static terms – although the inviting almost-smile on the faces of the mother and her baby must be noted. In this image, contrasting expressions of settlement, order, and home pride are marked

4.1 Bruce Davidson, *IRELAND. 1967. James Duffy and Sons Circus*, Gelatine silver print, Collection of the artist

and remarkable. The juxtaposition of the neat caravan, glamorous parents and well-turned-out children with the absent-minded dereliction of the surrounding housing estate confronts the viewer with an inquisition of convention and an inversion of type. In consequence, Davidson's images are eloquent in describing not only the social life of their *prima facie* subjects, but also the established society through which the travelling show moves. In the photograph's descriptive title, the family unit is first identified by place: *IRELAND*; then by time: *1967*; next by a line of showmen: *James Duffy and Sons Circus*. Ireland is pronounced in this sequence, emphasised in the taxonomy by capitalisation. This is the uniform index applied to each of Davidson's Duffy's shots. Thus, the family portrait is fixed within a decidedly nationed context by its title, in much the same way as the style of social housing or the vehicle registration plates indicate Ireland within the image. Even the deterioration that surrounds the pristine circus family and caravan has a peculiarly local specificity. Ireland the country is, then, seen through, or behind, Irish circus family subjects.

    Although Ireland might be revealed in this way for an individual viewer of the Duffy's images, Davidson himself believes ultimately in photography as a means of self-fashioning. He says: 'If I am looking for a story at all, it is in my relationship to the subject – the story that tells me, rather than that I tell.'[5] The suggested social commentary read from the family portrait reproduced above is, therefore, merely coincidental. The words beneath his images carry certain resonances for individual viewers that are subsequently transposed upon the pictures themselves. Truly, on reflection, little differentiates the Duffy's images from Davidson's other circus work. The smoking white-face dwarf he photographed while travelling through the scrubby meadows of Palisades, New Jersey, in 1958 could just as easily belong to Duffy's; the bleak anti-pastoral, semi-rural landscape seen behind him could just as well be Ireland, but for the instantly recognisable North American telegraph poles. Instead, it is the photographer's own identification with his subjects that is the apparent priority.

What, then, might the 34-year-old male photographer have seen of himself in his photograph of the Duffy's trapeze artist?

4.2 Bruce Davidson, *IRELAND. 1967. James Duffy and Sons Circus*, Gelatine silver print, Collection of the artist

The photograph reproduced at Fig. 4.2 is insistently physical. An intense connection with the trapeze artist is encouraged with the bold statement of the body and the sparseness of its surroundings, allowing the viewer to confront this circus artist almost face-to-face. Though costumed as woman, the planed and trained form of the performer is conditioned into a state of asexuality. Brutal sex acts are arguably synonymised with trapeze art in the rope, the bound feet, the cutaway costume that seems to gape at the groin, and the open mouth and concentrated brow of the woman, which co-ordinate to display an expression that could be ecstatic. Davidson was accustomed to meditating upon his sexualised subjects. When *Esquire* asked him to photograph topless entertainers in San Francisco in 1965, he commented: 'For me the true subject of these photographs was not these women's naked bodies but their endless loneliness.'[6] This worthy, but rather patronising, assumption about the erotic dancers is made amid a biographical introduction to a collection of Davidson's work published by Thames & Hudson in 1990. In an autobiographical essay entitled 'Life, Through my Eyes, Seen ...', Davidson writes of his own sense of loneliness and isolation as a child after his parents' divorce, the loss of his grandparents, and his mother's remarriage. Photography and its 'magic' became his solace and salvation – a means of travelling the world and seeing beautiful people on high-fashion catwalks and everyday people in city subway cars. The sexualised bodies of the topless dancers might thereby become something like a mirror for Davidson's own emotions; they become iconic repositories for the young man's feelings.

If this can be said of the topless dancers, then it might also be suggested that the trapeze artist performs a similar function for Davidson. Paul Bouissac reveals that in the circus system 'natural objects (humans, animals, artifacts) undergo a process of *iconization*' (original emphasis).[7] Davidson's trapeze artist becomes an illustrative case in point. Her pose, literally captured and exposed, takes the viewer far beyond earthly bodies. Although she is as stable as one might be deemed to be on her apparatus, her anxious expression is especially unsettling as she dangles in the darkest part of the photograph. Shadows seen in the big top and caught in print descend the greyscale from light, or somewhat lighter, to very dark indeed as the performer hangs in limbo. But up above the audience as an object of contemplation, she might assume more lofty significance. Her lean, almost wasted form, headdress and hairstyle, and her bound feet might refer us to mummified bodies – those exotic and eternally fascinating figures not beyond colonisation and cultural apprehension even in death – once they become thus iconised. More significantly, the aerialist might well be read as a visual quotation of Christian imagery, albeit a perversion of the religious scheme's iconography, as the sinewy body of the female figure performs the inverse crucifixion of Saint Peter. Davidson finished his biographical reflection in 1990 with a nearly affirmative, almost confident meditation on his corpus: 'But I think I have gone beyond my vision … in the heart of my own life, in the heart of other people's lives. Perhaps that is the most important thing I have done.'[8] The choice of 'vision' is particularly apt when looking upon the image of the trapeze artist as an example of Davidson's style. What the present viewer sees in her certainly cannot be bound within the confines of the big top tent.

The Image and the Vision: The Circus in Contemporary Irish Culture

'Thought takes the same form age after age,' wrote W.B. Yeats in 'The Theatre, The Pulpit, and the Newspapers'.[9] This chapter focuses on five late-twentieth-century texts in which the circus can be seen to take on the same form as Davidson's trapeze artist. Focused on the body of the female performer, these texts represent a trend in contemporary Irish writing that conflates sexual, sacred and circus images in the imagination of the young male narrator or principal actor. This recurrent, peculiarly specific means of dealing with sexual development and maturity displayed by male authors raised in, but dislocated from, the Irish Catholic faith has not been acknowledged until now. John Banville's *Birchwood* (1973), Paul Muldoon's 'Duffy's Circus' (*Mules*, 1977) and Seamus Deane's *Reading in the Dark* (1996) are comparable in the ways in which they constitute Irish political history and current affairs in sex scenes played out by circus characters. Contrastingly, Neil Jordan sought in his film *The Miracle* to push away the political, revealing instead the familiar and the personal through his Oedipal narrative set within the circus ring. Similarly, Seamus Heaney's poem 'Wheels within Wheels' (*Seeing Things*, 1991) revolves around an individual's exciting memories of the circus experience.

Banville offered a succinct explanation for the trend in interview, and the terms of his explanation have broad implications: 'To have been brought up in Ireland, in my time, was like being brought up in the circus – the Church, of course, being the ringmaster.'[10] Speaking specifically about his own work, Banville said that W.B. Yeats' 'The Circus Animals' Desertion' could act as an epigraph to *Birchwood* and cast the artist as fallible ringmaster within the exotic circus world.[11] Arguably, Banville misreads Yeats' poem in much the same way as Edna Longley – the critic's misapprehension of the poetic voice in

'The Circus Animals' Desertion' as 'ringmaster' was reviewed in the previous chapter. Banville's perhaps casual understanding of Yeats' poem allows for either himself as author or *Birchwood*'s aspiring artist narrator Gabriel Godkin to be positioned to usurp the role of the church as Ireland's ringmaster.

Such a profound, and yet at times deliberately inaccurate, appreciation for the poetry of W.B. Yeats is apparent in several of the primary works considered here. Muldoon's 'Duffy's Circus' was first published in an Arts Council Northern Ireland pamphlet, *Out of the Blue* (1973). The poet explained in interview that, at that time, 'I wouldn't have been as deeply into Yeats as I am now.'[12] Despite the fact that W.B. Yeats was 'not in the foreground' of Muldoon's imagination as he wrote about Duffy's, Michael Longley's poetic response 'Stilts' could not have been written without *Last Poems* in mind. 'Stilts' appeared in the collection *Man Lying on a Wall* (1976) and is dedicated to Muldoon.[13] The allusion to Yeats' 'High Talk' is clear within Longley's poem, which transforms the political situation of Northern Ireland into a circus by metaphor. Muldoon commented that in the early seventies, he and Longley 'were almost writing each other's poems. We were extremely close.'[14] The Juvenalian transpositioning of current affairs from the political arena to the circus ring is undertaken to great yet subtle effect in the poem that inspired 'Stilts', 'Duffy's Circus'. Deane, meanwhile, revises a recurrent figure in Yeats' poetry whose final appearance is made in *On the Boiler* (1939). The poet's Crazy Jane becomes the novelist's Crazy Joe in *Reading in the Dark*: a semi-autobiographical work, which charts the inverse relationship between a young boy's development into manhood and the worsening political situation in Northern Ireland over twenty-five years. Infused and confused by Catholic teaching, Deane's young male narrator is disturbed by local character Crazy Joe, who looks impatiently upon the child's immaturity: 'Copulate if you must. Get it over and done with. Then grow up.'[15] But Crazy Joe occupies a peculiar, unearthly position: his mental illness fixes him in the land of eternal youth. Arguably, this is where the boys who give voice to this chapter's focal texts long to remain – or better still, to where the grown men behind these voices give the impression of returning through childhood memory reconstituted in the circus image.

Neil Jordan's *The Miracle* shifts attentions decisively away from the political situation in contemporary Ireland. The few critics who have hitherto considered the role of the circus in the film have insisted upon the relationship between the sequences shot at Fossett's Circus and, again, the fleeting circus images in 'The Circus Animals' Desertion'. Kathleen Gallagher Winarski reads *The Miracle* as a redemptive transformation of Yeats' despair, enacted as Jordan stretches literary traditions to liberate his own fiction. According to Gallagher Winarski, the poet's elusive theme is constituted by the director who can capture real circus animals on film, thereby 'breathing new life into Ireland's stories of family and nation'.[16] However, Jordan himself denies the relevance of Yeats' late-style melancholia for his work.[17] Heaney, meanwhile, analysed another of Yeats' last poems, 'Long-legged Fly', in his essay 'The Makings of a Music: reflections on Wordsworth and Yeats' (1978). In this reading, Heaney commented on the deficiency of 'images' as a term consistently applicable to Yeats' vision:

> 'Long-legged Fly' is a poem that is absolute in its poetic integrity, that commands us both by the stony clarity of its sounds and the deep probes of its images, though 'images' is too weak a word, is somehow inaccurate: it is more that every element in the poem is at once literal and symbolic.[18]

Nevertheless, 'image' is the word that Heaney settles upon in his reflections on Yeats. It is used again in his essay, and so its sense is now tacitly understood as complicated, without the sign itself being replaced. Finally, this act of revisiting the image and refuting its terms, but maintaining the original as a kind of ghost, is of signal importance to the present argument.

Vision and Revision: The Circus as a Way of Seeing in Birchwood *(1973)*

Generically, Banville's *Birchwood* is classical tragedy, gothic *Bildungsroman*, and Big House novel combined. Its young male narrator, Gabriel Godkin, recounts the disintegration by degrees of his Protestant Ascendancy family and his country's communal descent into a kind of madness. Structurally, *Birchwood* is a triptych. Principal characters in the family saga bearing the weight of truly Christian names are gruesomely iconised in Parts I and III of the novel, 'The Book of the Dead' and 'Mercury'. Terrible violence on a near-biblical scale follows the revelation of an incestuous relationship between Gabriel's father, Joseph, and his aunt, Martha. Part II, 'Air and Angels', represents runaway Gabriel's reflective account of his time with Prospero's Magic Circus: the boy is driven into their company by his quest for his twin sister, Rose, who is, in fact, a figment of his malevolent aunt's imagination. In early drafts, the troupe was to be named Sordello's Magic Circus: in this case, allusions would have been to Dante's *Purgatorio* (1472) and to Robert Browning's narrative poem *Sordello* (1840). In interview, however, the author made clear that his plot depended upon the colonial activity of England in the time of Shakespeare: 'Our aristocracy was destroyed by Elizabeth I and her lieutenants.'[19] Banville turns to and borrows from Jacobean Shakespeare to name his magic and malevolent circus company in *Birchwood* in order to reflect upon the fallout of the violent history of aristocratic decline in Ireland. The function of Prospero's ethereal cast is to offset Gabriel's home life with images from a world that is just as sudden and crazy and spiteful and gay. The section's title is, of course, taken from John Donne's 'Air and Angels' (1633), a poem in which distinctly gendered atmospheres of heterosexual love are represented. There, women are seen first like angels by the eyes of the male voice: beautiful, lofty and divine. But those lovely, glorious things are soon undone for signifying nothing. Similarly, an exposure of false images is at the heart of *Birchwood*.

Despite references to drama and poetry of the seventeenth century, Banville has insisted that the time-place of the work is at once Famine Ireland, civil war Ireland and the Ireland of his 1950s childhood, but never in any explicit ways: 'Ireland,' he said, 'has a very long historical memory and that's why I tried to set the book in no particular time.'[20] Remarkably, then, the story of Prospero's Magic Circus cuts straight through a family history that we are invited to read as a miniature history of the modern Irish nation. As in Davidson's photograph of the family caravan at James Duffy's Circus, the state of the country is seen through a circus subject. The circus is, then, a way of seeing in *Birchwood*, and less a spectacle in itself. Banville's quite deliberate inexactness is further evidenced in letters exchanged between the author and his publisher Secker & Warburg's literary director David Farrer following submission of the first draft of *Birchwood*. Farrer wrote on 18 April 1972: 'If the novel has a fault, it is in the lack of signposting.' He continued with notes for particular pages of the manuscript, suggesting that, on page seven, Banville flag that the historical moment was nineteenth-century Ireland: 'It is important to date this novel. At first reading it wasn't until I got the reference to Queen Victoria, nearly halfway through, that I realised the setting was not contemporary.' Beside this comment, Banville has made a simple, handwritten annotation: it is marked with a cross.[21]

The author continued to resist the fixing of *Birchwood* in one historical place while adapting the novel for the screen with Thaddeus O'Sullivan and Andrew Pattman. Considering the 'look' of the film, O'Sullivan wrote in a letter dated 17 November 1981:

> The Civil War could be mis-interpreted [*sic*] by an audience as being the specifically intended backdrop to the story. No matter how stylised the

film is, people will always look for that kind of gap in which they can 'ground' the film. If this were to happen to Birchwood the universality (that is to say, the 'Irish universality') of the theme might be more difficult to achieve: we would have less freedom as a result. I am in fact trying to preserve that very quality of non-naturalism which is of such concern to you.[22]

It is perhaps because of this preference for 'non-naturalism' that Banville was comfortable in interview with citing precisely the historical source for his cast of unreal, supernatural circus performers. Prospero's Circus was most definitely:

> a circus I knew as a child when my family spent the summers by the seaside in Rosslare. It was a travelling circus that pitched its tent for a week in the centre of a field of chalets where we stayed. As I say in the novel, it was more a theatre than a circus: interspersed among the acrobatics and the clowning they played scenes from melodramas, by Boucicault and the like. There was an act in which a chicken was hypnotised – the hypnotist later came and sat in front of the stage and played the accordion. I went to every performance that week, seven performances at a shilling each – seven performances and possibly a matinee also. I was entranced.[23]

Banville went on to state in interview: 'Naturalistic theatre does not interest me. Theatre should be playful, raucous, instinctive, magical. I wrote the book at the time when magic realism seemed to many of us a way forward. […] It was a false dawn, of course, as we quickly came to realise.'[24] Therefore, the circus offered a credible set of characters and scenarios that would help situate *Birchwood* within the genre of magic realism, which, at that time, its author believed to be the future path of literature.

Banville's circus provides an external means of upset within the Godkin family from the outset of the novel. Gabriel's disturbed mother, Beatrice, accepts a troupe onto the Birchwood estate: its members appear indistinguishable from the tinkers who act as premonitions or ghosts of the starving peasantry wandering a landscape where the Famine took hold. Mother-in-law and matriarch Granny Godkin blasphemes in the name of the Holy Family on sight of these 'grotesque figures': 'O Jesus Mary and Joseph they'll murder us all!'[25] But the child Gabriel is far more disturbed by ideas of endogamous destruction and near self-harm. His sense of the uncanny, and an especially unsettling kind of *unheimlich*, the double, has origins within the Godkin family itself. Cousin Michael, product of the incestuous relationship between Gabriel's father and aunt, is the primary cause of Gabriel's anxiety: pointedly, both boys are named for archangels. It is the 'terrifying notion' (p. 98) of 'a phantom of myself' (p. 99) which compels the boy to run away with Prospero's Magic Circus.

Banville has commented on the certain ambiguity of the circus as children's entertainment:

> as a child at the circus I was transported by a sense of gleeful terror. You never knew whether the acrobat might fall off the high wire and be killed; the tent-pole might crack; the tent might be blown down, smothering us all. The circus is an image of violence barely contained. It is a little world within a world, barely controlled by its ringmaster – yes, the Church, or, if you like, the British Army, was ringmaster in those days.[26]

Gabriel's entry into the circus world is only permitted after he has thrown off the privilege of such childish toys as soldiers, tin drums and rocking horses: 'I broke them all, threw them all away. What were these paltry things compared to Birchwood, out of whose weeping walls I could knock the bright reverberations of fantasy?' (p. 34). This passage negates the value Walter Benjamin urgently placed in the objects of child's play in 'The Cultural History of Toys' (1928).[27] Gabriel's destruction of his soldiers and drums and the red rocking horse – military miniatures for the heir to an embattled estate – hints at a desire not to dominate, but to submit. This desire is satisfied for a time at Prospero's. Gabriel's part in this invading, occupying circus force performing in the name of Shakespeare's great coloniser is to play the role of Caliban in the ring. An act is contrived which opens with Gabriel's statement: '*Master, I am your slave, do with me what you could*' (original italics; p. 115). There seems to be something funny for the audience in seeing this well-spoken and, therefore, supposedly privileged young man apparently hypnotised into submission. Perversely, the metamorphoses which Gabriel subsequently performs – cock, snake, sea creature, bird, singer and dancer – give him a novel sense of freedom. This freedom depends upon fallacy, thereby conveying the complicated function of the circus within *Birchwood*. As in Ó Conaire's *Exile* and Seago's *Sons of Sawdust*, it is not a location without its troubles; certainly, it is not a place for children.

Birchwood's 'weeping walls' are marked with an invisible ink: the tears of those that have gone before and left their 'traces' of human depth behind them. Notably, certain episodes from 'The Book of the Dead' are repeated in 'Air and Angels', but that which was fantasy is revisioned in the form of a successively monstrous reality knocking about the canvas walls of the tent of Prospero's

Magic Circus. The trace of human depth in this alchemical location is an odd admixture of laughter with tears. Prospero's thereby unifies and animates two approximate Joycean concepts, one belonging to Stephen Dedalus and the other to Leopold Bloom. Without doubt, the circus in *Birchwood* does not provide such stuff as dreams are made on. Famously, Stephen cannot shake himself out of the fantastic nightmare that is Irish history: he is the crucible for grand, collective experience. Bloom's icon of personal history, pictured on the beach at 'Nausicaa', is less frequently recognised: 'Think you're escaping and run into yourself. Longest way round is the shortest way home. And just when he and she. Circus horse walking in a ring.'[28] The circus horse is the carrier of ambivalence and the vehicle for a perhaps melancholy, perhaps self-preserving accommodation of things as they happen – things that happen to be sexual. The circus image brings Bloom back to where he started out that morning – back to the place of sexual disturbance that is, even so, his point of origin that day. In joining Prospero's, the child Gabriel realises what the man Bloom only imagines.

As Banville remembered visits to the circus in his own childhood, he separated this world of performance from everyday life by considering its sexual potential:

> The circus has a strange erotic potential, an erotic energy, and that was what the authorities, Church and State, feared and discouraged: passionate energy of any kind. We were forced into meekness and quietude and a sinister sort of compliance. But energy, such as one encounters in the circus, encourages rebellion, resistance, and a Marx Brothers sort of anarchy. In the circus it looks as though real violence is being done – think of the clowns, how wild and uncontrolled they seem – how *rebellious*. And then there are those girls, in their corsets and sequins: posing and spinning in the powdery spotlights, what a dream-like eroticism they created. I know the circus didn't have any real similarity to our history of violence, of course. The circus was a life outside life. Yet it felt, for the duration of the performance, as uncontrollable, as makeshift, as potentially and gloriously anarchic as life itself.[29]

Banville indicated that the will to critique Ireland's history of violence and to recreate something of live performance's rebellious energy resulted in a unification of established cultural customs and radical political aims in a work that mocked the traditional Irish pastoral novel. Published in 1973, *Birchwood* offered a singular and yet unintentional response to the escalating Troubles. Banville remembered how expressive the circus had seemed in that moment:

As I look back at the novel, I see that it's quite political, but that was not my conscious intention. Northern Ireland was descending into horrors, and I was working in journalism at the time, dealing with reports of atrocities every night – I was a sub-editor, therefore I didn't report, only edited the reporters' work. So I suppose the anarchy and chaos of the circus offered a deep metaphor – but an *unintentional* metaphor, that I only recognised long afterwards.

The country was collapsing, it seemed. We thought we might well descend into absolute chaos and civil war. If the English army had withdrawn then, we would have seen internecine warfare on the scale of Bosnia.[30]

Banville narrates the prospect of his fellow countrymen transforming themselves, through internecine violence, into the kind of anarchic monster depicted by John Tenniel in his *Punch* cartoon, *Two Forces* (1881). According to Conor McCarthy, the ambivalence in Banville's perspective is apparent elsewhere in his writing. McCarthy argues influentially for the need to contextualise the novels of the 1980s and 1990s by placing them next to a discussion of Irish historiographical debate, thereby helping the critic to manage the tensions between realism and modernism, Irish and European literary traditions, the political optimism of the sixties and the nascent pessimism of the seventies which he sees as inherent to Banville's work. More broadly, this context helps McCarthy to accommodate, represent and negotiate in meaningful ways the 'moment of metanarrative crisis' at which these novels were written and published.[31] These tensions also operate throughout *Birchwood*, and it is, then, easy to appreciate Colm Tóibín's claim that, as a historical novel, it outstrips the work of any historian to become 'the most radical text in Irish revisionism'.[32] For Tóibín, the novel's melancholy lament for the repeated tragedy of Irish history is punctuated with loud bursts of 'dark laughter'.[33] Banville's laughter is truly disturbing, caused by an irresistible compulsion to repeat the past in a schizophrenic channelling of Irish history and historiographical debate, and ventriloquising of Irish literature.

Among the novel's most darkly comic scenes are Gabriel's rites of passage from childhood to adolescent maturity. These rites are generally marked by exposure to sex acts or sexual fantasies, which are frequently executed or expressed perversely. The boy is both passive voyeur and active participant in *Birchwood*'s sex scenes. In the opening section 'The Book of the Dead', his memories of early sexual activity are relayed with a mature tone proper to the retrospective account. Borrowing from L.P. Hartley's *The Go-Between* (1953),

Banville's narrator later insists: 'I was at that time an innocent lad to whom the dark damp side of life was still another country' (p. 130). But although the posture of this Housmanesque 'lad' towards that other country, the past, is self-conscious, Gabriel approaches his first participatory sexual experiences with Rosie, the farm girl, without a hint of anxiety. Rosie initiates an essential sequence of near-doublings, or faulty imitations. In early drafts of *Birchwood*, Banville tried out 'Maisie'[34] and variations on the name 'Bridget' for this character: 'Bridge', 'Bride' and 'Bríd' were all listed as possible alternatives.[35] But Rosie was the author's final choice. As Gabriel remembers feeling and fooling around with Rosie, he thinks upon an image of a 'Rose': a photograph, he is told by his biological mother Aunt Martha, of that invented long-lost sister. The photograph is, in fact, of his mother-substitute Beatrice. But the full significance of Rose and Rosie is almost insultingly blatant: both are, of course, diminutives of Rosaleen, that darkly beautiful icon of the aisling poem and cultural nationalism personified.

Gabriel's actual experiences with Rosie are communicated through incendiary language that is both indebted to Christian myth and clearly, if anachronistically, derived from psychoanalytic theory. As the children roll through the evening-time of a grassy wood, Rosie feels not floral like the rose, but like some far less romantic, no less symbolic species of fauna: her genitals are described as her 'furry damp secret' (p. 13). It is not shame that this son of Adam feels for his daughter-of-Eve sister, but rather pity: 'her delicate gash' is not the 'nice neat hole' the boy imagined; it is a 'wound' (p. 13). The boy reaches for what he thinks of as original ideas about the female body not via nature, but via culture – specifically, Christian religion. First, he thinks that the vagina is placed and functions like a second navel. He goes on: 'It must have been that chance encounter which left with me an abiding impression of the female as something like a kind of obese skeleton, a fine wire frame hung with pendulous fleshfruit, awkward, clumsy, frail in spite of its bulk, a motiveless wallowing juggernaut' (pp. 13–14). This description might be brought to bear on Davidson's asexual trapeze artist – the female form that has apparently escaped the paradoxical vessel of the 'obese skeleton' to become not 'awkward, clumsy, frail', but lithe, agile, and strong through her circus act. However, in so doing, the trapeze artist remains a strange fruit, transformed into something that is disturbing, troubling and meaningful; an icon that is neither one thing nor the other. Furry, damp and beastly, Rosie is neither conclusively plant nor animal and is left harbouring a secret. In this way, Banville forges the same genetic links relating Irishness and Irish ground to embody the motherland in miniatures of the politically aestheticised Rosaleens. The journalist John Waters explains in his parallel memoir of self and nation, *Jiving at the Crossroads* (1991), that among his generation: 'Many of us grew up to have almost a contempt for what was at best the womanly wonder of nature.'[36] If *Birchwood* is, for Colm Tóibín at least, the most radical revisionist text, produced in a context in which creative young men dislocated themselves from the contemptibly feminine earth, it is little wonder that Banville should poke fun at Rosie, the most recognisable form of cultural nationalism.

Sex scenes are a chief means of plot repetition in 'Air and Angels', but they are no longer approached with the same measure of assurance. Gabriel's seemingly consensual Laurie Lee-style tumblings and fumblings with Rosie become imbalanced as the farmer's daughter, Mag, lays herself out in the milking stalls for the circus boy who comes to collect her eggs. He considers the girl's apparent act of submission to be both petrifying and 'farcical' (p. 131). This time, Mag sounds like Magnus, the clown who is paternal substitute for Gabriel while he is on the road. Scared and almost nauseated by Mag's offering, Gabriel yields nonetheless and mechanically masturbates Mag while dealing with the melancholy sensation of his own semi-erect penis: 'that lugubrious puce stalk, my faintly pulsating blunt sword of honour' (p. 131). Gabriel is engaged by Mag's body as a child of a later generation might have been at the school nature table; he cultures the vocabulary of his discoveries as he describes the contrast between the 'shaggy black bush' outside with the soft silkiness of the 'sad secret' he believes she harbours at the indefinitely euphemistic 'in there' (p. 131). Something of the wondrous, emotional exuberance that accompanied his exploration of Rosie's body has evaporated; this is a child who has found and felt these objects independently before, and is less impressed when they are brought to his attention a second time. And yet, there is a significant addition to this sequence: Gabriel goes through the motions, until he provocatively concludes: 'how immaculate' (p. 131). The strange fruit into which all women were transformed after his encounters with Rosie recalls, of course, Eden and therefore the Old Testament and even, perhaps, the classical pagan world, but that taste is no longer the source of melancholy; now it is the image of the Holy Virgin that is created out of a void-like hole. The hole permits entrance into the immaculate for the circus boy Gabriel, who plays the cock of the ring and has been sent to collect Mag's eggs. Here, the common perspective on the dull disturbances of early sexual experience is inverted: it is the adolescent boy who strives for a take-away romantic memory with a pathetic parting kiss on the cheek. Mag's retort (as conceived by Gabriel) is redolent of odious cross-class cultural relations. Her repulsed reaction undercuts his vaunted notions of how he should conduct himself through heterosexual experience, and so he animates her irritation at his silly attempts to salvage them both as 'poor frail forked creatures' in familiarly beastly terms: she rears, snorts contemptuously, and flees across the farmyard (p. 131).

Despite Gabriel's memory of the scene, Mag's apparent control of their shared (if not mutual) sexual experience contrasts starkly with the helplessness of circus girl Ida. Ida is faced with diabolically piggish masculinity while blackberry-picking one autumn afternoon. Banville imagined this scene seven years after Heaney's *Death of a Naturalist* (1966) appeared; by now, the poem 'Blackberry Picking' from that collection is surely one of Heaney's best known: like Lee's *Cider with Rosie* (1959), its lines conserve that hellish feeling of lost summers and lost innocence. Set not in Heaney's late August but in autumn, Banville's crushing realisation that things have been spoiled is that much more explicit in theme and content. The novelist's simultaneous translation of actual events into legend is evidenced by recounted fantasies played out in the landscape through which Prospero's moved, which is inhabited by unfamiliar species: cannibalistic 'savage-fanged hermaphrodites' who signified the living's play 'with exaggeration as a means of keeping reality at bay' (p. 144). Readers are led to believe that the reality alluded to in this instance is the Famine, and Banville's depictions of Famine Ireland have much in common with Heaney's vision of its horrors as relayed in another *Death of a Naturalist* poem, 'For the Commander of the *Eliza*'. But Banville's countryside throws up another kind of monster that masquerades in human form. Three drunken English soldiers form a company of super-satyrs who hunt so-called '*nowghty girl*' Ida, while she sings nymph-like in among the briars (p. 146; original italics). Romantic Gabriel describes Ida not as naïve, but rather stricken with wonder at the 'complex and exquisite ciphers among which her life so tenuously hovered' (p. 122). The elevated and gentle demeanour resulting from her devotion to and fascination with her own world means nothing to the soldiers as they beat this not quite innocent, not properly naughty girl unconscious. When Ida is carried back to the circus to have her dead eyes closed by ringleader Silas, Gabriel believes that 'he had closed a door on a whole world' (p. 146). It is, perhaps, the world Gabriel entered through Mag's 'shaggy black bush' that is permanently closed off by the brutality mercilessly unleashed down among the blackberry bush.

There is a considerable degree of ambiguity in Banville's own explanation of the expressly '*unintentional* metaphor' for the 'anarchy and chaos' of Irish political history seen in *Birchwood*'s circus scenes. The novel is anti-nationalistic, but, at the same time, it challenges powerfully the record and legacy of English colonialism.[37] Significantly, the familiarly grotesque portrayal of these English soldiers causes further problems for any straightforward classification of *Birchwood* as a revisionist text. That their monstrosity should be demonstrated upon the body of a woman who belongs to Prospero's Magic Circus is crucially important. It must be understood that to conjure the mood of the circus in literature increases ideological tensions surrounding revisionism as a critical mode, since the circus contains that lament for something that is seldom (if ever) as good as memory imagines. There is still some investment in the effective and affective power of what was once promised, even if that remembered power is heightened only to undermine the reminiscing subject's present context. Indeed, the power of the circus to undermine the present is in its stability as a nostalgic concept that might well be distinct from its reality. It is, then, akin to childhood innocence as reviewed by the experienced adult. It is similar to sex, in the sequence of excited anticipation, climatic release, and melancholic afterthought.

Mademoiselle Murphy and the Wooden Woman: Paul Muldoon and Seamus Deane at Duffy's Circus

It was in the first issue of the *Irish Review* that Roy Foster famously and provocatively announced that: 'We Are All Revisionists Now'.[38] An extract from the unproduced Banville-O'Sullivan-Pattman screenplay of *Birchwood* appeared in the same publication. In the extract, Gabriel first sees the circus through the estate's garden wall:

> *Gabriel is at first anxious but then hears laughter, carts moving... Intrigued, he moves along the wall until he finds a gap he can climb up and see through. Instantly he sees the head of a stuffed tiger, its glassy eyes shining. It is a circus cage. Gabriel is shocked at this image, already familiar to him from his 'fairy-tale'. The wagon stops and Gabriel sees a dark-haired girl, Ada, sitting at the back swinging her legs provocatively, laughing and talking to someone off. She is beautiful and wears a colourful skirt and shawl. She looks in Gabriel's direction. Gabriel leaps down from the wall, listening. A man shouts and the wagon moves off.*[39]

Anxiety, beauty, danger, ardour (conveyed through the Nabokovian near-homonym 'Ada'), sex, death, and the shock of recognition: the attractive/repulsive circus fantasy is condensed in a few brief lines. The potential peril of the circus is aligned to the child's cautionary fairy-tale, as in the ambiguous idea of 'magic' seen through photographer Davidson's eyes. The treachery of its spectacles is caught in the glass eye of the stuffed tiger. Even though this scene places the actual circus in a state of exile beyond the garden wall, the powerful suggestion of this allegory is that the child's memory belongs to a fictitiously immature time before the Fall: the time when the child still has the agency to 'leap'. This exterior scene, shot from the perspective of the boy peeking through a gap in the garden wall, is juxtaposed with an interior, where the boy meets his father Joseph's eyes in the shaving mirror. In Scene 40, rain falls outside, perhaps unceasingly, while the father sings to amuse the child with an apparently familiar brand of menacing entertainment. The tension of waiting for the Fall in this world is almost unbearable – a tension that is palpable in Banville's original novel.

Despite the blatant failures of Joseph as a family man, Gabriel remains politely engaged in acts of awful hero worship throughout the novel, even at its bitter and grisly end. By contrast, Granny Godkin is well aware of her son's faults, and her awareness leads her to bestow Birchwood on her grandson. At that moment, Gabriel apprehends a 'new mythology' and sees Joseph, 'my invisible father' (p. 37), retreating from the supper table and into the surrounding shadows. Paul Muldoon looks upon a similarly spectral father in 'The Bearded Woman, by Ribera' (*Mules*, 1977):

I've seen one in a fairground,
Swigging a quart of whiskey,
But nothing like this lady
Who squats in the foreground
To suckle the baby,
With what must be her husband
Almost out of the picture.

Might this be the Holy Family
Gone wrong?

Her face belongs to my grand-da
Except that her beard
Is so luxuriously black.
One pap, her right, is bared
And borrowed by her child,
Who could not be less childlike.
He's ninety, too, if he's a day.

I'm taken completely
By this so unlikely Madonna.

Yet my eye is drawn once again,
Almost against its wishes,
To the figure in the shadows,
Willowy and clean-shaven,
As if he simply wandered in
Between mending that fuse
And washing the breakfast dishes.[40]

This poem, Muldoon's picture of 'the Holy Family / Gone wrong', might well be compared to the image Banville offers: Joseph and, not Mary, but Martha, produce, not Jesus, but his heralds, Gabriel and Michael. With this revision in mind, it is little wonder that Granny Godkin's appeal to Jesus, Mary and Joseph goes unanswered: in their absence, and in the substitutional presence of these false icons, family members meet terrible fates. 'Almost out of the picture', the male presence in Muldoon's poem interrupts the viewer's pleasure in the intimacy shared between the 'unlikely Madonna' and the boy who, in this portrait, 'could not be less childlike'. The presumed husband to the unlikely Madonna is seen, like Banville's invisible Joseph, as a 'figure in the shadows'.

Shadows are formative places for young imaginations. For the young male narrator of Seamus Deane's *Reading in the Dark*, the felt presence of God in the darkness of Duffy's Circus is a terrible thing, which sets the boy apart from the rest of the crowd. Catholic teaching parallels circus action in the second episode of the novel, 'Disappearances – September 1945', where lessons from church are illustrated by images at Duffy's. In the child's imagination, Hell is 'a deep place' that you fell into, 'turning over and over in mid-air until [...] you disappeared forever' (p. 7). Its dimensions are an inverse of the great height of the circus tent, which, in the child's eyes, is supported by poles that converge somewhere unknown and in the darkness beyond his field of vision – just as they do in Davidson's photograph of the trapeze artist. Also in the darkness, but only semi-obscured like the Bearded Woman's husband, is the star of Duffy's that season. A series of impressive acts lead to the final and spectacular disappearance of the magician Mr Bamboozelem: a feat that delights other members of the audience who, unfazed and unbamboozeled, claim to understand perfectly how the effect has been achieved. But the younger male 'I', confused by the image of the crying clown and relating the absence of a presence with lessons taught by strange and exciting religious authority, is left uneasy and doubtful of his brother's reassuring explanations made on behalf of the rapt crowd. The boy wonders: 'How could they all be so sure?' (p. 8).

Twenty years before Deane published *Reading in the Dark*, Muldoon took himself back to the big top in 'Duffy's Circus':

Once Duffy's Circus had shaken out its tent
In the big field near the Moy
God may as well have left Ireland
And gone up a tree. My father had said so.

There was no such thing as the five-legged calf,
The God of Creation
Was the God of Love.
My father chose to share such Nuts of Wisdom.

Yet across the Alps of each other the elephants
Trooped. Nor did it matter
When Wild Bill's Rain Dance
Fell flat. Some clown emptied a bucket of stars

Over the swankiest part of the crowd.
I had lost my father in the rush and slipped
Out the back. Now I heard
For the first time that long-drawn-out cry.

It came from somewhere beyond the corral.
A dwarf on stilts. Another dwarf.
I sidled past some trucks. From under a freighter
I watched a man sawing a woman in half.[41]

A certain frustration with the fallibility of authority figures in general is audible in Muldoon's male voice from the outset. He has tired of the sarcastically so-called 'Nuts of Wisdom' his well-meaning father imparts – fallen, presumably, from the tree in which his God sits. His reminiscence looks back to his father's lethargic dismay at the wilful redirection of devotion to the visiting circus in an image that brings God low before sending him up into the earthly heights of the tree branches. This father is a benevolent version of the shadowy man beside Ribera's Bearded Woman; his shadow is cast down from the first verse paragraph throughout dream-like 'Duffy's Circus', offering a clear example of the often-disquieting coexistence of the everyday and the transcendental in

Mules. But despite the son's cutting remarks, it is doubtful whether or not he is ready for the symbolic slip that takes place in the fourth paragraph, when he exits the Duffy's tent to find that an excess of carnival has spread out into the surrounding field. Both the significance of the 'rush' away from his father and the disorienting loss of that guardian's physical presence are reflected in the disruption of formal patterns established in the first three paragraphs, and the son's journey is set on a downward trajectory by the elusive phrase 'slipped / Out'. He too becomes diminutive, like Swift's Gulliver, even in relation to the two dwarves encountered beyond the corral. Recognising his own foreignness beyond the main tent enclosure, the boy hides himself under a freighter – a vehicle that carries the circus spectacle into town – to watch and learn how this world works.

Tim Kendall argues that 'Duffy's Circus' stands apart from the other poems in *Mules* that 'fuse – and confuse – sex and violence' because it 'introduces a poignant innocence'.[42] However, to accept Kendall's reading in relation to the voice that speaks the poem is to understand the critic's conclusion as misdirected and, ironically, naïve. Innocence in recollection must necessarily be dubious and feigned, as this male voice and Gabriel both know. Nevertheless, the confusion of sex and violence in this poem generates a striking political metaphor. Muldoon offered a possible reading of his own work when asked in interview about the exchange of circus images between himself and Michael Longley in the 1970s and, subsequently, about possible connections to W.B. Yeats' 'High Talk' and 'The Circus Animals' Desertion':

> Yeats was not in the foreground – what *was*, was politics. I think of it as more of a political poem. We use the term 'the political arena'. There's a figure called Wild Bill in the poem. Now, that might be Wild Bill Hickock or Buffalo Bill. But when the poem was written William Whitelaw was Secretary of State for Northern Ireland. He was dancing a 'rain dance' to have a particular effect on the political weather. 'Some clown' is some fool or some idiot in my part of the world, and the way I read his bucket of stars is primarily as some kind of explosion. This is not necessarily a definitive statement about the political situation in Northern Ireland, but it's certainly partaking in that. The young person sees what he perceives to be from the realm of the circus – 'the man sawing a woman in half'. This could be a revisiting of Kathleen Ní Houlihan. This is not the *key* or the *code* – you can read it without any of this at all. But you can't get more up front than a man sawing a woman in half – it's a violent partition. And that is at the heart of the Irish situation.[43]

As the final image of 'a man sawing a woman in half' is set within a political frame, the connections between Muldoon's poem *Birchwood* and *Reading in the Dark* become even stronger.

Banville's Gabriel excuses himself from the image sequence he creates out of his encounter with Mag: 'I began my journey a virgin and ended it still unsullied, but I am not ignorant of certain facts, and if here they create a somewhat twisted view of the basic acrobatic duet I insist that the warp is in the facts and not my recounting of them' (p. 130). The sex act is euphemised – 'twisted' and 'warped' – through the circus image of the 'basic acrobatic duet'. So, too, in 'Duffy's Circus'. The second line of paragraph four extends beyond the first, leading the boy towards his first experience of that paradoxically recognisable, yet unfamiliar, 'long-drawn-out cry'. The paradox is the inherited memory of something primal, inaudible to the speaker in 'Duffy's Circus' until this moment. That cry is a fitting non-verbal utterance to accompany the expression held on the face of Davidson's trapeze artist: the lips which part with actual effort, or imagined ecstasy. In the poem, it is comprehensively constituted in Muldoon's compound adjective, which sounds remarkably similar to the fall Joyce records on the first page of *Finnegans Wake*. The child does not participate in a prelude of masturbation, as in *Birchwood*, but is instead private audience to the great reveal: there is a man sawing a woman in half.

Muldoon's boy, obscured under the freighter, sees through the same eyes as the narrator of *Reading in the Dark*. It is in 1950, five years after his metaphysical troubles at Duffy's Circus, that Deane's child is first exposed to sex: a tinker man and woman are seen not in circus, but in sporting terms, 'wrestling on the floor' (p. 77). The boy's first reaction is visceral – he is about to vomit – but the disturbance soon manifests itself mentally. Heaney is recollected here, as Deane's narrator decides that whatever he has seen, he will say nothing: 'For ages afterwards, I could envisage them clearly, he butting back and forth on top of her, she writhing slowly, one leg in mid-air. I didn't know what I had seen, but I said nothing' (p. 78). Muldoon's image of the couple is similar, carrying a disambiguation of both literal and metaphoric meaning. At the moment of witness, both children do not appear to understand what they are seeing. Upon reflection, the circus and sporting metaphors of Banville, Muldoon and Deane allow their voices to flirt articulately with this image, without giving it its proper name.

The year after he sees the tinkers 'wrestling', Deane's narrator is implicated in the sexual fantasies of Crazy Joe: first in the adults-only art room of the public library, and then in a nearby park, where Joe acts as *seanchaí* and generates an Irish image of the French courtesan seen in the library on the pages of art history books. The ignorant boy who did not know what he had seen the tinkers doing becomes Joe's 'Caliban' (p. 82); by inference, Joe – who invests himself with the power to teach the child – becomes another Prospero. Concepts that belong to a religious imagination in the Duffy's episode are repeated here. Most significantly, disappearance is redefined in Joe's sex story, which comes from a place supposedly far more exciting than the church the boy visits 'every silly Sunday' with his 'daddy' (p. 85). The nationality of the luscious woman in the painting is hybridised so that she might become 'Mademoiselle Murphy' (p. 84); in the boy's imagination, she outstrips the now 'ordinary' local girl Irene Lecky. But Mademoiselle Murphy is relatable to the Poor Old Woman, since in Joe's story, she lures an engaged young man into a local field. Joe narrates how the young man and Mademoiselle Murphy lay in the strangely black grass (that is comparable to Mag's 'shaggy black bush'), but just when the bachelor thought he was to be privy to the beautiful woman's sad secret: 'wham! She's gone!' (p. 87). After this disappearance, the boy thinks he ought to laugh in the way that he did not feel able to do when Mr Bamboozelem vanished in the circus tent. But again, fantastic disappearance inspires doubtful emotions and he feels embarrassed that he 'didn't really know exactly what was supposed to happen, and maybe being gone was part of it' (p. 87). 'It', the child's classic euphemism for sex, complements Banville's 'in there'. But this is the *petit mort*, not the great eternal tumbling into Hell Deane's narrator has anticipated in the Duffy's tent. Going away occurs in place of the little death, and its impact is far more localised: it is only the bachelor's crotch that explodes. In this way, religious teaching, sexual intercourse and the circus are made to commingle with peculiarly Irish icons in the child's imagination.

Muldoon choreographs these elements to similarly startling effect in 'Duffy's Circus'. Readers are encouraged to look back on earlier spectacles through the peep-show frame constructed by the freighter: the assonantal elephants who troop across one another, expressing their efforts in a repeated stream of acute As and Es, or Wild Bill, whose Rain Dance 'Fell flat'. The circus comes to look like something quite different through more experienced eyes. When coupled with that hauntingly melancholic 'long-drawn-out cry', 'sawing' attains a verbal violence that is comparable to Gabriel's rough plugging of Rosie, or his finger's piston action in and out of Mag. Like dark, damp Rosie and like black, bushy Mag, the sawn woman is considered in natural terms, but is now lifeless: she is wooden – like a deadened statue hewn from God's tree, perhaps. By Muldoon's own suggestion, she is akin to Banville's Rosie, Deane's Mademoiselle Murphy and to cultural nationalism's dark Rosaleen, since she is the figure of Kathleen Ní Houlihan – or better still, Yeats' Cathleen ni Houlihan. Kendall is mistaken by his own impression of 'Duffy's Circus', an impression that he subsequently applied to *Mules* as a collection: 'that life is more bizarre and freakish than anything even a circus can offer'.[44] In fact, the relative value of what the voice sees within the circus compound is not given; there is no tangible attribution of more or less in terms of the bizarre or the freakish. Indeed, these adjectives are too strong for the subtleties of emotional reaction implied through 'Duffy's Circus' – a poem that creates a Northern Irish microclimate as it places the political arena under the big top. Rather, Muldoon poses the questions of similarity, equivalence and repetition that preoccupy the boys in *Birchwood* and *Reading in the Dark*. Like Banville, he seems to suggest that the circus might be 'as uncontrollable, as makeshift, as potentially and gloriously anarchic as life itself'.[45] The circus, then, is a locus of reflection, and it is possible that those things seen within and without the ring are *as* incredible as each other.

A Particularly Irish Circus Image: Neil Jordan's The Miracle (1991)

In the early 1990s, national broadcaster RTÉ considered that the circus had a role to play in uniting Ireland. Fossett's National Circus won the privilege of becoming the venue for primetime Saturday night variety show *The Big Top*, as the station tried, apparently, to counter claims that it was 'too Dublin-centred'.[46] This comment, made by an anonymous contributor to *Circus* magazine, signifies certain divisions in contemporary Irish society. Similarly, although using a spatial metaphor that transforms circles with centres into spheres, Barra Ó Séaghdha appreciates that the force of Fintan O'Toole's journalism in the early 1990s derived from an understanding of Irish society as 'essentially bipolar'.[47] According to Ó Séaghdha, O'Toole's reporting set up binary oppositions between rural/urban, quaint/normal, Catholic/secular, nationalist/internationalist, traditional/modernising, uncritical/critical, immobile/mobile, Ireland/America and past/future in his readings of culture, politics and society in Celtic Tiger Ireland. These binaries operated to dispel 'the recalcitrant realities of land, nationality and religion' and thereby fill 'the space vacated by the old dissolving certainties'.[48]

More than eighty years on from Yeats' 'The Theatre, the Pulpit, and the Newspapers', and his powerful denunciation of 'those enemies of life, the chimeras' manufactured by the Catholic Church and the Irish media, radical changes in journalism in the 1970s and 1980s meant that the vehemently disparaging tone of the poet-politician had been widely adopted in the Irish press and on the radio.[49] Its full force was frequently turned upon the church and the faith of its followers. *Jiving at the Crossroads*, John Waters' memoir of growing up and away from the prospects of employment as a farm hand, a shop boy, or a psychiatric hospital warden in Castlerea, County Roscommon, and towards the country's capital, Dublin, is also dependent on Ó Séaghdha's oppositions. Waters offers a factual correlate to Banville's *Birchwood* and Deane's *Reading in the Dark* as he charts the related and remarkable changes in mid- to late twentieth century Ireland through a work that coheres around his own family story. He devotes particularly sensitive attention to images of women. In that moment, women's bodies, what they do, and what to do with them were preoccupying subjects of contemporary religious and political debate. Waters records this disorientating period of political, social and cultural upheaval and its effects on women, remarking that, in many ways, 'the nation was still trammelled in the embrace of the irrational'.[50]

In 1983, amendments to the Constitution regarding restrictions on abortion signalled profound ideological schisms between and within the Catholic Church and Irish state. The following year, on the afternoon of 31 January 1984, fifteen-year-old Ann Lovett left school in Granard, County Longford and made her way to a local grotto devoted to the Virgin Mary. There, alone, she gave birth to a baby boy. The child died at the shrine and his mother soon afterwards. Later that spring, one young woman from County Kerry was deemed responsible for two counts of infanticide. Joanne Hayes, pregnant for the third time by a married man, delivered of herself what she believed to be a stillborn baby in a field beside her family farm in Abbeydorney on 12 April 1984. She buried the infant first in hay, and then, after she had wrapped the child in paper and plastic bags, in a nearby pool. Two days later, a baby with multiple stab wounds was washed up on the seashore near Caherciveen. The ensuing police investigation into the Caherciveen baby's murder was monstrously confused: gardaí believed that this was the child who Joanne had admittedly killed. Her family signed statements to the effect of concealing the infant death by throwing the body in the sea. After a blood test proved that the Caherciveen baby could not have been Joanne's child and the body of the Abbeydorney baby was found on the Hayes family farm, attentions turned to the cause of the death of the infant Joanne had truly borne. Following three months of hearings, the tribunal report of the Kerry Babies Case claimed in October 1985 that Joanne had strangled her child, although no pathologist had found evidence of this. This was beside the point. In this Ireland, where rapid social change was undercutting the country's constitutional foundations, she had become, in the popular consciousness and in the words of investigative journalist Nell McCafferty, 'a woman to blame'.[51]

Amid all this, there was a great release of Catholic fervour in the summer of 1985 as statues of the Virgin Mary had been seen to be moving all over Ireland.

Waters makes a powerful suggestion in *Jiving at the Crossroads* that is reminiscent of Walter Benjamin's own conception of the past, not as objective and historic, but instead subjective and collective. Waters writes: 'The past is made up, not of dates and names and battles and conquests as in the history books, but of images, colours, tastes and longings from our everyday lives.'[52] The rhetorical force of this statement is cumulative, shifting from body to mind, or heart: from what we see in 'images' to what we feel as 'longings'. In between there are somewhat more physical, tangible objects: 'colour' and 'taste'. The effect of placing sight and taste in between 'images' and 'longings' subordinates bodily sensations and bodies themselves to larger concepts. The consuming embrace of those things sensed by the eye and the mouth by the infinite possibility of 'images' and distracting abstract of 'longings' holds fast here. Sensual images are seen as approximate to religious icons: casts of those figures revered by the Catholic tradition that are set within a sacred context full of colour, taste and smell. Such a description of sensuality in the Catholic Church brings it close to the circus tent – a proximity made most obvious in Neil Jordan's *The Miracle*.

Critic Philip French counted *The Miracle* among his favourite films in an end-of-year round-up review for *The Observer* – an article for the English newspaper in which he all-too-easily claims Irish director Jordan as one of 'half-a-dozen of our most remarkable movie-makers'. However, French is correct to appreciate and identify the particularly fine observations Jordan makes in his characters, which make *The Miracle* a picture of 'individuality and distinction on local subjects'.[53] The film might be manoeuvred into the position of social commentary, since recent, traumatic events in Irish current affairs might appear to be replicated in the plot. It has already been shown that the age and relative inexperience of teenage mothers was a preoccupying subject in Ireland in the mid- to late 1980s, and *The Miracle* resonates with this preoccupation: it is the story of the return of American actress Renee to the seaside town of Bray where, as a touring singer in her late teens, she met musician Sam, and mothered, then abandoned their child Jimmy after the breakdown of their relationship; she is sympathetically understood as having been 'too young' to have stayed behind.[54] However, any sustained pursuit of this line of argument would counter the express wishes of Jordan. In an interview given to *The Washington Post* around the time of the US release of *The Miracle* in July 1991, the director commented: 'By and large my preoccupations are more personal than political. More emotional.'[55] Therefore, social constructs of the present country are seen only incidentally and in the background of the film – for example, in people's hairstyles and clothing, and in their leisure pursuits. Its soundtrack is not pop, soul and rock-and-roll, but the compositions of Hoagy Carmichael and the lyrics of Alberto Testa. Jordan's effort is, then, to create a study of personal and emotional subjects that are in some ways out of time, if not timeless, through sensitive deployment of sounds and images that were considered classic, if not outdated, by 1991.

Though *The Miracle* refuses to be fixed in time, it is definitively located in a place. Comparable to Thaddeus O'Sullivan's concept of the 'Irish universality'[56] represented in Banville's *Birchwood*, Jordan's own production notes describe his film as 'particularly Irish' and state that its 'Irishness' was constituted in its representation of male/female relationships.[57] Predominantly, *The Miracle* explores these fundamental – and fundamentally Irish – male/female relationships through the character of adolescent Jimmy. The film is an Oedipal narrative of desire in which the boy obsessively pursues Renee, the mother he presumed dead, who responds to her son's increasingly forceful advances with increasing ambivalence. Jordan's subtle, sophisticated study of the emotional complexities bound up in encounters between Jimmy and Renee takes place between live performance venues: a seaside dance hall, a city theatre, a parish church, and the Fossett's Circus tent. These locations are generously full of images that come to frame the narrative. It is notable that the dance hall and the parish church belong to the real world of lived experience; these are familiar and unimpressive locations where Jimmy works alongside Sam, and in which he challenges the efforts of his father and the promise of his faith. The theatre and the circus, meanwhile, are transposed from life to coexist in Jimmy's imagination, transforming his intangible emotions into vivid images. Tellingly, the theatre is where Renee works, and the circus is where Jimmy's fantasies about her are set. But the religious icons and circus images that feature separately as markers of distinct stages in his development towards a better-informed state of self-consciousness combine to produce the film's final sequence. Arguably, the simultaneous use of religious icons and circus images, which enables correspondences with Banville and Muldoon, lends *The Miracle* a considerable degree of its Irish specificity.

Jordan went back to Ireland, and back to his own childhood, after a run of professional disappointments in Hollywood. The director explained in interview why Bray, County Wicklow, was his chosen location for *The Miracle*:

It's very simple. My mother grew up in Bray. I spent time there as a child. It's been a convenient backdrop to a number of my films. It's always had that strange element of fantasy against the general greyness of Irish life.[58]

Strangely fantastic Bray is cast as a version of Tír na nÓg: dissimilar from the mystical vision of that mythical place that is seen in Jim Sheridan's *Into the West* (1992), and rather more robust and tawdry. The locations of leisure, pleasure and entertainment between which the story is set are the concrete means by which the special effort required to secure eternal youth is made apparent. Women work particularly hard to arrest the appearance of age. It is Miss, 'Not Mrs, boy', Strange who fascinates Jimmy and his friend Rose as they walk along the promenade. Renee believes that she 'lost it a long time ago' – according to Rose, her hands betray that she is much older than she looks. Renee is associated with a time that is long before her own in her style. Before they speak, Jimmy thinks that given the general cool of her red lipstick, sunglasses and 'old-fashioned' stockings, her desirability must derive from the fact that she is French. In this misconception, Renee is seen like the hybrid Mademoiselle Murphy of Crazy Joe's imagination in *Reading in the Dark*. But the pathos inherent within attempts to defer age and maturity are calmly recognised and easily accommodated by Jordan as plausible, personal narratives of desire. There is no suggestion in actress Beverly D'Angelo's characterisation of Renee that the desire to return to a past self has overtaken her, nor any hint of her visible surrender to a time that has gone. She is perfectly composed in the classic fashions of forties film stars, which coordinate with the twenties popular jazz and sixties bossa nova performed by Jimmy on saxophone and piano to indicate the attractive and expressive potential of the outmoded. In her, then, are seen the desires of the male author who looks upon her: Jordan is conveyed through the image of Renee, just as Davidson reveals himself through his photography.

Chiefly, it is Renee who produces the contemplative mode of *The Miracle*, which Elizabeth Butler Cullingford has accurately, if uncertainly, described as 'oddly reverent'.[59] Oddly reverent is apt, since it connects the way in which D'Angelo is styled – both in performance and appearance – to the habit in which Waters continues to use the language of Catholic devotion to express the novel and exciting articulacy his generation found in popular icons. Jimmy often watches Renee swimming, and, accordingly, this lead actress and new-found object of adolescent fascination becomes, in a certain sense, a secular Star of the Sea. This association is reinforced by the recurring group of holidaying nuns who, so beautifully directed to imply a child-like delight, rush towards the water in their swimming hats and full-length bathing suits – costumes that are suitably muted counter symbols to the loud leotards sported by the female acts at Fossett's which leave nothing to the imagination. Renee is further secured by the recurrent use of Hoagy Carmichael's 'Stardust' (1927). Mitchell Parish's lyrics trail images of a lost paradise garden out of the lover's dreams and into the world of musical performance. 'Stardust' is often heard in scenes where D'Angelo is costumed in sequined garments. Accordingly, she embodies her own memory of 'the years gone by' when she stood, like Gabriel Godkin, literally demurred beside the garden wall – just inside Eden, or just on the other side of that immovable symbol of lost innocence.

The circus, as both a real event and an imagined location, provides Jordan with images that give form to the unuttered narrative of Jimmy's desire: to lose his innocence to Renee. The director elaborated in interview on his decision to give Fossett's such a prominent role in *The Miracle*: 'At the circus, there's the possibility of enacting a real and a fantasy event […] Selfishly, I suppose, I just chose what I could from the circus. I just wanted to create images.'[60] As he related the cinematic influences that determined how the circus was made to appear in his film – Fellini's *La Strada* (1954), Carol Reed's *Trapeze* (1956) and Tod Browning's *Freaks* (1932) – Jordan emphasised the popular image of the circus as something 'slightly sinister' or 'slightly "other"'; especially in 'the small and closed society of Ireland, performers are almost inevitably from strange and "other" backgrounds – [there's] always something almost orientalised about them.'[61] Out of his mind's eye, Jordan develops a circus image that has features in common with Davidson's photograph of the trapeze artist at Duffy's Circus: the slightly sinister, the 'almost orientalised'. The extent to which Fossett's, as filmed for *The Miracle*, could be considered sinister is arguably limited. Nevertheless, its slight 'other'-ness and exotic potential, especially within the Irish context, are deployed to great effect, and alternative correspondences with Davidson can be found in Jordan's deliberate co-ordination of sexual suggestion and religious expression within the circus image.

In scenes filmed during 'real' circus performances, Jordan makes effective frames out of human bodies or circus apparatus to develop the plot. Jimmy is seen playing the saxophone alongside a bored-looking clown through the legs of a contortionist who bends over backwards to pick up a rose with her teeth. At a more advanced stage in Jimmy's pursuit of Renee, the same contortionist is seen firing an arrow with her feet into a crudely shaped plasticine heart. These frames draw attention to Jimmy, indicating that his narrative of experience is manufactured out of conventions. They are, in themselves, complex structures, founded upon the woman and her actions in performance, which signal the drive of this peculiar narrative as they elide the obviously sexual with clichéd icons of the banally romantic: the rose and the heart.

Unspoken truths are realised and wishes are fulfilled through the circus as constructed in Jimmy's dream-space. Banville's definition of the sexual charge of that performance space, which constituted 'a life outside life', is worth repeating here: 'The circus has a strange erotic potential, an erotic energy [...] there are those girls, in their corsets and sequins: posing and spinning in the powdery spotlights, what a dream-like eroticism they created.'[62] In filming the dream sequences Jordan wrote for his character, cinematographer Philippe Rousselot allows his camerawork to appear self-consciously naïve, transforming human faces into types or icons of themselves. Jimmy's first circus dream stages the son's primary, sexual fascination with his mother: Renee is cast as an aerialist, dressed in a sequined bustier to perform her routine; her son masters the *corde lisse* apparatus. Throughout the couple's performance, 'Stardust' is heard non-diegetically, played off-key by an unseen saxophonist. Renee smiles down at Jimmy in an illuminated inversion of an earlier dream, or memory, in which her silhouette is framed with the fringes of what is first taken to be a miniature theatre or promenading parasol, but soon understood to be the decoration on the infant Jimmy's pram. Intercut with these shots are moments from a sequence in which Jimmy's father Sam is burnt alive. First, a photograph of Sam catches light, and then flames spread to the man himself, who is lying in a single bed.

These dreamed images appear to resolve the Oedipal phase of Jimmy's development, a resolution necessarily postponed until the return of his mother. The result is the second circus dream, the desexualised content of which belongs to the more mature latency phase. The sequence reveals another aspect of Jimmy's emotional response to Renee's return: the unfulfilled hope for a reunion between mother and father. It is presented in the dress circle of Dublin's Olympia Theatre where his mother takes on the role of Frenchy in a stage adaptation of Hollywood Western *Destry Rides Again* (1939). Jimmy has followed Sam and watched from a distance as his father tries to persuade Renee against making future visits to Bray. As Jimmy's eyes close sleepily, curtains lift on an open-air, seaside tableau in which Renee and Sam flank two kneeling circus elephants. His mother is outfitted as a saloon girl, while his father is dressed as a Mexican bandolero. Though symbolising adversarial communities in the folklore of the American West, the pair hold hands and bow together gracefully. Bouissac argues that circus families refuse to hint at 'any kind of dysfunction', and Jimmy manufactures for himself that same functioning unit out of the circus trope.[63] Seen in his family picture, framed in the symbolic logic of the traditional circus, his parents smile to an audience applauding them from elsewhere – apparently, they are with Jimmy in the dress circle, since the hands that clap for this reunion overlap with the son's sleeping face. When he wakes he is alone again, save for the cleaning lady sweeping between the seats, too late to enjoy his parents' performance and to join in with the audience's elated response.

Jimmy's companion, the aspiring writer Rose, is equipped with skills which enable her to interpret these dream sequences in the mode of the psychoanalytic literary critic. Rose deconstructs their significance according to basic principles that she has learnt in an advanced alphabet of narrative theory, which she also uses to write her own original fantasies. In turn, she delivers her lessons to Jimmy as they eat chips and ice creams, walk the promenade, or ride the seaside rollercoaster. Rose ornaments her vocabulary with excessive words and arch phrases that erupt into her conversations with Jimmy to disrupt the manner in which two teenagers might be expected to talk: 'pellucid' and 'gauche' are fine examples. It is in this vein that Rose describes from behind the bars of the circus animal lorries her advancing plan to seduce Jonner, the brutish animal trainer, and thereby orchestrate the final sequence of the film. Jonner is cast as Caliban for comic effect, and he could just as well speak the lines of mastery and surrender uttered by Gabriel Godkin in the circus ring as Rose works to tame him through the inflictions of sexual frustration and humiliation. But in a scene shot in the animal lorries, Rose occupies an ambivalent position: there, she perhaps deliberately inverts her civilising intentions as she is equated with the animals that Jonner commands and coerces into performance. In this way, Jordan's very definite rejection of critical opinions aligning his use of the performing animal with W.B. Yeats' 'The Circus Animals' Desertion' becomes apparent. The Fossett's animals are not like Yeats' past 'theme'; nor are they Banville's fateful and fated objects of reflection: the stuffed tiger and Albert the monkey who belong to Prospero's Magic Circus. Jordan sees in his circus animals living, vital beings who offer him dramatically ironic images, and his characters appear in these moments of identification in complex and negative terms.

In interview, the director commented: 'At a circus you have tents; a series of cages; the vehicles. They house both people and animals. It's a place where wonder, fantasy, magic have to be chained and put in cages.'[64] This lamentable recognition of the need to contain and limit the reach of wonder, fantasy and magic bears striking resemblance to Yeats' review of his own sense of the power of the artist in 'The Theatre, The Pulpit, and The Newspapers': 'I had spoken of the capricious power of the artist and compared it to the capricious movements of a wild creature, and *The Independent* [*sic*], speaking quite logically from its point of view, tells me that these movements were only interesting when "under restraint".[65] Yeats cannot have known that the point of view of the *Independent* aligned exactly with that of the famed circus proprietor Frank Bostock, who wrote in 1903 (the same year in which the poet published his essay responding to and lamenting the logical perspective of the newspaper) about what his 'public does not know': that 'the tamed animal is a chimera of the optimistic imagination, a forecast of the millennium'.[66] Jordan communicates his own un-rosy view of the caged animal through his aspiring artist Rose, who is caged at the circus. His unwitting return to Yeats is even more complete, as Bostock's symbolic chimera is mated with chimeras of the Catholic Church. For in her caged setting, Rose is also associated with the nuns she observes and narrates as they paddle and splash in the sea: 'Nuns remain children longer than most […] It's to do with their lifetime's confinement.' According to Rose, nuns maintain their childhood beyond the expected time because they are 'married to a man they never meet'. That Jesus Christ should not be named outright and his proper sign should be replaced with the humbler concept of 'man' indicates the gentle irreverence with which Catholicism is viewed throughout *The Miracle*. This act of verbal substitution works like the lower-case 'g' for 'god' in *Birchwood*, and the upper case for the father's doctrinal 'Nuts of Wisdom' in 'Duffy's Circus'. But, importantly, Jordan's script casts forward a poignant, if naïve reflection on Rose as she is seen behind the circus bars. The inference is that, in being wedded to an absence, nuns stay children because they remain intact, and immaculate, in marriage. Rose is confined by the role she has given herself in Jimmy's present narrative of desire, within which her virginity and, by standard implication, her childhood are coincidental sacrifices. Both Catholic practices of devotion and adolescent sexual drives are, then, caught within the circus frame.

Prevailing critical approaches to *The Miracle* are arrested at the Oedipal phase of Jimmy's sexuality, and thereby fail to attend to both the dreamt circus form that represents his fantasies of deliverance and the real circus image that represents Rose's sexual experience. Carole Zucker's reading falls short in this regard. She lauds Jordan enthusiastically for entering 'untrammelled territory' in his 'postmodern fairy tale' and for exploring 'a dark recess of the mind that has not been substantially addressed in thousands of years of folklore and fairy tales, although Oedipus is an obvious exception'.[67] Zucker's reading is deficient, too, as it fails to appreciate the possibility that the conventional elements of Jordan's narrative are indebted to Irish literary traditions. Toni O'Brien Johnson has persuasively demonstrated how Irish literature's most famous parricide, J.M. Synge's Christy Mahon, is typical of medieval tales, and considers that his entertainment value for the coastal community of *The Playboy of the Western World* is derived from his concretisation of the archetypal struggle between youth

and age – a contest hitherto confined to the oral tradition both within the setting
of Synge's play and the context of its production. Synge parallels the archetypal
struggle between Christy and Old Mahon with that between Pegeen and the
Widow Quin as they vie for Christy's attention – Pegeen more energetically than
the Widow. Elements of this tripartite male–female relationship are also explored
by Jordan in *The Miracle*, most notably in Rose's absent-minded disappointment
at Jimmy's lack of interest in her as sexual partner. 'Gauche', one of Rose's
prize words, is used disparagingly to dismiss the rather trashy and predictable
narrative Jimmy invents for Renee before he realises her actual story. But gauche
is an adjective that might just as easily catch Rose herself in the cross-fire of her
attempts to wound his image of Renee: she snaps cattily that it is probably the
menopause that makes the older woman emotional.

Rose's resolution to seduce, and thereby 'humanise', Jonner doubles in
force after Jimmy promises that he will try to 'work' on his jealousy. Instead,
he remains preoccupied with Renee. The ambivalent, ambiguous mood in
which Rose is seen in relation to Jonner lends to the uncertain tone of *The
Miracle*. Zucker is quite incorrect in her statement that Jordan did not produce
a sex scene until he filmed the extravagant sequences involving Julianne
Moore and Ralph Fiennes in his adaptation of Graham Greene's *The End of
the Affair* (1999): their couplings convey confidence, assurance, and a wealth
of sexual experience.[68] Jordan's first sex scene is, in fact, played out by Rose
and Jonner on the hay-strewn floor of the Fossett's tent. It is less sophisticated,
but considerably more affecting. Rose and Jimmy discuss the humanising
plan before it is enacted. Jimmy asks Rose if it will hurt, and Rose says, quite
calmly, that it will. The intimation of the pain of a girl's first sexual experience
communicates two levels of discomfort, the physical and the emotional. In
what Jordan subsequently films, Rose is seen wooden and distracted as Jonner
pumps energetically at her: visually, the scene recalls Muldoon's 'man sawing a
woman in half'. Sexual pleasure is not supposed to be the end, but instead the
means by which Rose sets the spectacular final sequence of the film in motion.
But what she imagines before and narrates after the event in Jimmy's company
has quite a different tenor. Rose becomes akin to Gabriel Godkin in his
review of sexual experiences with Rosie and Mag, as it is not the girl's sense of
practicality, but rather her romantic bent that are conveyed in her descriptions.
However, her overblown images are devoid of any of Gabriel's mawkishness or
melancholy: Rose sees herself in classical terms with her hair spread out across
the floor like a seashell. Conclusively, she owns the revisioned moment when
Jimmy suggests that her crown might have been more like a fan: 'Whose hair
was it? *My* hair – like a seashell – on the hay.' The girl sees herself after the fact

as Venus, goddess of love, not as a conventional coquette and certainly not as an icon of cultural nationalism.

The disjuncture between the recorded image of the lived moment and the repetition of that moment in memory and as words allows the Rose/Jonner sex scene to be read as Romantic drama, at least as that genre is defined by O'Brien Johnson in relation to the plays of Synge. In reading Victor Hugo, she sees that the grotesque appears in Romantic drama as the vital foil for the sublime; the grotesque finds its correlate in the comic, while the sublime is associated with the awesomely dramatic.[69] To inject comedy into what is, ostensibly, a serious inquisition of morality is an action Jordan performs in *The Miracle*. Walking past the circus animal cages, Jimmy describes his mother's acting style as both comic and tragic. Rose pitches the central 'story to do with love' involving father, mother and son between tragedy and farce on the seaside rollercoaster. In even simpler terms, when Jimmy says that he is no longer 'sad' at the end of the film, that makes Rose 'happy'. The mood of the film is, then, indefinite, or blurred. In his preface to the first published edition of *The Well of Saints* (1905), Yeats described the almost magical power that the masterful playwright had over the use of idiomatic language in resonant terms. For Yeats, Synge made 'word and phrase dance to a very strange rhythm' that 'blurs definition, clear edges, everything that comes from the will, it turns imagination from all that is of the present, like a gold background in a religious picture, and it strengthens in every emotion whatever comes to it from far off, from brooding memory and dangerous hope'.[70] In the final sequence of *The Miracle*, Jimmy seeks relief from his anxieties in the parish church. He turns to plaster icons in the hope that they will turn his imagination away from his present concerns. These are the same icons to whom Rose has made irreverent devotions on his behalf, euphemistically asking in mischievous tones that they help him to win Renee in sexual conquest – her 'you know' is similar to Gabriel's 'in there' and the 'it' of *Reading in the Dark*. But at that moment, Jimmy renounces his faith in their power; in the instant, Rose gives him 'no reason to believe'. The passive, dispassionate saints, who are akin to his saintly-yet-defeated father Sam, stare blankly out at Jimmy, but at once seem to share the knowledge of 'The Statues' that inspired one of Yeats' *Last Poems*: 'Empty eyeballs knew / That knowledge increases unreality, that / Mirror on mirror mirrored is all show'.[71] In more contemporary terms, Jordan's statues are seen up against the spirit of the age as consolidated by Waters in *Jiving at the Crossroads*: their force as intercessors and articulate advocates on behalf of the faithful has been overpowered by other secular images more ready and better able to turn the imagination away from the present time.

Jordan explains that while Jimmy might look to the church in desperation: 'he finds no answer within the space of the church or the world it represents. But he does find it in his girlfriend's sense of fun – in her imagination – in their mutual imaginations which are allowed to run riot.'[72] Returning to 'The Theatre, the Pulpit and the Newspapers', Yeats argued that the theatre – that drama – was 'the most immediately powerful form of literature, the most vivid image of life'.[73] It stood, then, in opposition to life's enemies as they are instituted in the pulpit and the press. Transforming drama as a noun into its adjective, Jordan is a director keenly aware of the power of theatricality – the dramatic – in the images he creates, and looks for cinematographers who are 'willing to use colour and light and shade in a way that is consciously unrealistic'.[74] The final opposition staged in *The Miracle* is not between the pulpit and the theatre; instead it is between the pulpit and the circus. Jimmy's imagination literally runs riot at the close of the film, as Rose, through her ambiguous self-sacrifice, releases the animals that embody his brooding memory and dangerous hopes. In place of a miracle, the incredible presence of a circus elephant appears in the church aisle, freed from its cage by Rose, as promised, with the keys she has stolen from Jonner as he pumped thoughtlessly away at her. Her act of revenge – Jordan's own 'anarchic, untrammelled gesture' – is at once an act of devotion to Jimmy.[75] Upon exiting the church, he finds himself within a kinematic scene in which circus animals run comically wild on the promenade. Men rush after them, trying to recapture the llamas and lions, the horses and ponies, the zebras and monkeys that scatter across the seafront in place of the child-like nuns. And yet, despite the comic exuberance of this scene, *The Miracle*'s final narrative note is deliberately off-key; to talk in simple terms of sadness and happiness is, at this point, unsatisfactory. Rose has given herself up to two boys in one act; there is no real resolution for Jimmy or his parents. Both nuns and animals will be returned to their habitual lives in the convent or at the circus. But in this wonderfully upsetting moment of symbolic equivalence that has sprung from the anxieties of juvenile sexuality, a fundamental belief that once belonged to Synge is displayed: 'The gaiety of life is the friction of the animal and the divine.'[76]

A Double-Take of Feeling: Seamus Heaney's 'Wheels within Wheels' (1991)

Friction gives essential force to Seamus Heaney's poem 'Wheels within Wheels'. Like Banville's Gabriel, like the narrators of Muldoon's poem and Deane's autobiographical novel, and like Jordan's Jimmy, the meditations of Heaney's voice upon sexual awakening in 'Wheels within Wheels' run tangential to the circus image. And just as in the work of his contemporaries, the circus is a means by which religious icons are brought down to earth. The poem appears towards the close of Part I of *Seeing Things*.[77] The progress of the speaking self takes place across three sections obviously marked as chapters in this narrative of experience; structurally, then, it is comparable to the movements indicated in Banville's novel and Muldoon's poem. Fundamentally, similarities in form and content that are apparent in each of these contemporary Irish texts belong to past literary traditions that flash up in moments of recognition. This includes traditions more recently established by Heaney himself, consolidated in the potatoes, and mud, and an image of the Irish pastoral that is at once menacing and beguiling:

I

The first real grip I ever got on things
Was when I learned the art of pedalling
(By hand) a bike turned upside down, and drove
Its back wheel preternaturally fast.
I loved the disappearance of the spokes,
The way the space between the hub and rim
Hummed with transparency. If you threw
A potato into it, the hooped air
Spun mush and drizzle back into your face;
If you touched it with a straw, the straw frittered.
Something about the way those pedal treads
Worked very palpably at first against you
And then began to sweep your hand ahead
Into a new momentum – that all entered me
Like an access of free power, as if belief
Caught up and spun the objects of belief
In an orbit coterminous with longing.

II

But enough was not enough. Who ever saw
The limit in the given anyhow?
In fields beyond our house there was a well

('The well' we called it. It was more a hole
With water in it, with small hawthorn trees
On one side, and a muddy, dungy ooze
On the other, all tramped through by cattle).
I loved that too. I loved the turbid smell,
The sump-life of the place like old chain oil.
And there, next thing, I brought my bicycle.
I stood its saddle and its handlebars
Into the soft bottom, I touched the tyres
To the water's surface, then turned the pedals
Until like a mill-wheel pouring at the treadles
(But here reversed and lashing a mare's tail)
The world-refreshing and immersed back wheel
Spun lace and dirt-suds there before my eyes
And showered me in my own regenerate clays.
For weeks I made a nimbus of old glit.
Then the hub jammed, rims rusted, the chain snapped.

III

Nothing rose to the occasion after that
Until, in a circus ring, drumrolled and spotlit,
Cowgirls wheeled in, each one immaculate
At the still centre of a lariat.
Pepetuum mobile. Sheer pirouette.
Tumblers. Jongleurs. Ring-a-rosies. *Stet*!

In recycling his own stock images, the poet not only approximates 'Wheels within Wheels' to the biographical record of theatre history made by W.B. Yeats in 'The Circus Animals' Desertion', but also, and quite literally, turns the earlier poem upside down: Heaney's circus scene closes rather than opens the three-part narrative. Vitally, Heaney's hybrid poetic sensibility generates its own kind of literary revival in the poem. Specifically, Wordsworth and Yeats are both reflected in the three spots of time picked out in the miniaturised *Künstlerroman* represented by the poem. Fiona Stafford believes that Heaney's definition of the 'adequacy' of poetry developed out of his dual appreciation of Wordsworth and Yeats; adequacy 'combines lyrical satisfaction with clear-sighted understanding of a world in which pain and suffering *almost* predominate'.[78] Indeed, the pain and suffering of exile from the first place is almost overwhelming in the central section of 'Wheels within Wheels'. The necessity of substitution for the pleasures that belonged to the beginning is dubiously, unsatisfactorily recognised – and, ultimately, realised – through circus images that are almost inadequate.

'Wheels within Wheels' can be aligned with three prose pieces published or broadcast by Heaney in the 1970s: 'Omphalos' (1978), 'Reading' (1973) and 'Rhymes' (1974) were first collected under the title 'Mossbawn' for the volume *Preoccupations* (1984). Mossbawn was Heaney's first place, and on reflection, he asserts the influence, not of Yeats, but of Joyce in creating its image in his memory: in the beginning is the word 'omphalos'. The Ancient Greek for navel here signifies the pump outside the child Heaney's back door: 'a slender, iron idol [...] marking the centre of another world'.[79] In *The Nets of Modernism* (2010), Maud Ellmann examines the significance of the navel for Joyce: 'The navel signifies the exile of the infant from its first home in the mother's body, which induces the hunger for home – nostalgia – that motivates odysseys ancient and modern.'[80] Truly, Heaney appears almost overwhelmed by nostalgia in the voyage he made in 1978 around his remembered self at Mossbawn. Ellmann goes on to demonstrate that the figure of the navel is complex: it is both hole and net, and the possibility of entrapment within this feminised original place is also sensed keenly in 'Mossbawn'. This theme connects Heaney's essay to Banville's *Birchwood*, most firmly in the suggestion of another world that the novel's narrator Gabriel believes he enters through his sexual experiences with Rosie and Mag. In 'Mossbawn', Heaney describes his first experience of swimming in the moss-hole with another boy. He apprehends this memory as a ritual of initiation, of betrothal to the 'watery ground and tundra vegetation' surrounding his family farm.[81] This union is ordained in the shadow of Church Island, but the location of Christian religion is kept at bay. Instead, it is the point of origin, the omphalos – named in the language of the classical world, and from some pagan space where idols were forged of iron, not turned from wood or cast in plaster – that is close at hand.

In the lecture 'Among Schoolchildren' (1983), Heaney speaks of the integration of the 'Me. And me now.' enabled through – indeed, dependent upon – reading Joyce.[82] But the title of this lecture is taken from Yeats' 'Among School Children' (1926). Notably, where Yeats keeps concepts of 'School' and 'Children' quite separate, Heaney revises that title to elide the person with the institution he revisits in the poem. As a signal of assimilation, 'Schoolchildren' marks a more complete process of incorporation than the hybrid, hyphenated compound 'school-children' would have done, perfectly expressive of the fraught duality presented by the learning experience. Heaney places himself and his audience within Yeats' construction of 'the world of routine, the reliable world of agreed behaviour: smiles, embarrassment, courtesy, desks and nuns' in order to confront, through a narrative of his own experience, the 'challenge and liberation' of learning.[83] Stanza VII of Yeats' poem is confounded by the power of images – specifically, the Catholic nun's icon and the reverent mother's child – to 'break hearts'; women, it seems expressly and problematically, are most susceptible to this power. Heaney pays no attention to these specifics. Instead he takes from 'Among School Children' an effect that is consolidated along the lines of Davidson's pride in the power of having gone beyond his own vision. He finally suggests:

> the necessity of an idea of transcendence, an impatience with the limitations of systems, a yearning to be completely fulfilled at all levels of our being […] to arrive at a final place which is not the absence of activity, but is, on the contrary, the continuous realisation of all the activities of which we are capable.[84]

But these specifics of gender are important. The union of nuns and mothers returns us to *The Miracle*. Jimmy's anxious, half-hearted prayers are the preliminary to Jordan's final sequence in which images of immovable, dispassionate religious icons are overtaken by the animation of living circus animals. The animals are released from their own limited systems (which are constituted in their cages) by Rose, who has held on to a plan and harboured a private belief that the circus image – in Jordan's words, the space in which 'both a real and a fantasy event might be enacted' – will relieve Jimmy and fulfil his immediate need to return to his initial emotional state: in the end, he is no longer 'still sad'. Neither his mother nor the church could hope to provide this kind of relief. Certainly, it is only temporary and only adds another set of images to those systems that have already failed, but the circus animals are nonetheless distracting in the instant.

Similarly, 'Wheels within Wheels' strives ultimately to regain the original feeling that inspires the poem. According to Stafford, *Seeing Things* is energised by an 'active quest for meaning'.[85] The notion of the quest is most important. Ellmann is paraphrasing Henry James as she defines the condition of the modernist Odysseus: he has gone back other, and to other things. Perhaps the condition of the postmodern Odysseus is to go through the exertions of the active quest, to remain dissatisfied and unfulfilled, but to maintain the pretence that one can go back uncannily unchanged. In 'Wheels within Wheels', that quest is ultimately unfulfilled. Indeed, early drafts of 'Wheels within Wheels' included the pessimistic truth-teller's blatant phrase: 'Everything comes too late.'[86] The poem fails to get back to its starting lines, but fails self-consciously. In spite of a matured state of disbelief, paradoxically, it is miraculous as per the definition of the miracle given by the chorus of Heaney's *The Cure At Troy* (1990): 'Call miracle self-healing: / The utter, self-revealing / Double-take of feeling.'[87] The poem makes its revealing double-take by looking at a place that, through magic, illusion and grinding physical repetition, gives the impression – and the impression only – of the continuous realisation of all the activities of which we are capable. It does so by looking, again, at the circus.

'Wheels within Wheels' begins with a fascinated engagement with the mechanics of things. The 'I' who as a boy turned the bicycle upside down and unnaturally, nonsensically pedalled with his hands is braver than Deane's narrator in his love of disappearance. The spokes, hub and rim of the wheel are blurred into humming transparency by the boy's actions, which collapse the boundaries between and confuse the functions of various parts of the wheel. As the human hand and the pedal treads become one figure, the bicycle is personified not as other, but as self. In earlier versions, that personification was also gendered, and suggestively so. One manuscript draft reads: 'When I learned the pleasure of hand-pedalling/~~An upside-down ladies bicycle~~.'[88] The friction between two bodies, which is felt in 'the first real grip', is pleasing, perhaps, as it functions to produce one of a series of images running through *Seeing Things* that Stafford has termed 'self-generated'.[89] But the coincidence of 'real' with 'grip' is an early warning sign. In Banville's novel, 'grip' is the 'great word' of Gabriel's father: "*Grip*," he said softly. "It's your only man."' (p. 91). At that moment, for a moment, the father becomes in his son's eyes like the stuffed tiger of the *Birchwood* screenplay: an animation that does not simply signal the awesome power of the living wild beast. Prospero's tiger is a dead thing, dragged out at the circus, whose terrible force is nothing but an illusion which inspires brief moments of unsubstantiated pleasure.

The upset of such phony resurrections is also felt in 'Wheels within Wheels'. In Heaney's poem, 'grip' has sexual potential, but the coupling that occurs between individual and machine is onanistic. Onanism, in fact, signals the impossibility of self-generation: it is, perhaps, an aesthete's act, since it is undertaken to no end other than the production of finite pleasure. More locally, it is certainly a wasteful, grievous sin. Nevertheless, the poem works in that vein towards its own version of Muldoon's 'long-drawn-out cry', although it is seen rather than heard in the metaphysical observations concluding Part I. Here, the child is like the Mossbawn pump, at once marking a new point of entry and outlet for that which is identified through a process of divination;

the language of these final lines slips between the disciplines of science and religion. At this moment, Heaney's speaker shares with Deane's narrator a sense of excitement derived from religious conception. In the poem, it is the devotional abstract of belief that lifts those objects embodying belief into an active equation with the human weakness of longing – one of those abstract nouns of subjective experience taken by Waters as constitutive of history.[90] And longing is a painful thing, admitted into this child's orbit in the instant of this imagined union.

The conceit of the bicycle carries us back to *Birchwood*. Gabriel inserts into his record of the night his grandfather died a memory that is 'hardly worth mentioning': Granda Godkin taught him how to ride a bike (p. 58). Transition through this rite of passage belongs to that rather hackneyed order of 'the things we normally do' to signify a functional, ordinary childhood; a visit to the circus might also figure there. Characteristically, there seems to be an urgent need in Banville's novel to revise that popular image; the author chooses finally to represent the reality of this order through dysfunction and physical pain. Initially, Gabriel's experience is frightening, then exhilarating, then transcendent: 'I felt a kind of *click*, I cannot describe it, and the bike was suddenly transformed [...] The taut spokes sang. I flew!' (p. 58). The memory is more acute since this moment of flight is complemented by comic violence and the grounding pain that follows: the crossbar knocks the child in the crotch; the back wheel runs over his foot; Granda Godkin is too preoccupied with a twisted hip to congratulate his grandson.

Heaney's 'I' seems to have mastered the bicycle to the extent that the normal practice of riding the machine is no longer of interest: 'enough was not enough'. Unaided, he is inspired to turn the machine upside down in a deliberate act of dysfunction, made in the hope of being newly productive. But the primary feeling of 'love' for the bicycle is consequently dulled in Part II, as a place beyond the family home – 'The well' – is introduced: it is also loved. Grammatically, this dirty paradise is built concentrically: it is constituted as a gap in the verse paragraph, bound in parentheses and crowned with a special, lofty sign whose frame of quotation marks belies its real self. Here, the urgent, active and wilful destruction of Part I is replaced by the deterioration of things. Deterioration occurs through ill-conceived attempts to prolong that first delight through coupling the two loved things, well and wheel. At first, the effect produced from placing the machine in the 'dungy ooze' is 'world-refreshing'. Time turns backwards as the young boy is made younger still by the 'regenerate clays'. Earth and sky confuse themselves as this spinning Adam makes 'a nimbus of old glit'. And so, the land appears, at first, male: spunky, as it sprays the speaker with itself. But 'glit' – a now obsolete term, the Oxford English Dictionary explains, for greasy or slimy matter or, in medical history, a morbid discharge from the urethra – signals the end of this beginning.

The hard suddenness of past surprise is recollected in the faulty sequence of events: the hub that 'jammed', the rims that 'rusted', and the chain that 'snapped'. The private performance of this trick cyclist is over, while the Edenic image of Adam's beasts tramping over the well is interrupted by a more local set of images that figure the land as woman. In this way, Heaney's description of Muldoon's poetic imagination might equally well be applied to his own. It is an imagination produced by two distinct cultures: 'fathered by the local subculture on the mothering literate culture of schools'.[91] This is a version of the 'Mossbawn' moss-pool, that place of shared male experience, initiation and betrothal which is remembered as the first place, before the schoolroom invested an initially resistant Heaney with the poetic language necessary to articulate its memory so artfully. But at the same time, this upsetting image of the land is arguably mothered on the literacy of cultural nationalism, since it is made through the same scheme of language that Gabriel uses to describe Rosie's genitals – the 'baleful orifice' the boy had, until that moment of lived experience, mistaken for a second navel. But it is made distinct, as Heaney excises anything of Gabriel's insincere sympathy from his description: the well, surrounded by prickly hawthorns and tramped-over ooze, is a 'hole', not a pitiable and suggestive 'wound'.

The seemingly unkempt figure in the landscape of Part II is reminiscent of *The Midnight Verdict* (1993) and Heaney's translation of Brian Merriman's women who remain unfertilised by a spunkless generation: 'like flowers in a bed / Nobody's dibbled or mulched or weeded / Or trimmed or watered or ever tended.'[92] Both the translation and the original are equally divested of romantic images of women: they are figured as wild, rapacious and ruthless sexual beings. Real, and not allegorical, women appear in Part III of 'Wheels within Wheels': they are circus cowgirls, marrying up with the seemingly unhusbanded cattle in Part II. More broadly, their Wild West costumes pick up on a theme common to Muldoon's depiction of 'Duffy's Circus', where readers can imagine one model for the poet's Wild Bill stalking the 'corral', and Jimmy's final dream in *The Miracle*, where viewers see *Destry* star Renee and Mexican bandit Sam fantastically reunited. Further, the gendering of the circus as a female space that is apparent in Jordan's film is also undertaken here. In Heaney's poem, the conventionally titillating and impersonal representation of female sexuality in cowgirl form provides an acceptable, instantly effective substitute for the lonely play that went before. Again, women's bodies in a circus context are subject to a familiar process of animation: these performers are in a state of human to animal metamorphosis as cowgirls. Moreover, the voice derives a comparable pleasure from concentricity: these performing women are imagined as gaudy, brilliant repetitions of the 'slender, iron idol' that was the Mossbawn pump. In prose, the pump marked the 'omphalos', the navel of the earth. The connection to the first place is broken when the child goes to school. In the poem, school is replaced with circus. As the 'still centre of a lariat', Heaney's cowgirls are icons of perpetual motion spun out of a poetic imagination that is no longer fixed within the natural world. It now derives from the complex symbolism of Yeats, as the girls represent revisions of Loïe Fuller, whose ribbon dancing is remembered in Part II of 'Nineteen Hundred and Nineteen' (1921). Here, though, Loïe's ribbons are tied to another scheme of imagery. The performers are seen backlit by immortal light and, like Banville's Mag, are conceived of as immaculate by the juvenile gaze that rests upon them. Like Jordan's Renee, these spotlit women are secular icons, immaculately haloed by their circus apparatus and at the centre of memory's focused devotion. Once more, church and circus collapse into a single order of images that excels in reproducing and elevating the cliché that it is *this* that makes the world go round, as ecstasies of sex, faith and circus are all understood as being dependent upon concentration and control.

In his Royal Society lecture 'Feeling into Words' (1974), Heaney defines how the technique of poetry involves:

> not only a poet's way with words, his management of metre, rhythm and verbal texture; it involves also a definition of his stance towards life, a definition of his own reality. It involves the discovery of ways to go out of his normal cognitive bounds and raid the inarticulate: a dynamic alertness that mediates between the origins of feeling in memory and experience and the formal ploys that express these in a work of art.[93]

Normal cognitive bounds are exceeded in Part III of 'Wheels within Wheels' as the narrative 'I' evacuates the final scene; the near-wordless, physically spectacular circus space is raided as a trove for inarticulacy. Inarticulacy is also immediately apparent in the successive breakdown of phrases that make images. Fulsome descriptions in Parts I and II, and the climactic build of Part III's first sentence are ultimately replaced by finite couplings or single words that flash up in pictures of past experiences. The language of Benjamin's fifth concept of history, which acts as an epigraph to this chapter, is unconsciously echoed here: the poem signs off in defiance of the notion that images of the past, and all that they inspire, might be seen once and once only.

The terminal '*Stet!*' is shrill. This unusual word might be imitative of the kind of commanding vocabulary, tone and diction heard in phrases conventionally uttered by the circus ringmaster who conducts his artists – the cowgirls, the tumblers, and the jongleurs, maybe – with precision and force to manufacture the entertaining image. 'Stet' means, of course, 'let this stand', and the sexual pun cannot be ignored. The function of the impressive punctuation mark might usefully be compared to the raindrops that made 'exclamation marks' all over the shirt of Deane's narrator after a terrifyingly confusing encounter in which Crazy Joe explains sex and sexuality in a peculiarly Irish context (p. 89). However, '*Stet!*' does not simply euphemise the physical, sexual effect on the spectator. The term is a common annotation in mechanical printing, indicative that a previous correction or deletion in a proof or manuscript should be cancelled. It is, then, a sign that resists revision, without denying it outright. Neil Corcoran understands the tension between moving forward and pulling back in *Seeing Things* as a striking balance 'between scepticism and yearning'.[94] In 'Wheels within Wheels', what the speaker thought was lost is, in fact, retrieved through this sequence of images. Within Heaney's final exclamation point is something of the force of Beckett's Krapp, full of fire and longing at recordings and remembrances of things past. Ultimately, the poetic voice seems to be resigned to mettle tarnishing. In '*Stet!*', Heaney's great reveal is the self collected and uncorrected. It becomes the word, which transfixes generations of that self, and which remains beyond the grasp of Gabriel Godkin, whose story ends in silence.

But permanent longing is let stand by another voice that comes from somewhere out of the frame. Italicised like Gabriel's Caliban lines, '*Stet!*' belongs to someone else – perhaps to the same speaker of that foreign phrase '*perpetuum mobile*'. This intervention exemplifies the troubling habit identified by Stafford in the Heaney of *Seeing Things*, in which it appears that the poet adopts 'the voice of twentieth-century irony, questioning illusions of the past'.[95] This transforms the poem into a dialogue, and Stafford's apprehension of the ironic suggests the possibility of performance. The dramatic intervention of the other voice that speaks in the absence of an 'I', or any other clear subject of interrogation, brings this concentrated poem to the point of consummation. This is a paraphrase of Heaney's own reading of Yeats' 'Long-legged Fly', and it is intended to manage the state of inadequacy in which a reader of 'Wheels within Wheels' is left: we are brought to the point of consummation, but are not carried beyond it. Despite the climactic exclamation, the goal of this narrative of desire and the return to the original feeling is deferred as the substitution of circus cowgirls for the wheel in the well interrupts images that are self-generated. This external voice brings us back to those worshipped images of Yeats' 'Among School Children' that appear as 'self-born mockers of man's enterprise'.[96] Heaney's last word, which might easily be taken as symbolic of the triumphant recapture of the spirit of the first place, might instead deny the possibility of transcendence.

The final speech act of 'Wheels within Wheels' is, then, comparable to the final sequence of *The Miracle*. Just as the release of the circus animals substitutes any divine intervention, and, as a temporary distraction from present tension, is recognised as a means by which a brief return to the first state of being not 'still sad' might be effected, the revolutions in the circus ring that are revelations in 'Wheels within Wheels' appear to bring the poem's speaker back to himself, at least. Heaney gives no value to this return: it is neither good nor bad, but simply longed for. For Joyce's Bloom, the ambivalence of self-reflection is similarly contained: it is the circus horse walking in the ring. Heaney, who singles Joyce out as the figure who made the 'integration' of his Irish literary heritage possible, marks out his ring with Rosies.[97] The imagery of 'Wheels within Wheels' is like Davidson's photography, as it conveys the story of the self: the making of the music, which is, at once, the making of the man. It repeats the course of the journey undertaken in prose form in the 'Mossbawn' essays and in 'Among Schoolchildren', indicating that one of Heaney's preoccupations was the search not for an idol, but for an image within which to contain the two literary traditions from which his poetic imagination was produced. Having done with school in the essays, he settles in the poem – briefly – on the circus: an image that is recognisable in a flash, and that thereby sends us back to the past in our active quest for its own meaning, and our own feeling.

CHAPTER 5

Conclusion: 'All tales of circus life are highly demoralising.'

T his book has explored the place of the circus in twentieth-century Irish culture. I began researching this subject in 2012 and, since then, have kept a close watch on the activity of traditional and contemporary circus troupes performing in Ireland today. This conclusion reveals how suggested continuities appear not only between circus fictions and circus history, but also how they might connect the imagined circuses of Joyce and Heaney, of Yeats and Banville, of Synge and Parker with current circus practice. It does so by detailing the work of two very different companies – Ireland's National Circus, Fossett's, and Belfast-based Tumble Circus – whose shows provoke questions worthy of further critical consideration.

The impact of the global financial crisis was seen incidentally at Fossett's Circus in March 2013.[1] A traditional range of family entertainments was performed on a Saturday afternoon on the Clane Road in rural County Kildare beside a busy branch of European budget supermarket Lidl, an unfinished housing development, and Behan's Maxol service station. Looking out across the Clane Road, the eye takes in a stretch of the River Liffey, Cupidstown Hill, and the distant Wicklow mountains. Fossett's – Ireland's state-funded, self-proclaimed National Circus – celebrated their 125th birthday in 2013: an anniversary that dictated the contents of the season's programme in various ways.[2] In all, nineteen people and animals were involved in action inside the tent. Ten principal actors performing a total of twenty-one distinct roles commanded the attentions of a small audience. Ring mistress Marion Fossett led the troupe consisting of a juggler, a tightrope walker, a contortionist and hoop dancer, an illusionist and his assistant, Otto the clown, the Chinese aerialist and acrobat Wang Dan, and the multi-talented Machine Brothers. They were joined in the ring by two miniature ponies: the animals appeared during the interval for younger members of the audience to ride. No other animals performed. Male members of the company acted as ushers before the show began; female members of the company sold popcorn and were on hand for children's face painting. During the show, Marion Fossett emphasised the historical aspects of the programme as Fossett's celebrated its '125th continuous season'.³ Acts displaying traditional skills and apparatus were set to a soundtrack of tinny recordings that ranged throughout eighteenth- and nineteenth-century compositions including Handel's 'Hallelujah Chorus' (1741), Beethoven's 'Ode to Joy' (1824) and Thomas Arne's setting of 'Rule, Britannia!' (1740).

Entirely, this show was offered as captivating evidence of the troupe's enduring popularity. There were, perhaps, twenty-five members of the audience in a big top capable of seating hundreds. Nonetheless, like the troupe itself, diverse nationalities were represented in the audience to this supposedly celebratory performance of Ireland's National Circus. It is interesting to meditate on the low level of attendance at such a significant event during Ireland's decade of centenaries – a preoccupation that mirrors an exchange between Oona Frawley, Peter Gray and Emily Mark-FitzGerald at the close of the conference, 'Irish Studies and the Dynamics of Memory' (2015), which offered an academic perspective on the popularity of and public engagement with events marking the Easter Rising of 1916. Frawley's contributions were particularly pertinent to this discussion, as she emphasised (a little patronisingly) that 'we must not forget' that it would be those commemorations enacted by 'ordinary people' that would be of lasting significance.⁴

Far from giving Fossett's something to celebrate, 2013 signalled the start of serious financial trouble. The company suffered a net loss of €5,000 in their 125th year and was forced into a state of examinership in 2014 after it was revealed that it had failed to pay VAT for the past eight years. Circuit Court President Justice Raymond Groarke presided over hearings in February 2015 and his comments perhaps indicate the gap that Helen Stoddart has seen emerging 'between *the* circus and circus'.⁵ Lamenting the fact that Fossett's was facing 'an uphill struggle' to survive, Judge Groarke added: 'This company has been in existence for 127 years and is a part of all our childhoods.'⁶ It seems, then, that the circus is just too nostalgic to fail.

For contemporary troupe Tumble Circus, the programmes of established state-supported, family-run outfits such as Fossett's are outdated and out of touch with the realities of Irish life – especially Irish urban experience. Kenneth Fanning and Tina Segner founded Tumble in 1998 in Dublin. For them, the kind of fantastic escapism one might imagine the traditional circus offered in past decades no longer seems to cut it in these hard times. The troupe invokes the spirit of Mikhail Bakhtin's carnivalesque, as they quote freely from a review attributed to *The Irish Times* that describes their work as 'turning the circus tradition upside down'.[7] Tumble work to reach new audiences with their brand of 'dysfunctional family entertainment'.[8] Their distinctive style of absurd circus encourages a cynical response from its spectators towards the social norms upon which they comment through circus art. Now based in Belfast, Tumble spends much of the year touring the fringe theatre circuit in Europe and Australia. They enjoy somewhat wider-spread appeal, as they usually perform in black box studios within theatres, public and community arts venues. Their recent creations, *Death or Circus: modern life is rubbish* (2012) and *Damn the Circus: a show about physical poetry and annoying reality* (2013), seem to delve back in twentieth-century theatre history: both shows play with a Weimar aesthetic in the performers' Brechtian attitudes, original music and comic song parodies, and a red-and-black, electric candle-lit cabaret set design. Notably, touring information for *Damn the Circus*, which was presented in the Samuel Beckett Theatre at Trinity College Dublin as part of the Dublin Fringe Festival 2013, concludes with a quotation attributed to Beckett: 'Theatre is just shadows and mirrors. In the circus the blood is real.'[9]

Tumble do not only take their cue from (experimental) theatre. The influence of rockabilly and other renascent underground roots music cultures is also discernible in their style. Their costumes – such as they are – celebrate the fashionable outcast: Fanning, Segner and accompanying harpist Ursula 'all the way from the Falls' Burns sport animal prints, which are combined with sexy, luxurious materials worn casually and naturally to undercut any formal glamour sequins, silk or velvet might connote.[10] Dramatic make-up and tousled hair finish a contemporary look that is intended to attract audiences who might not otherwise patronise the circus.

In this attitude, Fanning and Segner announce themselves as outsiders with the will to 'reinvent Irish Circus' and their own identities. They are billed respectively as 'Kenneth Fall, the carny god and saviour of Africa' and 'Tina Machina, the Queen of Sweden and new age white witch of circus'.[11] The confusion of national identities that they encourage is reminiscent of Ó Conaire's George Coff and Seago's true-born Irish-Mexican-American cowboy.

The Tumble team embrace their capacity to shock. The majority of the audience at one of the first showings of *Death or Circus* at The Mac Belfast in November 2012 were children brought to the Saturday afternoon matinee at a local theatre by parents who were, perhaps, unsuspecting of just how adult its themes and content would be. The performance – explicitly classed by the company as theatre – asks its audience in production notes to challenge what is deemed acceptable in and by society. In so doing, Tumble's professed hope is to alleviate anxiety by irritating social and political reality: 'to disturb, take over, inspire change and mostly remind people that they are not alone'.[12] This profession of faith has been lucrative: where Fossett's receive support from Arts Council Ireland, Tumble benefit from the patronage of Culture Ireland, suggesting that the public fund has replaced the royal patent as a mark of cultural distinction.[13] The sense of community Tumble wishes to foster through a parodic representation of social angst and anxiety accounts for their treatment of more universally applicable personal conflicts such as identity politics and, like Jordan's *The Miracle*, male/female relationship dynamics. In this way, Tumble presents a vision of contemporary Ireland that is comparable to that envisaged earlier by Fintan O'Toole in *The Ex-Isle of Erin* (1996). O'Toole endeavours through that collection to betray a widespread concern in the years of the Celtic Tiger: that Ireland should set aside questions over nationality, sovereignty and identity 'as sites of confusion'.[14] The real question to be answered was perceived, at that moment, to be how Ireland might 'surf the global waves without drowning in a flood tide of blandness and amnesia'.[15] It seems that Tumble Circus is still riding that wave.

Paul McErlane's photograph of Tumble performing at the 2013 Belfast Festival at Queen's (Fig. 5.1) records a moment in a mimed acrobatic routine. This routine dealt with a complex of (male) emotions released after a man discovers that he has fathered a child: Segner performed the charade of an unplanned pregnancy, while Fanning's forced smiles and anxious grimaces communicated his displeasure to the audience. Segner adopted various challenging positions, sliding in and out of precarious holds; Fanning's stance towards her was menacingly negligent. Throughout this book, the prevalence of texts preoccupied with circus, or circused, women has been noted, and Tumble's acrobatic routine might be considered against these various representations of the place of women in a circus context, as it prioritises a woman's meaningfulness from a male perspective over the woman herself. The actual, physical and emotional experience of Segner's pregnant character was ignored in favour of an exploration of the response to her pregnancy by Fanning as father, which was played for comic effect. The *Death or Circus* aerial display represents another provocative and ironic example of this. Segner tumbled from the rigging of the theatre, while Fanning mockingly narrated her movements with an offensive script that revealed anxieties over the manufacture and control of cultural representations of women still prominent and prevalent in and beyond twenty-first-century Ireland. The barbs of these

5.1 Paul McErlane, 'Tumble Circus Perform in Belmont Park during the 2013 Ulster Bank Belfast Festival at Queen's', 2013, Digital image

anxieties might be inflicted upon female targets, but Tumble's suggestion is that they are emblematic of more general failures in society:

> *Segner in white vest and animal-print pants winds the silk around her; pulls her body to the top of the lighting rig. Fanning stands by to the right, holding a support rope taut in his right hand. He apes nonchalance while speaking into a microphone. The mike is close to his lips; his breathing heavy. Ursula plays something Weimar-esque on the harp. Fanning starts to narrate:* Circus women are amazing – we used to revere women. But now we mostly use them to sell candy floss and popcorn. *Segner's shadows are split; prismatic; like a diorama. Fanning:* You're fat and you're ugly and everyone hates you. So stop eating…SEX, SEX, SEX, SEX, SEX, SEX, SEX, SEX, SEX, SEX: *(The parents in the audience fidget; the younger children have not understood and the older children do not giggle.)* you're not getting enough, you're doing it wrong, so why not marry your best friend's girlfriend? *Segner's eyes seem to me the most muscular part of her whole body – they are clearly working hard, but not with outward focus. Her mouth too: less composed than the rest of her. She scrambles away from his voice towards the ceiling. Fanning:* Have a baby: it's a natural way to live your life! (Terms and Conditions apply) *Savita Halappanavar: her story broke this week. Segner falls abruptly out of the knot, winds down to the ground and lies looking at the ceiling she has just left. Fanning stands on her stomach, calls for respect, then stuffs the microphone into his underpants. Applause.*[16]

As the muse of rubbish modern life, Segner comes to symbolise the plainly depressing – that is, the minimal advances that have been made in deconstructing the prohibitive divisions constructed out of that primary differentiator, gender. More particularly, urgent local situations are perhaps implied in Fanning's record of female experience. Tumble performed *Death or Circus* in Belfast on the day that 12,000 protestors met in Dublin's Parnell Square to demonstrate their outrage at the news story of 31-year-old dentist Savita Halappanavar; the young woman's name is noted above in the transcript. Halappanavar died of septicaemia and organ failure in University Hospital Galway on 28 October 2012 after doctors refused to remove the child she had miscarried. Her death was first reported by journalists Kitty Holland and Paul Cullen on the *Irish Times* front page on 14 November 2012. As Fanning caustically joked on a small studio stage in Belfast that having a baby was the natural way to live one's life, thousands voiced anger at the news that Halappanavar's death could have been prevented had she been granted the abortion for which she and her husband had pleaded. Tumble's project is, then, similar to that of Joyce in *Ulysses* and Friel in *Crystal and Fox*, in that the history, politics and culture of Ireland are all implicated within their circus acts; they are similar to Davidson's Duffy's photographs and to Banville's *Birchwood*, in that the state of Ireland is seen from within the circus space.

Many acts featured in the *Death or Circus* programme reappeared in Tumble's *Damn the Circus*. A performance of this work was attended at axis Ballymun, Dublin, in December 2014. Again, the audience were, for the most part, families with young children. It was evident that many of the patrons were from the surrounding area and enjoyed access to what Fanning, with his tongue firmly in his cheek, called in his introduction 'Ballymun's most highly advanced and state-of-the-art arts centre'.[17] axis is situated at the heart of a centre for regeneration of the notoriously challenged area of Dublin's northside, a stone's throw from the glossy glass building that is home to the forward-thinking team behind Ballymun Civic Centre and across the road from the ominous-looking Towers bar and Town Centre shopping centre (scheduled for demolition in 2018) that belong, very much, to another time and another Ballymun, so politicians might hope. axis is, then, appropriately named. However, Tumble's decision to cancel performances in this curious pivot-point of a venue scheduled for the following day due to lack of audience suggests that the attraction of *Damn the Circus* was somewhat limited in this context. It would seem that enchanting an audience remains as much of a challenge for both avant-garde Tumble in urban Dublin and traditional Fossett's in rural Kildare in the 2010s as it was for Paddy O'Flynn on western roads in the 1930s.

Acts repeated from *Death or Circus* for the axis audience reveal that it is not only, nor specifically, Irish circus that is reinvented through Tumble's performances. Irish culture more broadly is subject to acts of revision. *Damn the Circus* picked up what was once standard practice for top-class traditional circus performers like Johnny Patterson: the comic representation of local history, local characters and local issues. W.B. Yeats was subject to macabre exaggeration in the acrobatic routine 'The Isle of Balbriggan'. His ballad 'The Lake Isle of Innisfree' (1888) was turned inside out by Segner and Fall as they capered to the discordant harping of Burns. The ballad was co-opted specifically to deride the infamous Irish mother-and-son relationship; both parties in that relationship ended up dead, but not quite buried, in Tumble's parodic revision, which is inevitably reminiscent of Synge's *The Playboy of the Western World*, and now, perhaps, *The Miracle*. Collateral damage was wrought upon the reputation of another 'corny' Celtic industry, as Burns narrated the acrobatic duo's performance: 'The mother danced a *Riverdance* of grief all the way to his grave and she climbs into the grave in an attempt to touch his soul – oh! he loved her, he loved her, his mother from Balbriggan – oh! he killed her!' Here, Fanning broke character to attack Burns, verbally and physically: 'You killed this show with your Celtic fusion, Celtic *Riverdance*!' he cried, as effects of the Yamaha keyboard made his comedy blows ridiculously audible for the audience, in a scene which returns us to Lynne Parker's production of *Heavenly Bodies* at the Peacock in 2004.[18]

Adrienne Monnier presented 'the true epigraph' for *Ulysses* in her essay 'The Humanism of Joyce' (*c*.1931): 'That which is above is as that which is below, and that which is below as that which is above.'[19] This inversion occurred unwittingly, perhaps, at Fossett's Circus, where Handel and Beethoven blasted out of loudspeakers. It is deliberately enacted at Tumble Circus, where no effort is made towards distinguishing between 'high' and 'low' culture – this is evident from the Yeats–*Riverdance* equation described above. Banal aspects of contemporary society also offer Tumble rich material. Fanning's monologue on a visit to pawnbroking chain Cash Converters is exemplary. In the performer's imagination, the shop is populated by single mothers trading in second-hand jewellery and teenagers longing to become techno icons who are looked upon by Fanning's persona from the Country and Western CD section: 'I'm waiting for a 14-year-old to change that world, but there's Dolly Parton, with her curvy Southern Belle cowgirl body […] it's voodoo and it's erotic.'[20] Leaving the American South for Ireland's North, *Damn the Circus* continued the project of *Death or Circus*, as it confronted audiences with the 'darker themes' of Belfast's troubled history.[21] A cardboard box was painted up to read 'TNT: a present from Belfast', while a clowning routine represented the factions of Northern Irish life as they are manifest now in a younger generation.[22] Segner as clown performed the role of Bobby the Steek – 'steek' being a colloquial term, defined by contributors to BBC Northern Ireland's *Voices* project as:

> Approximate translation of the English 'chav' but has been around longer. Typically dresses from head to foot in sportswear (but avoids exercise at all costs), with a baseball [cap] tilted as far back on the head as possible without falling off, lots of chunky gold jewellery including at least 6 sovereign rings, chainsmokes [*sic*], talks with a distinctive nasal tone and a particularly strong Belfast accent and aspires to own a souped-up Corsa or Nova. Also steek or smicker.[23]

As society looks cynically upon these troublesome young men, Fanning and Segner's circus action generated its own entertaining definition:

> *Soundtrack: The Smiths, 'Heaven Knows I'm Miserable Now'. Fanning is crying as he dresses in the absurd guise of* DR BONZO, *children's entertainer: nose, clown shoes, wig, boa. His tricks all fail. Segner appears dressed in tracksuit bottoms and baseball cap: she is* BOBBY THE STEEK. BOBBY *calls* DR BONZO *on the phone*: Hullo, yeh, it's Bobby the Steek asking for his kid's birthday … It's for the community … It's a piece of piss … Aye, in Ballyhackamore … DR BONZO *signs up for the gig.* BOBBY: Art's crap! BOBBY *lays into him with a cricket bat, especially his face and crotch.* DR BONZO: Three years in Le Coq! I was in the same class as Borat! I've played the Lurgan International Arts Festival! BOBBY (to audience): More? AUDIENCE: YEAH! *The Yamaha keyboard produces the sound of the blows.*[24]

Routines such as this exemplify the ways in which Tumble's work confronts contemporary social and political issues that are both specific to Ireland and familiar worldwide. In this way, their work represents another kind of 'Irish universal': a concept that has been instructive throughout this book, first articulated by film director Thaddeus O'Sullivan when referring to Banville's *Birchwood*. The same might also be said of Fossett's Circus. Their interaction with current affairs is less obvious and less conscious, but the sensitive patron cannot help but appreciate certain facts about modern life when attending a Fossett's performance. Both shows pose, in their own way, urgent yet familiar questions about Ireland today. This study has aimed to show that using the circus as a conveyor of these old pressing questions is not something new, but it is in recognising this tradition that this study achieves its own novelty.

By closing this book with a review of two circuses working in Ireland at the start of the twenty-first century, the field of critical enquiry opens up. There is, as yet, no consolidated cultural history dedicated to the circus in Ireland. Here, historical material relaying something of the circus itself has woven in and out of analyses of literary texts and works of visual art concerned, primarily, with family life. In expanding the historical frame, other fascinating performers whose lives have been uncovered might be considered in detail: the Irish Giant Patrick Cotter, for instance, who performed at Sadler's Wells in the late eighteenth century alongside dancing dogs and learned pigs, magicians and other human curiosities; or the Hanlon Lees Brothers: an acrobatic troupe from Manchester immensely proud of their Irish heritage, who took the

American and European circus worlds by storm in the nineteenth century.[25] These historical figures might be read in a tradition of circus performance that, as well as encompassing the acts discussed here, also extends to 1980s Northern Ireland, and the positive work of the Belfast Community Circus, which was founded in 1985 by Donal McKendry and Mike Moloney with a remit 'specifically to bring together young people from both Protestant and Catholic communities'.[26] Belfast Community Circus continues to devise street theatre for Belfast's annual Festival of Fools, which celebrated its fifteenth anniversary in spring 2018. Producing an oral history of this venture would offer a fascinating perspective on community-building through cultural activity in Northern Ireland, which might, in turn, be supplemented with material from holdings that represent amateur, artistic and commercial histories of the circus in the Republic. The RTÉ and Irish Film Institute Archives are particularly promising resources, from which the changing fortunes of the circus and its relevance in Irish life might be better understood. Certainly, these films would complement the breadth, diversity and richness of circus texts and circus sources covered in this book that is drawn from manuscripts, sketchbooks, ephemera and rare publications held at institutions in England, Ireland and the United States. The remarkable range of material collected here is, in itself, indicative of the significance of the work this project has already done.

But the principal aim of this historicist literary study has been to demonstrate that the circus as theme, metaphor or setting offers writers and visual artists an ideal medium through which to assess complexities of individual and collective experience in modern and contemporary Ireland. It began with Joyce's *Ulysses*, and with Mr Bloom's resolute appreciation for the fact that: 'All tales of circus life are highly demoralising.'[27] That intriguing word 'demoralising' has been an inspiration: pitched somewhere between the status of adjective and verb, it emanates ambiguity. Mr Bloom's understanding denies the purposeful force and good intentions of such works as Amye Reade's *Ruby; or how girls are trained for a circus life. Founded on fact* (1890), as it does not simply suggest that the circus in literary form is a cause of moral panic. Instead, it tempers the atmosphere that is sensed most keenly throughout all the tales of circus, or circused, life that are told in *Ulysses*: they are dispiriting, disheartening, disorienting and disintegrating. Despite clear evidence in the form of Ó Conaire's *Exile* that Joyce was not the innovator of this mood, it can be supposed that his demoralising tales have been of the widest influence on the later generations of artists considered in this book. The terminal perspectives offered self-consciously in Yeats' 'The Circus Animals' Desertion', Friel's *Crystal and Fox* and Banville's *Birchwood* are fine examples of how putting one's own life 'on show' through the circus trope can be terribly demoralising.

However, many of the primary works considered here communicate feelings and moments of fragmentation and discontinuity in terms that are not simply, or necessarily, pejorative. It is in reaching this conclusion that this book has refined and advanced arguments made with regards to Irish culture in broad terms by leading critics, including Declan Kiberd, Luke Gibbons, Seamus Deane and Colin Graham. The idea of the circus in certain texts allows for accommodation of acute disappointment and exciting promise at once. This accommodation is made perhaps unconsciously in Edward Seago's *Sons of Sawdust*, where his robust prose is faced with sentimental sketches of his circus friends. It is performed provocatively by Johnny Patterson in *Heavenly Bodies*: behind the quick-witted comic that is Parker's Mephistophelean clown stands an individual actor whose life ended rather more pathetically than anyone has yet been willing to admit. But there is something extra – something almost transcendent – in Joyce's circus writing that is not seen clearly again until we reach the circus images of Heaney. Appropriately, it is 'Wheels within Wheels' (*Seeing Things*, 1991) that brings us back to the acute poignancy of lost promise that is preserved in the form of a knowing, and yet disinterested, little boy. The poet sets us on the quest for a 'double-take of feeling', which mimics that of Mr Bloom as he catches sight of his son Rudy for the first-last time at the close of 'Circe'.[28] But the poem also revels in the power of incorporating loss, as it refuses to revise that feeling out of its orbit. Heaney used an important expressive compound in his review of Paul Muldoon's *Mules* (1977) and the particularly emblematic achievement of the poem 'Centaurs', which he believed shows 'simply the process of the image's life-history'.[29] Conclusively, then, the same might be said of this study, and of the Irish circus image.

Endnotes

Introduction

1 *Circus*, vols 2–17, Circus Association of Ireland, 1990–2000.

2 *Circus*, vol. 2, Winter 1990, p. 2. Hereafter, citations to this volume are given in the main body of the text.

3 Clairol advertised on the back cover of *Circus*, p. 6 (Winter 1992–3); Woodchester Farm Finance advertised on the back cover of *Circus*, vol. 2, Winter 1990.

4 *Circus*, vol. 15, Summer 1998, p. 3.

5 'Irish Circuses Y2K', *Circus*, vol. 17, Autumn 2000, pp. 11–12.

6 Agnes Sullivan, 'The End of the Strolling Players', *Circus*, vol. 17, pp. 15–21.

7 Helen Burke, 'Jacobin Revolutionary Theatre and the Early Circus: Astley's Dublin Amphitheatre in the 1790s', *Theatre Research International*, vol. 31, no. 1, March 2006, pp. 1–16, http://dx.doi.org/10.1017/S0307883305001859 [accessed 15 October 2012].

8 Harry Bradshaw, 'Johnny Patterson, the Rambler from Clare', *Dal gCais*, vol. 2, 1986, pp. 73–80, http://www.clarelibrary.ie/eolas/coclare/music/johnny_patterson_bradshaw2.htm [accessed 15 October 2012].

9 Kenneth Fanning and Tina Segner, Production notes for *Death or Circus*, Tumble Circus, http://www.tumblecircus.com/shows-acts/death-or-circus [accessed 24 March 2015] (para. 4 of 4).

10 Helen Stoddart, *Rings of Desire: circus history and representation* (Manchester: Manchester University Press, 2000). Hereafter, citations are given in the main body of the text.

11 Róisín Kennedy, 'The Circus Has Come', in *Masquerade and Spectacle: the circus and the travelling fair in the work of Jack B. Yeats*, ed. Róisín Kennedy (Dublin: National Gallery of Ireland, 2007), p. 66.

12 Edward Seago, *Sons of Sawdust, with Paddy O'Flynn's Circus in Western Ireland* (London: Putnam, 1934), p. 36.

13 Lynne Parker, 'Showtime: the strategy of mischief in the plays of Stewart Parker', in *The Dreaming Body: contemporary Irish theatre*, ed. Melissa Sihra and Paul Murphy (Gerrards Cross: Colin Smythe, 2009), pp. 43–54 (p. 49).

14 Personal interview with John Banville, Dublin, 30 September 2014. Reprinted by kind permission of John Banville.

15 Luke Gibbons, *Transformations in Irish Culture* (Cork: Cork University Press in association with Field Day, 1996), p. 10.

16 Colin Graham, *Deconstructing Ireland: identity, theory, culture* (Edinburgh: Edinburgh University Press, 2001), p. 155.

17 Seamus Deane, *Strange Country: modernity and nationhood in Irish writing since 1790* (Oxford: Clarendon Press, 1997), pp. 17–18.

18 Graham, *Deconstructing Ireland*, p. 23.

19 Deane, *Strange Country*, p. 2.

20 Graham, *Deconstructing Ireland*, p. 55.

21　Paul Bouissac, 'When Failure Means Success: the staging of a negative experience', in *Semiotics at the Circus* (Berlin and New York: De Gruyter Mouton, 2010), pp. 127–32 (p. 127).

22　Declan Kiberd, *Ulysses and Us: the art of everyday life in Joyce's masterpiece* (New York and London: Norton & Company, 2009), p. 11.

23　Consider Cheryl Herr's 'Plays and Pantomimes in Joyce's Dublin' in *Joyce's Anatomy of Culture* (Urbana and Chicago, IL: University of Illinois Press, 1986), pp. 96–135, and the approach of many of the essayists collected in *Roll Away the Reel World: Joyce and cinema*, ed. John McCourt (Cork: Cork University Press, 2010). Crowley's article '"Between Contemporaneity and Antiquity": Katie Lawrence and the music hall scaffold of "Circe"' (*Hypermedia Joyce Studies*, vol. 9, no. 2, 2008, http://hjs.ff.cuni.cz/archives/v9_2/essays/crowley.htm [accessed 16 July 2014]) reflects several points of comparison between our approaches to Joyce.

24　Biographical details derived from Bradshaw, 'Johnny Patterson, the Rambler from Clare', pp. 73–80.

25　Article 41.1.1, The Constitution of Ireland, http://www.irishstatutebook.ie/en/constitution [accessed 10 July 2014].

26　Fintan O'Toole, *The Ex-Isle of Erin: images of a global Ireland* (Dublin: New Island Books, 1997), p. 223.

27　Graham, *Deconstructing Ireland*, p. 93.

28　Tim Youngs, 'Introduction', in Tim Youngs (ed.), *Travel Writing in the Nineteenth Century: filling in the blank spaces* (Cambridge: Cambridge University Press, 2012), pp. 1–18 (p. 2).

29　Gerald Dawe, 'A Hard Act: Stewart Parker's *Pentecost*', in *The Rest Is History* (Newry: Abbey Press, 1998), pp. 59–69 (p. 68).

30　Ibid., p. 69.

31　Samuel Beckett, *Waiting for Godot*, in *The Complete Dramatic Works* (London: Faber, 2006), pp. 34–5.

32　For arguments positing Shakespeare's Captain Macmorris as the earliest known Irish character written for the English stage, see John Goodby, *Irish Poetry Since 1950: from stillness into history* (Manchester: Manchester University Press, 2000), p. 153; Rebecca Steinberger, *Shakespeare and Twentieth-Century Irish Drama: conceptualizing identity and staging boundaries* (Aldershot: Ashgate, 2008), p. 22.

33　Graham, *Deconstructing Ireland*, p. 5.

34　Thaddeus O'Sullivan, Letter to John Banville, 17 November 1981, Dublin, Trinity College Dublin Archives and Manuscripts, MSS 10252/3/13/2: Banville Literary Papers.

35　Neil Jordan, Production notes for *The Miracle*, quoted in Carole Zucker, *The Cinema of Neil Jordan: dark carnival* (London: Wallflower Press, 1998), p. 87.

36　Dennis O'Driscoll with Seamus Heaney, '"Time to be dazzled": *Seeing Things*', in *Stepping Stones: interviews with Seamus Heaney* (London: Faber, 2009), pp. 317–44 (p. 323).

37　Paul Muldoon, 'Duffy's Circus', *Poems, 1968–1998* (London: Faber, 2001), l. 12, p. 66.

38　O'Driscoll with Heaney, 'From Home to School', in *Stepping Stones*, pp. 3–33 (p. 3).

CHAPTER 1 Joyce's Family Circus

1　James Joyce, *Ulysses*, ed. Jeri Johnson (Oxford: Oxford University Press, 1998; repr. 2008), p. 649. Hereafter, citations to this edition are given in the main body of the text.

2　James Joyce, *Finnegans Wake* (London: Penguin Books, 1992; repr. 2000), p. 307. Hereafter, citations to this edition are given in the main body of the text.

3　Thomas Frost, *Circus Life and Circus Celebrities* (London: Tinsley Brothers, 1875), p. 119.

4　*Patterson's Great London Circus Songster: only original Irish clown*, DeWitt's Song and Joke Book Series, no. 241, 1878, p. 3.

5   Bradshaw, 'Johnny Patterson, the Rambler from Clare', pp. 73–80 (p. 75).

6   *Patterson's Great London Circus Songster*, p. 10

7   The Oxford English Dictionary isolates the first recorded use of the usually pejorative term 'Oirish' in an article published in March 1862 by the *Caledonian Mercury*.

8   *Patterson's Great London Circus Songster*, p. 49.

9   James Joyce, *Stephen Hero*, ed. Theodore Spencer, revd edn (London: Grafton Books, 1986), p. 101. Hereafter, citations to this edition are given in the main body of the text.

10 Janet M. Davis, *The Circus Age: culture & society under the American big top* (Chapel Hill, NC: University of North Carolina Press, 2002), p. 48 and p. 52.

11 *Patterson's Great London Circus Songster*, p. 20.

12 James Lloyd, *My Circus Life* (London: Douglas, 1925), p. 27.

13 Bradshaw, 'Johnny Patterson, the Rambler from Clare', pp. 79–80.

14 Ibid., p. 79.

15 Marilynn Richtarik, *Stewart Parker: a life* (Oxford: Oxford University Press, 2012), pp. 292–3.

16 Stewart Parker, *Heavenly Bodies*, in *Plays: 2* (London: Methuen, 2000), Act Two, p. 91.

17 Stewart Parker, *Spokesong*, in *Plays: 1* (London: Methuen, 2000), Act One, p. 2.

18 Richtarik, *Stewart Parker: a life*, p. 291.

19 Personal email correspondence with Marilynn Richtarik, 10 February 2014.

20 S. Theodore Felstead, *Stars Who Made the Halls: a hundred years of English humour, harmony and hilarity* (London: Werner Laurie Ltd, 1947), p. 15.

21 Harry Clifton, 'Pulling Hard Against the Stream (Do Your Best For One Another)' (London: Hopwood & Crew, *c.*1867).

22 Paul Bouissac, *Semiotics at the Circus* (Berlin and New York: de Gruyter Mouton, 2010), p. 121.

23 Donal Maguire, *The Singing Clown*, in *Masquerade and Spectacle: the circus and the travelling fair in the work of Jack B. Yeats*, ed. Róisín Kennedy (Dublin: National Gallery of Ireland, 2007), p. 46.

24 Paddy Woodworth, 'Foreword', in J.M. Synge, *Travels in Wicklow, West Kerry and Connemara* (London: Serif, 2009), pp. 7–15 (p. 2). Hereafter, citations to this edition are given in the main body of the text.

25 James Joyce, 'Subjugation', in *Occasional, Critical and Political Writing*, ed. Kevin Barry (Oxford: Oxford University Press, 2000; repr. 2008), pp. 4–11 (p. 6).

26 'El Niño Farini', Victoria and Albert Museum biography, http://www.vam.ac.uk/content/articles/e/el-nino-farini [accessed 15 July 2014] (para. 7 of 7).

27 John Turner, *Historical Hengler's Circus* (Formby: Lingdales Press, 1989), 5 vols, Vol. I, p. 5.

28 Mary Power, 'The Discovery of *Ruby*', *James Joyce Quarterly*, vol. 18, no. 2, Winter 181, pp. 115–21.

29 Amye Reade, *Ruby; or How Girls are Trained for a Circus Life. Founded on fact* (London: Trischler & Company, 1890), n.p. Hereafter, citations to this edition are given in the main body of the text.

30 Margot Norris, *Virgin and Veteran Readings of Ulysses* (New York: Palgrave Macmillan, 2011), p. 92.

31 Jennifer Burns Levin, '"Ruby pride of the on the floor naked": fetishizing the circus girl in Joyce's *Ulysses*', *Joyce Studies Annual*, 2009, pp. 125–58.

32 Power, 'The Discovery of *Ruby*', p. 120.

33 Caroline Nobile Gryta, 'Who Is Signor Maffei? And Has *Ruby: the Pride of the Ring* Really Been Located?', *James Joyce Quarterly*, vol. 21, no. 4, Summer 1984, pp. 321–8 (p. 321).

34 Ibid., p. 325.

35 Ronan Crowley, '"Between contemporaneity and antiquity": Katie Lawrence and the music hall scaffold of "Circe"', *Hypermedia Joyce Studies*, vol. 9, no. 2, 2008, http://hjs.ff.cuni.cz/archives/v9_2/essays/crowley.htm [accessed 16 July 2014] (para. 2 of 31).

36 Davis, *The Circus Age*, p. 150.

37 Ibid., p. 150.

38 Geraldine Higgins, *Heroic Revivals from Carlyle to Yeats* (New York: Palgrave Macmillan, 2012), p. 106.

39 M.W.D., '"The Circus": the new adventures of Charlie Chaplin', *Observer*, 18 March 1928, p. 22.

40 Christine Froula, *Modernism's Body: sex, culture, and Joyce* (New York: Columbia University Press, 1996), p. 156.

41 Seamus Deane, *Strange Country: modernity and nationhood in Irish writing since 1790* (Oxford: Clarendon Press, 1997), p. 144.

42 Richard Ellmann, 'Appendix: Joyce's Trieste Library', in *The Consciousness of Joyce* (Toronto and New York: Oxford University Press, 1977), pp. 97–134.

43 Helen Stoddart, *Rings of Desire: circus history and representation* (Manchester: Manchester University Press, 2000), p. 5.

44 Terry Eagleton, *Walter Benjamin, Or Towards a Revolutionary Criticism* (London: Verso, 1981), p. 148.

45 Stoddart, *Rings of Desire*, p. 7.

46 Adrienne Monnier, 'The Humanism of Joyce', in *Joyce's Ulysses and the French Public*, trans. Sylvia Beach (1931), *Kenyon Review*, vol. 8, no. 3, Summer 1946, pp. 430–44 (p. 443), http://www.jstor.org/stable/4332775?seq=1 [accessed 1 September 2014].

47 'Rabelais and Joyce prove that there may be something in seminal fluid and faecal matter. The thing is to have genius. James Joyce has it. What bad luck that he isn't French! He is English. Or rather, he is Irish. And the Irish are Celtic. No Anglo-Saxon has ever been capable of writing *Ulysses*' (present author's translation). P. Demasy, 'Un Nouveau Rabelais', *Chronique de Paris*, 14 February 1930, n.p.; clipping in James Joyce – collection of papers, 1897–1971 (bulk 1902–1949), New York, The Henry W. and Albert A. Berg Collection of English and American Literature, New York Public Library.

48 Burns Levin, 'The Circus Girl in Joyce's *Ulysses*', p. 127.

49 Terry Eagleton, *Heathcliff and the Great Hunger: studies in Irish culture* (London: Verso, 1995), p. 303.

50 Ibid., p. 304.

51 Marcel Brion, 'Les Grandes Figures Européennes: James Joyce, Romancier', *Gazettes des Nations*, 3 March 1928, p. 4; clipping in James Joyce – collection of papers, 1897–1971 (bulk 1902–1949), New York, The Henry W. and Albert A. Berg Collection of English and American Literature, New York Public Library.

52 Jean Carrère, 'Mussolini et La Littérature: Mussolini et Alessandro Manzoni', *Gazettes des Nations*, 3 March 1928, p. 3; clipping in James Joyce – collection of papers, 1897–1971 (bulk 1902–1949), New York, The Henry W. and Albert A. Berg Collection of English and American Literature, New York Public Library.

53 Jared Becker, *Nationalism and Culture: Gabriele D'Annunzio and Italy after the Risorgimento* (New York: Peter Lang, 1995).

54 Sarah Crompton, 'Samuel Johnson Prize 2013: Lucy Hughes-Hallett is a revelation', *Telegraph*, 4 November 2013, http://www.telegraph.co.uk/culture/books/booknews/10425909/Samuel-Johnson-Prize-2013-Lucy-Hughes-Hallett-is-a-revelation.html [accessed 5 November 2013].

55 Nick Higham, 'The 2013 Samuel Johnson Prize', *Today*, BBC Radio 4, 5 November 2013.

56 'Behind the clowning and his great talent for storytelling it seems there is a cheerful stoicism. But on the contrary, the backdrop to the verbal torrent of *Ulysses* is a sad hallucination and a morose pleasure. The essential character of Rabelais' spirit is its fearlessness; he considers the body with amusement and not with horror. *Ulysses* strikes me, as it has struck others, as a product of suffering, of a sentiment of almost insupportable oppression. [...] Despite the biting precision of his phrases, his stunning mastery of beauty, his sardonic humour – things

that everyone can appreciate – the author of *Ulysses* gives me the impression of an enslaved mind, rather than a fearless spirit' (present author's translation). Desmond MacCarthy, 'Le Roman Anglais d'Après-Guerre (1919–1929)', *Revue de Paris*, 7 May 1932, p. 148; clipping in James Joyce – collection of papers 1897–1971 (bulk 1902–1949), New York, The Henry W. and Albert A. Berg Collection of English and American Literature, New York Public Library.

57 Davis, *The Circus Age*, p. 237.

58 Eagleton, *Heathcliff and the Great Hunger*, p. 317.

59 Alan Read, 'The Manual Labour of Performance', Lecture, Anatomy Theatre, King's College London, 16 October 2012.

CHAPTER 2 **Imagined Communities at the Irish Circus**

1 Luke Gibbons, *Transformations in Irish Culture* (Cork: Cork University Press, 1996), p. 40.

2 Following an exhibition of his artwork at the Irish Museum of Modern Art in summer 1993, an article about Hinde and his Cicorama was published in *Circus*, vol. 8, Winter 1993/4, p. 30.

3 John Hinde, 'Preparing for the show', in *British Circus Life*, ed. Eleanor Smith (London: Harrap & Company Ltd, 1948), pp. 136–48 (p. 138).

4 Ibid., p. 136.

5 John Hinde, 'A Visit to Dublin', in *British Circus Life*, pp. 149–51 (p. 149).

6 Ibid.

7 Ibid., p. 151.

8 Gibbons, *Transformations in Irish Culture*, p. 40.

9 John T. Koch (ed.), *Celtic Culture: a historical encyclopedia*, 5 vols (Santa Barbara: ABC-CLIO, 2006), vol. I, p. 1013; Pádraigín Riggs and Norman Vance, 'Irish Prose Fiction', in *The Cambridge Companion to Modern Irish Culture*, ed. Joe Cleary and Claire Connolly (Cambridge: Cambridge University Press, 2005), pp. 245–66 (p. 248).

10 Pádraic Ó Conaire, *Exile*, trans. Gearailt Mac Eoin (London: Peter Owen, 2009), p. 6. Hereafter, citations to this translation are given in the main body of the text.

11 Conrad M. Arensberg and Solon T. Kimball, *Family and Community in Ireland*, 3rd edn (Ennis: Clasp Press, 2001), p. 217. Hereafter, citations to this edition are given in the main body of the text.

12 Benedict Anderson, *Imagined Communities*, revd edn (London: Verso, 2006).

13 Ernest Renan, *The Poetry of the Celtic Races*, trans. William G. Hutchinson (1896; Port Washington: Kennikat Press, repr. 1970), pp. 61–83 (p. 81).

14 Biographical information from 'Pádraic Ó Conaire: man and statue', www.galwaycity museum.ie/listen-and-learn/man-statue [accessed 21 January 2015], and Mac Eoin, 'The Author', in *Exile*, pp. 5–6 (p. 6).

15 A publication history of Ó Conaire's short stories is available from the James Hardiman Library, NUI Galway, at http://nuiarchives.blogspot.co.uk/2012/02/padraic-o-conaire. html [accessed 21 July 2014].

16 Pádraic Ó Conaire, *Field and Fair*, trans. Cormac Breathnach (Cork: Mercier Press, 1966).

17 Liam O'Flaherty's *Shame the Devil* (1934) is quoted in Brendan McGowan, 'Introduction', in Pádraic Ó Conaire, *Seacht mBua an Éirí Amach – Seven Virtues of the Rising*, trans. Diarmuid de Faoite (Galway: Arlen House, 2016), pp. 27–8.

18 David Lloyd, *Anomalous States: Irish writing and the post-colonial moment* (Dublin: Lilliput Press, 1993), p. 96.

19 Pádraic Ó Conaire, *Deoraíocht*, 3rd edn (Cló Talbot: Dublin, 1973), p. 16. I am sincerely grateful to Martin Dyar for providing me with literal translations from the Irish in June 2018.

20 William Booth, *In Darkest England and the Way Out* (London: Charles Knight, repr. 1970), pp. 10–11.

21 Ó Conaire, *Deoraíocht*, p. 16. Translation of the Irish made by Martin Dyar, June 2018.

22 Pádraigín Riggs, 'Pádraic Ó Conaire's London: a real or an imaginary place', in *The Irish Writing London*, ed. Tom Heron, 2 vols (London: Bloomsbury, 2013), vol. I, pp. 84–97 (n. 11, p. 97).

23 Flora Tristan, *London Journal: a survey of London life in the 1830s*, trans. Dennis Palmer and Giselle Pincetl (London: George Prior Publishers, 1980), pp. 135–6.

24 Ibid., p. 135.

25 Lloyd, *Anomalous States*, p. 150.

26 Charles Dickens, *Bleak House* (London: Penguin Classics, 1985; repr. 1996), p. 13.

27 Thomas Carlyle, 'Chartism', in *Irish Migrants in Britain, 1815–1914: a documentary history*, ed. Roger Swift (Cork: Cork University Press, 2002), pp. 37–8.

28 Helen Stoddart, *Rings of Desire: circus history and representation* (Manchester: Manchester University Press, 2000), p. 142.

29 Sigmund Freud, 'Three Essays on the Theory of Sexuality: infantile sexuality', in *On Sexuality: three essays on the theory of sexuality and other works*, trans. James Strachey, ed. Angela Richards (Harmondsworth: Penguin Books, 1977), pp. 88–126 (p. 99).

30 Pádraic Ó Conaire, 'Little Marcus's Nora', in *The Woman at the Window*, trans. Eamonn O'Neill (Cork: Mercier Press, 1966), pp. 53–67 (p. 64).

31 Franz Kafka, 'A Hunger Artist', trans. Edwin Muir, in *The Complete Short Stories*, ed. Nahum N. Glatzer (London: Allen Lane, 1983), pp. 268–77 (p. 277).

32 Maud Ellmann, *The Hunger Artists: starving, writing & imprisonment* (London: Virago Press, 1993), p. 16.

33 Samuel Beckett, *Molloy*, ed. Shane Weller (London: Faber & Faber, 2009), p. 23.

34 Ó Conaire, *Deoraíocht*, p. 126.

35 Details of Krause's study and the *Telegraph* articles appear in James Vernon, 'The Humanitarian Discovery of Hunger', in *Hunger: a modern history* (Cambridge, MA: The Belknap Press, 2007), pp. 17–40.

36 Ibid., p. 43.

37 Ellmann, *The Hunger Artists*, p. 5

38 Vernon, *Hunger: a modern history*, p. 33.

39 Paige Reynolds, *Modernism, Drama, and the Audience for Irish Spectacle* (Cambridge: Cambridge University Press, 2007), p. 134.

40 Ibid.

41 Townsend Walsh, 'Clowns', in *Love of the Circus*, c. 1900, Townsend Walsh Papers, New York, New York Public Library, Manuscripts and Archives Division, Astor, Lenox, and Tilden Foundations, MSS Col 3213.

42 Stewart Parker, *Heavenly Bodies*, in *Plays: 2* (London: Methuen, 2002), Act One, p. 115.

43 Kafka, 'A Hunger Artist', p. 276.

44 Cormac Ó Gráda, *Black '47 and Beyond: the Great Irish Famine in history, economy, and memory* (Princeton: Princeton University Press, 1999), pp. 221–2.

45 Ó Conaire, *Deoraíocht*, p. 90. Translation of the Irish made by Martin Dyar, June 2018.

46 Kafka, 'A Hunger Artist', p. 275.

47 Thomas Frost, *Circus Life and Circus Celebrity* (London: Tinsley Brothers, 1875), p. 257.

48 Barbara Gibson, 'Carlos and Patricia MacManus Interview Transcript – Tape 1' (F13636): Side A, in *Oral History of the Circus*, 2003, London, British Library. Carlos MacManus' maternal grandparents were Frank and Clara Paulo. MacManus and his wife were both involved in the circus: he as an animal trainer and harness maker, she as a performer in the ring.

49 See Maurice Moynihan (ed.), *Speeches and Statements by Éamon de Valera: 1917–1973* (Dublin: Gill & Macmillan, 1980), p. 466.

50 Rupert Croft-Cooke and Peter Cotes, *Circus: a world history* (London: Paul Elek Ltd, 1976), pp. 108–9.

51 Ibid., p. 109.

52 Horace Shipp, 'Edward Seago', in *Edward Seago: a painter in the English tradition* (London: Collins, 1952), pp. 15–47 (p. 15).

53 Ibid., p. 21.

54 See HRH The Prince of Wales, 'Foreword', in James Russell, *Edward Seago* (Farnham: Lund Humphries and Portland Gallery, 2014), n.p.

55 *The Circus: a delightful day with the circus folk* (London and Barcelona: Green Trefoil Ltd and Euredit, 196-?), published as part of the IDEABOOKS series.

56 Jack Yeats, *The Circus Dwarf*, 1912, Oil on canvas, Private collection, Ireland. Exhibited at the National Gallery of Ireland during *Masquerade & Spectacle: the circus and the travelling fair in the work of Jack B. Yeats*, 18 July–11 November 2007.

57 Edward Seago, *Circus Company* (London: Putnam, 1933), p. 208.

58 Ibid., p. 209.

59 Edward Seago, *Sons of Sawdust* (London: Putnam, 1934), p. 13. Hereafter, citations to this work are given in the main body of the text.

60 Seago, *Circus Company*, p. 209.

61 Colin Gleadell, 'Seago Rides Again', *Telegraph*, 3 June 2014, http://www.telegraph.co.uk/luxury/art/35292/art-sales-royal-favourite-edward-seago-rides-again.html [accessed 27 January 2015].

62 Seago, *Circus Company*, p. 5.

63 Anthony Trollope, *An Autobiography*, ed. David Skilton (London: Penguin Books, 1996), p. 46.

64 William Makepeace Thackeray, *The Irish Sketch Book, 1842* (Belfast: Blackstaff Press, 1985), pp. 140–1.

65 Ibid., p. 142.

66 Ibid., p. 144.

67 J.M. Synge, *Travels in Wicklow, West Kerry and Connemara* (London: Serif, 2009), p. 82.

68 Ibid.

69 J.M. Synge, *The Playboy of the Western World*, in *The Playboy of the Western World and Other Plays*, ed. Ann Saddlemyer (Oxford: Oxford University Press, 1998), Act 3, ll. 631–3, p. 146.

70 Anne Byrne, 'Introduction to the Third Edition', in Arensberg and Kimball, *Family and Community in Ireland*, pp. I–CI (p. I).

71 David Herlihy, 'The Making of the Medieval Family: symmetry, structure, and sentiment', *Journal of Family History*, vol. 8, no. 2, 1983, pp. 116–30. Paraphrased in Ellmann, *The Hunger Artists*, p. 80.

72 Synge, *The Playboy of the Western World*, Act 3, ll. 572–3, p. 144.

73 Gibson, 'Interviewer Transcript: Violet Sandow interview', Tape 1 (F9178): Side A, 2001.

74 Smith (ed.), *British Circus Life*, p. 116.

75 Ibid.

CHAPTER 3 Irish Circus History and Ireland's Theatrical Heritage

1 Samuel Beckett, *Waiting for Godot*, in *The Complete Dramatic Works* (London: Faber, 1990; repr. 2006), pp. 34–5.

2 Line reference to Stewart Parker, *Heavenly Bodies*, in *Plays: 2* (London: Methuen, 2002), Act One, p. 95. Personal interview with Owen Roe, Dublin, 29 September 2014.

3 Personal interview with Roe, 2014.

4 Paul Muldoon, 'Yeats and the Afterlife', four lectures, Clark Lecture Series, University of Cambridge, 19–29 January 2015.

5 Samuel Beckett, *The Letters of Samuel Beckett*, ed. Martha Dow Fehsenfeld, Lois More Overbeck, Dan Gunn and George Craig, 3 vols to date (Cambridge: Cambridge University Press, 2009–14).

6 David Lloyd, 'Republics of Difference: Yeats, MacGreevy, Beckett', *Field Day Review*, Vol. 1 (2005), pp. 43–70.

7 Gerald Dawe, 'Hearing Things: Samuel Beckett's William Butler Yeats', Samuel Beckett Summer School, Trinity College Dublin, 13 August 2014.

8 Ireland's ambassador to the United Kingdom, Daniel Mulhall, described W.B. Yeats as 'Ireland's greatest poet' in advance of the London launch of Yeats2015: a year of international celebrations to mark 150 years since the poet's birth. Quoted in press release, 'London Launch Yeats2015', http://www.yeatsday.com/yeatsday-2015/ [accessed 24 February 2015] (para. 3 of 16).

9 Astley was first instituted as 'father of the modern circus' in *The Book of Days*, ed. Robert Chambers (London: W. & R. Chambers, *c.* 1869).

10 Charles Dibdin quoted by Speaight in *A History of the Circus*, p. 34.

11 Helen Burke, 'Jacobin Revolutionary Theatre and the Early Circus: Astley's Dublin Amphitheatre in the 1790s', *Theatre Research International*, 31:1 (March 2006), pp. 1–16 (p. 1), http://dx.doi.org/10.1017/S0307883305001859 [accessed 15 October 2012].

12 Ibid., p. 2.

13 Helen Stoddart, *Rings of Desire* (Manchester: Manchester University Press, 2000), p. 71.

14 Articles from the *Press* are quoted in Burke, 'Jacobin Revolutionary Theatre and the Early Circus', p. 9.

15 W.B. Yeats, 'Dramatis Personae', in *Autobiographies* (Dublin: Gill & Macmillan, 1955), pp. 383–458 (p. 409).

16 W.B. Yeats, Lady Gregory and Edward Martyn, *Manifesto for the Irish Literary Theatre* quoted in Lady Gregory, *Our Irish Theatre: a chapter in autobiography* (New York and London: G.P. Putnam's and Sons and the Knickerbocker Press, 1913), p. 9, http://digital.library.upenn.edu/women/gregory/theatre/theatre.html [accessed 19 November 2014].

17 Ibid., p. 8.

18 W.B. Yeats, 'An Irish National Theatre', in *Explorations* (London: Macmillan, 1962), pp. 114–18 (p. 115).

19 Yeats, 'Dramatis Personae', p. 399.

20 Yeats, 'An Irish National Theatre', p. 117.

21 Jack B. Yeats, Letter to Thomas MacGreevy, 21 March 1927, Dublin, Trinity College Dublin Archives and Manuscripts, MSS 10381/84/1-2. Reprinted by kind permission of United Agents LLP on behalf of Caitríona Yeats.

22 Jack B. Yeats, Letter to Thomas MacGreevy, 12 September 1933, Dublin, Trinity College Dublin Archives and Manuscripts, MSS 10381/119. Reprinted by kind permission of United Agents LLP on behalf of Caitríona Yeats.

23 Ian Walsh, *Irish Experimental Theatre: after W.B. Yeats* (Basingstoke: Palgrave Macmillan, 2012), p. 2.

24 John Purser, *The Literary Works of Jack B. Yeats* (Gerrards Cross: Colin Smythe, 1990), p. 34.

25 Jack Yeats, 'Indigo Height', *New Statesman and Nation*, 8 December 1926; noted in Calvin Bedient, *The Yeats Brothers and Modernism's Love of Motion* (Notre Dame: University of Notre Dame Press, 2009), p. 356, n. 28.

26 Bruce Arnold, *Jack Yeats* (New Haven, CT and London: Yale University Press, 1998), p. 98.

27 Ibid., p. 95.

28 Jack Yeats, *Sligo* (London: Wishart, 1930), p. 34.

29 Ibid., p. 60.

30 Anthony Roche, *Contemporary Irish Drama: from Beckett to McGuinness* (Dublin: Gill & Macmillan, 1994), p. 115.

31 Purser, *The Literary Works of Jack B. Yeats*, p. 28.

32 Lloyd, 'Republics of Difference', p. 48.

33 Helen Stoddart, *Rings of Desire*, p. 99.

34 Henri Bergson, *Laughter: an essay on the meaning of the comic*, trans. Cloudesley Brereton and Fred Rothwell (London: Macmillan, 1911), p. 37.

35 Hilary Pyle, *Jack B. Yeats: a biography* (London: Routledge & Kegan Paul, 1970), pp. 118–19.

36 Lloyd, 'Republics of Difference', p. 65.

37 W.B. Yeats, 'High Talk', in *The Poems*, ed. Daniel Albright (London: Everyman, 1992), pp. 390–1.

38 W.B. Yeats, 'Long-legged Fly', in *The Poems*, ll. 9–10, p. 386.

39 Samuel Beckett, *The Unnamable*, ed. Steven Connor (London: Faber, 2010), p. 134.

40 W.B. Yeats, 'The Circus Animals' Desertion', in *The Poems*, pp. 394–5.

41 Quoted in Pyle, *Jack B. Yeats*, p. 63.

42 Edna Longley, *Yeats and Modern Poetry* (Cambridge: Cambridge University Press, 2013), pp. 30–31.

43 Pyle, *Jack B. Yeats*, p. 163.

44 Patricia Goldstone, 'Director's Notes', in the programme for *The Circus Animals' Desertion* (September 1974), Dublin, Trinity College Dublin Archives and Manuscripts, Mun/Soc/Players/9/140, n.p. Reprinted by kind permission of Patricia Goldstone.

45 Ibid., n.p.

46 Jack Yeats, *Sligo*, p. 60.

47 Paul Durcan, 'The Beckett at the Gate', in *Going Home to Russia* (Belfast: Blackstaff Press, 1987), pp. 55–62 (ll. 31–6, p. 58).

48 Ibid., ll. 19–21, p. 61.

49 Ibid., l. 23, p. 61.

50 Paul Durcan, 'The Lion Tamer', in *Jumping the Train Tracks with Angela* (Dublin: Raven Arts Press, 1983), p. 92.

51 Durcan, 'The Beckett at the Gate', ll. 7–15, p. 58.

52 Richard McMinn, 'Duffy's Circus in the Fifties', *Circus*, vol. 10, Winter 1994, pp. 22–4 (p. 24).

53 'Duffy's Circus', *Circus*, vol. 11, Summer 1995, p. 14.

54 Luke Gibbons accounts for this widespread trend in 'The Myth of the West in Irish and American Culture', in *Transformations in Irish Culture* (Cork: Cork University Press, 1996), pp. 23–35.

55 Photograph caption, 'Bibi Baskin and Marion Fossett (1993)', *RTÉ Stills Library*, https://stillslibrary.rte.ie/indexplus/image/2036/009.html [accessed 8 May 2015] (para. 2 of 2).

56 Astley's bicentennial celebrations at Fossett's are detailed by an anonymous writer in *Circus*, vol. 11, Summer 1995, p. 13.

57 'Fossett's Circus: our story', http://www.fossettscircus.com/story.html [accessed 26 February 2015] (para. 2 of 10).

58 'Obituary: Teddy Fossett', *Circus*, vol. 15, Summer 1998, p. 3.

59 'Fossett's Circus: our story' (para. 7 of 10).

60 Fintan O'Toole, 'How Poetry Joins Dramatic Action', *Guardian*, 29 November 1990.

61 Elmer Andrews, *The Art of Brian Friel: neither reality nor dreams* (New York: St Martin's Press, 1995), p. 110.

62 Ibid.

63 Desmond Rushe, 'Kathleen Mavourneen, Here Comes Brian Friel', *The Word*, February 1970, pp. 12–15; reprinted in *Brian Friel in Conversation*, ed. Paul Delaney (Ann Arbor, MI: The University of Michigan Press, 2000), pp. 79–88 (p. 85).

64 Brian Friel, *Crystal and Fox* (Oldcastle: The Gallery Press, 1984; repr. 2014), Act One, Episode Two, p. 26.

65 Ibid.

66 John Boyd, 'Soundings: interview with Brian Friel', BBC Radio 4 Northern Ireland, 2 August 1970, transcript in *Brian Friel in Conversation*, pp. 89–97 (p. 95).

67 James Mateer, *A Life on the Open Road* (Bangor: Edyplus Publications, 1996).

68 Friel, 'The Set', in *Crystal and Fox*, p. 8.

69 Beckett invents the concept of perceivedness in his notes for *Film* (1964). It is possible for his characters to exist within or without an angle of perceivedness, which might induce anguish or even agony.

70 Geraldine Higgins, *Brian Friel* (Tavistock: Northcote House Publishers, 2010), p. 21.

71 Andrews, *The Art of Brian Friel*, p. 105.

72 Friel, *Crystal and Fox*, Act One, Episode Two, p. 36.

73 Andrews, *The Art of Brian Friel*, p. 69.

74 Giovanna Tallone, 'Brian Friel's Fox Melarkey and Frank Hardy', *Hungarian Journal of English and American Studies*, vol. 5, no. 1, 1999, pp. 25–46 (p. 37).

75 Gilles Deleuze, *Francis Bacon: the logic of sensation*, trans. Daniel W. Smith (London: Continuum, 2003; repr. 2012), pp. 35–6.

76 Ibid., p. 50.

77 Tallone, 'Brian Friel's Fox Melarkey and Frank Hardy', p. 27.

78 F.C. McGrath, 'Friel and the Irish Art of Lying', in *Brian Friel's (Post)Colonial Drama: language, illusion, and politics* (Syracuse: Syracuse University Press, 1999), pp. 13–48 (p. 38).

79 Ibid., pp. 21–2.

80 Scott Boltwood, *Brian Friel, Ireland, and the North* (Cambridge: Cambridge University Press, 2007), p. 77.

81 P.J. Mathews, *Revival: the Abbey Theatre, Sinn Féin, the Gaelic League and the Co-operative Movement* (Cork: Cork University Press, 2003), p. 14.

82 Brian Friel, 'The Theatre of Hope and Despair', in *Brian Friel: essays, diaries, interviews, 1965–1999*, ed. Christopher Murray (London: Faber, 1999), pp. 15–24 (p. 16).

83 Fintan O'Toole, 'The Man from God Knows Where', *In Dublin*, 28 October 1982, in *Brian Friel in Conversation*, pp. 168–77 (pp. 168–9).

84 Eavan Boland, 'Brian Friel: Derry's playwright', *Hibernia*, 16 February 1973, in *Brian Friel in Conversation*, pp. 112–16 (p. 115).

85 Warner Berthoff, 'The Analogies of Lyric: Shelley, Yeats, Frank O'Hara', in *Literature and the Continuances of Virtue* (Princeton: Princeton University Press), pp. 223–73 (p. 243).

86 Brian Friel, 'The Illusionists', originally published in the *Saturday Evening Post*, 6 April 1963; collected in *Selected Stories* (Oldcastle: Gallery Press, 2005), pp. 71–82.

87 Ibid., p. 73.

88 Flann O'Brien, *Faustus Kelly*, in *Plays and Teleplays*, ed. Daniel Keith Jernigan (Dublin: Dalkey Archive Press, 2013), Act One, pp. 45–6.

89 Ibid., p. 46.

90 George Moore, 'A Play-House in the Waste', in *The Untilled Field* (Gerrards Cross: Colin Smythe, 1976), pp. 223–39 (p. 234).

91 Ibid., p. 227.

92 Friel, *Essays, Diaries, Interviews*, p. 23.

93 Rushe, 'Kathleen Mavourneen, Here Comes Brian Friel', p. 81.

94 Personal interview with Roe, 2014.

95 'Quotes', *An Audience with Hal Roach*, dir. Ian McGarry, Emdee 2000 Productions, 1988, http://www.imdb.com/title/tt1410224/?ref_=ttqt_qt_tt [accessed 27 November 2014] (para. 6 of 45).

96 Ibid. (para. 45 of 45).

97 Ibid. (para. 5 of 45).

98 Personal interview with Roe, 2014.

99 Ibid.

100 Paul Brady, 'Nothing But the Same Old Story', frontispiece in Liz Curtis, *Nothing But the Same Old Story: the roots of anti-Irish racism* (London: Information on Ireland, 1984), n.p.

101 Paul Brady, 'Nothing But the Same Old Story', in *Bringing It All Back Home: the influence of Irish music*, dir. Philip King, Hummingbird Productions, 1991, Episode 1.

102 Brady, frontispiece in *Nothing But the Same Old Story*, n.p.

103 Personal interview with Roe, 2014.

104 Stewart Parker, *Northern Star*, in *Plays*, Act Two, p. 81.

105 Stewart Parker, *Dramatis Personae: a John Malone memorial lecture* (Belfast: John Malone Memorial Committee, 1986), p. 17.

106 Lynne Parker, 'Showtime: the strategy of mischief in the plays of Stewart Parker', in *The Dreaming Body: contemporary Irish theatre*, eds Melissa Sihra and Paul Murphy (Gerrards Cross: Colin Smythe, 2009), pp. 43–54 (p. 45).

107 Parker, *Heavenly Bodies*, Act Two, p. 142.

108 Personal interview with John Banville, 30 September 2014.

109 Personal interview with Roe, 2014.

110 Parker, *Heavenly Bodies*, Act One, p. 95.

111 Ibid., Act Two, pp. 154–5.

112 Personal interview with Roe, 2014.

113 Quoted in 'Notices of the Press', *Patterson's Great London Circus Songster*, DeWitt's Song and Joke Book Series, no. 241, 1878, p. 4.

114 Personal interview with Roe, 2014.

115 Parker, *Dramatis Personae*, p. 6.

116 Marilynn Richtarik, *Stewart Parker: a life* (Oxford: Oxford University Press, 2012), p. 293.

117 Gerald Dawe, 'A Hard Act: Stewart Parker's *Pentecost*', in *The Rest is History* (Newry: Abbey Press, 1998), pp. 59–69 (p. 68).

118 Personal interview with Roe, 2014.

119 Parker, 'The Strategy of Mischief', p. 53.

120 Personal interview with Roe, 2014.

121 Speaight, *A History of the Circus*, p. 165.

122 Hinde, 'The Journey to Belfast', pp. 136–48.

123 Matthew Lloyd, 'The Royal Hippodrome, Victoria Street, Belfast', *Arthur Lloyd: the music hall and theatre history site*, http://www.arthurlloyd.co.uk/BelfastTheatres.htm#hippodrome [accessed 17 November 2014].

CHAPTER 4 Revisioning the Circus

1 Walter Benjamin, 'On the Concept of History', in *The Selected Writings of Walter Benjamin*, ed. Michael Jennings, trans. Rodney Livingston et al., 4 vols (Cambridge: The Belknap Press, 2001–3), vol. IV, pp. 389–400 (p. 390).

2 Bruce Davidson, *Bruce Davidson* (London: Thames & Hudson, 1990), p. 1.

3 Ibid., p. 6.

4   Jennifer A. Watts, 'Strangers in a Strange Land', in Jennifer A. Watts and Scott Wilcox, *Bruce Davidson/Paul Capanigro: two American photographers in Britain and Ireland* (New Haven, CT: Yale University Press, 2014), pp. 17–43 (pp. 37–8).

5   'Bruce Davidson', *Magnum Photos*, http://www.magnumphotos.com/C.aspx?VP3=CMS 3&VF=MAGO31_9_VForm&ERID=24KL53ZTH6 [accessed 20 May 2013] (para. 1 of 5).

6   Davidson, *Bruce Davidson*, p. 6.

7   Paul Bouissac, *Semiotics at the Circus* (Berlin and New York: de Gruyter Mouton, 2010), p. 36.

8   Davidson, *Bruce Davidson*, p. 9.

9   W.B. Yeats, 'The Theatre, the Pulpit and the Newspapers', in *Explorations* (London: Macmillan & Co., 1962), pp. 119–23 (p. 121).

10 Personal interview with Banville, 2014.

11 Ibid.

12 Personal interview with Paul Muldoon, 29 January 2015.

13 Michael Longley, 'Stilts', in *Collected Poems* (London: Jonathan Cape, 2006), p. 102.

14 Personal interview with Muldoon, 2015.

15 Seamus Deane, *Reading in the Dark* (London: Vintage, 1997), p. 189. Hereafter, citations to this edition are given in the main body of the text.

16 Kathleen Gallagher Winarski, 'Neil Jordan's *Miracle*: from fiction to film', in *Contemporary Irish Cinema: from The Quiet Man to Dancing at Lughnasa*, ed. James MacKillop (Syracuse: Syracuse University Press, 1999), pp. 98–108 (p. 98).

17 Personal interview with Neil Jordan, 10 June 2014.

18 Seamus Heaney, 'The Makings of a Music: reflections on Wordsworth and Yeats', in *Preoccupations* (London: Faber, 1984), pp. 61–78 (p. 77).

19 Personal interview with Banville, 2014.

20 Ibid.

21 David Farrer, Letter to John Banville, 18 April 1972, Dublin, Trinity College Dublin Archives and Manuscripts, MSS 10252/3/10: Banville Literary Papers.

22 Thaddeus O'Sullivan, Letter to John Banville, 17 November 1981, Dublin, Trinity College Dublin Archives and Manuscripts, MSS 10252/3/13/2: Banville Literary Papers. Reprinted by kind permission of Thaddeus O'Sullivan.

23 Personal interview with Banville, 2014.

24 Ibid.

25 John Banville, *Birchwood* (London: Picador, 1998), p. 24. Hereafter, citations to this edition are given in the main body of the text.

26 Personal interview with Banville, 2014.

27 Walter Benjamin, 'The Cultural History of Toys', in *The Selected Writings of Walter Benjamin*, ed. Michael Jennings, trans. Rodney Livingston et al., 4 vols (Cambridge: The Belknap Press, 2001–3), vol. II, pp. 113–16.

28 Joyce, *Ulysses*, p. 360.

29 Personal interview with Banville, 2014.

30 Ibid.

31 Conor McCarthy, *Modernisation, Crisis and Culture in Ireland, 1969–1992* (Dublin: Four Courts Press, 2000), p. 82.

32 Colm Tóibín, 'Introduction', in *The Penguin Book of Irish Fiction*, ed. Colm Tóibín (London: Penguin, 1999; repr. 2001), pp. ix–xxxiii (p. xxxi).

33 Ibid., p. xxxi.

34 John Banville, *Birchwood* Manuscript, Dublin, Trinity College Dublin Archives and Manuscripts MSS 10252/3/3: Banville Literary Papers, p. 3. Reprinted by kind permission of John Banville.

35 Ibid., p. 38. Reprinted by kind permission of John Banville.

36 John Waters, *Jiving at the Crossroads* (London: Transworld Ireland, 2011), p. 85.

37 Personal interview with Banville, 2014.

38 Roy Foster, 'We Are All Revisionists Now', *The Irish Review*, vol. 1, 1986, pp. 1–5.

39 John Banville and Thaddeus O'Sullivan with Andrew Pattman, '*Birchwood*: extracts from the screenplay', *The Irish Review*, vol. 1, 1986, pp. 65–73 (p. 72).

40 Paul Muldoon, *Poems, 1968–1998* (London: Faber & Faber, 2001), pp. 57–8.

41 Ibid., p. 66.

42 Tim Kendall, *Paul Muldoon* (Bridgend: Seren, 1996), p. 53.

43 Personal interview with Muldoon, 2015.

44 Kendall, *Paul Muldoon*, p. 53.

45 Personal interview with Banville, 2014.

46 'Fossett's Circus', *Circus*, vol. 8, Winter 1993/4, p. 5.

47 Barra Ó Séaghdha, 'The Celtic Tiger's Media Pundits', in *Reinventing Ireland: culture, society and the global economy*, eds Peadar Kirby, Luke Gibbons and Michael Cronin (London and Sterling, VA: Pluto Press, 2002), pp. 143–59 (p. 149).

48 Ibid., pp. 154–5.

49 Yeats, 'The Theatre, the Pulpit and the Newspapers', p. 119.

50 Waters, *Jiving at the Crossroads*, p. 152.

51 Nell McCafferty, *A Woman to Blame* (Cork: Attic Press, 1985).

52 Waters, *Jiving at the Crossroads*, pp. 33–4.

53 Philip French, 'The Best of 1991: ghosts of high returns', *Observer*, 29 December 1991, p. 39.

54 *The Miracle*, dir. Neil Jordan, Shock DVD, 2011.

55 Hal Hinson, 'The "Miracle" of Neil Jordan', *Washington Post*, 14 July 1991, p. G1.

56 Trinity College Dublin MSS 10252/3/13/2.

57 Neil Jordan, production notes, *The Miracle*, quoted in Carole Zucker, *The Cinema of Neil Jordan: dark carnival* (London: Wallflower Press, 2008), p. 87.

58 Personal interview with Jordan, 2014.

59 Elizabeth Butler Cullingford, *Ireland's Others: ethnicity and gender in Irish literature and popular culture* (Cork: Cork University Press, 2001), p. 252.

60 Personal interview with Jordan, 2014.

61 Ibid.

62 Personal interview with Banville, 2014.

63 Bouissac, *Semiotics at the Circus*, p. 83.

64 Personal interview with Jordan, 2014.

65 Yeats, 'The Theatre, the Pulpit and the Newspapers', p. 122.

66 Frank C. Bostock, *The Training of Wild Animals*, ed. Ellen Velvin (New York: Century Co., 1917), p. 185.

67 Zucker, *The Cinema of Neil Jordan*, p. 89.

68 Ibid., p. 138.

69 Toni O'Brien Johnson, *Synge: the medieval and the grotesque* (Gerrards Cross: Colin Smythe, 1982), p. 2.

70 W.B. Yeats, 'Preface to the First Edition of *The Well of the Saints*', in J.M. Synge, *The Playboy of the Western World and Other Plays*, ed. Ann Saddlemyer (Oxford: Oxford University Press, 1998), pp. 52–6 (p. 53).

71 W.B. Yeats, 'The Statues', in *The Poems*, ed. Daniel Albright (London: Everyman, 1992), pp. 384–5 (ll. 20–22, p. 384).

72 Personal interview with Jordan, 2014.

73 Yeats, 'The Theatre, the Pulpit and the Newspapers', p. 119.

74 Brian McIlroy, 'Interview with Neil Jordan', *World Cinema 4: Ireland* (Tronbridge: Flicks Books, 1989), pp. 114–18 (p. 115).

75 Personal interview with Jordan, 2014.

76 J.M. Synge, 'A Rabelaisian Rhapsody', in *Collected Works: III: Plays Book I*, ed. Ann Saddlemyer (London: Oxford University Press, 1968), pp. 183–6 (p. 186).

77 Seamus Heaney, 'Wheels within Wheels', in *Seeing Things* (London: Faber, 1991), pp. 46–7.

78 Fiona Stafford, 'Introduction', in *Local Attachments: the province of poetry* (Oxford: Oxford University Press, 2010), pp. 1–30 (p. 13).

79 Seamus Heaney, 'Mossbawn', in *Preoccupations*, pp. 17–27 (p. 17).

80 Maud Ellmann, 'Introduction: what hole?', in *The Nets of Modernism: Henry James, Virginia Woolf, James Joyce, and Sigmund Freud* (Cambridge: Cambridge University Press, 2010), pp. 1–13 (p. 4).

81 Heaney, 'Mossbawn', p. 19.

82 Joyce, *Ulysses*, p. 168.

83 Seamus Heaney, *Among Schoolchildren: a lecture dedicated to the memory of John Malone* (Belfast: John Malone Memorial Committee, 1983), p. 10.

84 Ibid., p. 16.

85 Fiona Stafford, 'Seamus Heaney and the Caught Line', in *Starting Lines in Scottish, Irish, and English Poetry: from Burns to Heaney* (Oxford: Oxford University Press, 2000), pp. 292–327 (p. 310).

86 Seamus Heaney, 'Wheels within Wheels', Dublin, National Library of Ireland MS 49,493/95 (Folder 1): MS drafts for poems included in *Seeing Things*, Sheet A. Reproduced by kind permission of the Heaney Estate.

87 Seamus Heaney, *The Cure at Troy* (London: Faber, 1990), p. 77.

88 Seamus Heaney, 'Wheels within Wheels', Dublin, National Library of Ireland MS 49,493/95 (Folder 1) (cont.): MS drafts for poems included in *Seeing Things*, Sheet C. Reproduced by kind permission of the Heaney Estate.

89 Stafford, 'Seamus Heaney and the Caught Line', p. 324.

90 Waters, *Jiving at the Crossroads*, p. 34.

91 Seamus Heaney, 'The Mixed Marriage: Paul Muldoon', in *Preoccupations* (London: Faber, 1984), pp. 211–13 (p. 212).

92 Seamus Heaney, *The Midnight Verdict* (Oldcastle: Gallery Press, 1993), p. 29.

93 Seamus Heaney, 'Feeling into Words', in *Preoccupations*, pp. 41–60 (p. 47).

94 Neil Corcoran, *The Poetry of Seamus Heaney: a critical study* (London: Faber, 1998), p. 163.

95 Stafford, 'Seamus Heaney and the Caught Line', p. 316.

96 W.B. Yeats, 'Among School Children', in *The Poems*, pp. 261–3 (Part VII, l. 8, p. 263).

97 Heaney, *Among Schoolchildren*, p. 10.

CHAPTER 5 Conclusion: 'All tales of circus life are highly demoralising.'

1 Matinee performance, *Fossett's 125th Anniversary Tour*, Clane Road, Co. Kildare, Saturday 16 March 2013.

2 Craig Redmond, 'Arts Council Ireland funding', in *Ring of Cruelty II: the use of animals in circuses in Ireland* (Captive Animals Protection Society, 2012), www.irishcircuses.org/ringofcruelty2 [accessed 11 October 2012], pp. 40–6 (p. 40).

3 Transcript, *Fossett's 125th Anniversary Tour*, Clane Road, Co. Kildare, Saturday 16 March 2013.

4 Oona Frawley, Roundtable Discussion, Thursday, 2 April 2015, part of 'Irish Studies and the Dynamics of Memory', Radboud University, Nijmegen, The Netherlands, 31 March – 2 April 2015.

5 Helen Stoddart, *Rings of Desire: circus history and representation* (Manchester: Manchester University Press, 2000), p. 28.

6 Justice Raymond Groarke, quoted in Ray Managh, 'Fossett's Circus Faces "Uphill Struggle To Survive"', *Irish Examiner*, 13 February 2015, http://www.irishexaminer.com/business/fossetts-circus-faces-uphill-struggle-to-survive-312383.html [accessed 24 March 2015] (paras 9–10 of 18).

7 The original *Irish Times* article could not be traced. However, this quote is used variously on publicity literature. For example, see: 'Family Super Saturday in the Marketplace Theatre, Armagh, N. Ireland', *Tumble Circus*, http://www.tumblecircus.com/calendar [accessed 7 May 2015] (para. 2 of 2).

8 Kenneth Fanning and Tina Segner, 'Death or Circus: modern life is rubbish', *Tumble Circus*, http://www.tumblecircus.com/shows-acts/death-or-circus [accessed 24 March 2015] (para. 3 of 4).

9 Fanning and Segner, '*Damn the Circus*: 2013 touring information', *Tumble Circus*, http://www.tumblecircus.com/wp-content/uploads/2013/07/Damn-the-Circus-Touring-Info-2013.pdf [accessed 7 May 2015], footer.

10 Eleanor Lavan, 'Transcript: *Damn the Circus*, 5 December 2014, axis Ballymun, Dublin', 5 December 2014.

11 Fanning and Segner, 'Production notes *Death or Circus*', http://www.tumblecircus.com/shows-acts/death-or-circus [accessed 24 March 2015] (para. 1 of 4).

12 Ibid., para. 3 of 4.

13 Fanning and Segner, 'About Tumble Circus', *Tumble Circus*, http://www.tumblecircus.com/about [accessed 7 May 2015] (para. 5 of 6).

14 Fintan O'Toole, *The Ex-Isle of Erin: images of a global Ireland* (Dublin: New Island Books, 1997), p. 12.

15 Ibid., p. 22.

16 Eleanor Lavan, 'Transcript and Personal Observations: *Death or Circus*, The Mac, Belfast', 17 November 2012.

17 Kenneth Fanning introducing *Damn the Circus*, recorded in Lavan, 'Transcript: *Damn the Circus*', 2014.

18 Ibid.

19 Adrienne Monnier, 'The Humanism of Joyce', in 'Joyce's *Ulysses* and the French Public', trans. Sylvia Beach (1931), *Kenyon Review*, vol. 8, no. 3, Summer 1946, pp. 430–44, http://www.jstor.org/stable/4332775?seq=1 [accessed 1 September 2014], p. 443.

20 Lavan, 'Transcript: *Damn the Circus*', 2014.

21 Fanning and Segner, Production notes for *Death or Circus*, *Tumble Circus*, http://www.tumblecircus.com/shows-acts/death-or-circus [accessed 24 March 2015] (para. 4 of 4).

22 Lavan, 'Transcript: *Damn the Circus*', 2014.

23 'Spide' and 'Steek', in *Voices: Northern Ireland*, BBC Online (2005–6), http://www.bbc.co.uk/northernireland/voices/atilazed/s.shtml [accessed 24 March 2015].

24 Lavan, 'Transcript: *Death or Circus*', 2012, and Lavan, 'Transcript: *Damn the Circus*', 2014.

25 For an introduction to the life of Patrick Cotter, see G. Frankcom and J.H. Musgrave, *The Irish Giant* (London: Duckworth & Co. Ltd, 1976). Although the Hanlon Brothers were born and raised in their very earliest years in the north of England, second son George was proud to claim his Irish heritage in the brothers' biographical memoir, *Mémoires et Pantomimes des Frères Hanlon Lees* (n.p., Paris, 1879), cited by John McKinven in *The Hanlon Brothers: their amazing acrobatics, pantomimes, and stage spectacles* (Glenwood: David Meyer Magic Books, 1998), p. 1.

26 Stoddart, *Rings of Desire*, p. 61.

27 Joyce, *Ulysses*, p. 431.
28 Seamus Heaney, *The Cure at Troy* (London: Faber, 1990), p. 77.
29 Seamus Heaney, 'The Mixed Marriage', in *Preoccupations* (London: Faber, 1984), pp. 211–13 (p. 212).

Bibliography

Primary Sources

Banville, John, *Birchwood* (London: Picador, 1998)

Banville, John, and Thaddeus O'Sullivan with Andrew Pattman, '*Birchwood*: extracts from the screenplay', *The Irish Review*, vol. 1, 1986, pp. 65–73, http://www.jstor.org/stable/29735251 [accessed 18 August 2014]

Beckett, Samuel, *The Complete Dramatic Works* (London: Faber & Faber, 1990; repr. 2006)

—, *The Letters of Samuel Beckett* (eds) George Craig, Martha Dow Fehsenfeld, Dan Gunn and Lois More Overbeck, 3 vols to date (Cambridge: Cambridge University Press, 2009–14)

—, *The Unnamable*, ed. Steven Connor (London: Faber & Faber, 2010)

Booth, Charles, *Life and Labour of the People in London*, 9 vols, 3rd edn (London and New York: Macmillan & Co., 1902)

Booth, William, *In Darkest England and the Way Out* (London: Charles Knight & Co. Ltd, 1970)

Bostock, Frank C., *The Training of Wild Animals*, ed. Ellen Velvin (New York: Century Co., 1917)

Bowen, Elizabeth, *People, Places, Things: essays by Elizabeth Bowen*, ed. Allan Hepburn (Edinburgh: Edinburgh University Press, 2008)

Browne, Joseph, *The Circus: or, British Olympicks. A satyr on the ring in Hide-Park* (London and Westminster: n.p., 1709)

Carter, Angela, *Nights at the Circus* (London: Vintage, 1994; repr. 2006)

Circus: a delightful day with the circus folk (London and Barcelona: Green Trefoil Ltd and Euredit, 196–?)

Davidson, Bruce, *Circus* (London: Steidl, 2007)

Deane, Seamus, *Reading in the Dark* (London: Vintage, 1997; repr. 2011)

Delaney, Paul (ed.), *Brian Friel in Conversation* (Ann Arbor, MI: The University of Michigan Press, 2000)

Dickens, Charles, *Bleak House* (London: Penguin Classics, 1985; repr. 1996)

—, *Hard Times* (London: Penguin Classics, 1995; repr. 2003)

Duncan, John, *Bonfires* (Brighton, Belfast and Göttingen: Photoworks, Belfast Exposed Photography and Steidl, 2008)

Durcan, Paul, *Going Home to Russia* (Belfast and Wolfeboro, NH: The Blackstaff Press, 1987)

—, *Jumping the Train Tracks with Angela* (Dublin and Manchester: Raven Arts Press and Carcanet New Press, 1983)

Edward Seago, 1910–1974: paintings and watercolours (London: Marlborough Fine Art Ltd, 1978)

Fossett, Robert, *Spangles and Sawdust: circus ways and circus days* (Great Britain: n.p., 1938)

Friel, Brian, *Crystal and Fox* (Oldcastle: The Gallery Press, 1984; repr. 2014)

—, *Brian Friel: essays, diaries, interviews, 1965–1999*, ed. Christopher Murray (London: Faber & Faber, 1999)

—, *Selected Stories* (Oldcastle: The Gallery Press, 2005)

Gaskell, Elizabeth, *Mary Barton* (Oxford: Oxford University Press, 2006; repr. 2008)

Gore, Montague, *On the Dwellings of the Poor and the Means of Improving Them*, 2nd edn (London: James Ridgway, 1851)

Gregory, Augusta, *Our Irish Theatre: a chapter in autobiography* (New York and London: G.P. Putnam's Sons and the Knickerbocker Press, 1913), http://digital.library.upenn.edu/women/gregory/theatre/theatre.html [accessed 19 November 2014]

Grimm, Jacob and Wilhelm, *The Complete Grimm's Fairy Tales* (London: Routledge & Kegan Paul, 1975)

Heaney, Seamus, *Among Schoolchildren: a lecture dedicated to the memory of John Malone* (Belfast: John Malone Memorial Committee, 1983)

—, *The Cure at Troy* (London: Faber & Faber, 1990)

—, *Death of a Naturalist* (London: Faber & Faber, 1966; repr. 1969)

—, *Finders Keepers: selected prose 1971–2001* (London: Faber & Faber, 2002)

—, *The Midnight Verdict* (Oldcastle, Co. Meath: The Gallery Press, 1993)

—, *Seeing Things* (London: Faber & Faber, 1991; repr. 2002)

—, *Preoccupations* (London: Faber & Faber, 1984)

Jordan, Neil (dir.), *The Butcher Boy*, Warner Home Video, 2007

—, *The Dream of a Beast* (London: John Murray, 2005)

— (dir.), *The Miracle*, Shock DVD, 2011

—, *Night in Tunisia* (London: John Murray, 2004)

— (dir.), 'Not I', in *Beckett on Film*, Blue Angel Films/Tyrone Productions for Radio Telefís Éireann and Channel 4, 2001

—, *The Past* (London: John Murray, 2005)

—, *Sunrise with Sea Monster* (London: John Murray, 2004)

Joyce, James, *A Portrait of the Artist as a Young Man*, ed. Seamus Deane (New York: Penguin Books, 1992; repr. 2003)

—, *Dubliners*, ed. Jeri Johnson (Oxford: Oxford University Press, 2000)

—, *Finnegans Wake* (London: Penguin Books, 1992; repr. 2000)

—, *Haveth Children Everywhere: fragment of* Work in Progress (London: Faber & Faber, 1931)

—, *Occasional, Critical, and Political Writing*, ed. Kevin Barry (Oxford: Oxford University Press, 2000; repr. 2008)

—, *Pomes Penyeach* (London: Faber & Faber, 1966; repr. 1991)

—, *Selected Letters of James Joyce*, ed. Richard Ellmann (London: Faber & Faber, 1975; repr. 1992)

—, *Stephen Hero*, ed. Theodore Spencer, revd edn (London: Grafton Books, 1977; repr. 1986)

—, *Ulysses*, ed. Jeri Johnson (Oxford: Oxford University Press, 1998; repr. 2008)

Kafka, Franz, *The Penguin Complete Short Stories of Franz Kafka*, ed. Nahum N. Glatzer (London: Allen Lane, 1983)

Lardinois, Brigitte, and Val Williams (eds), *Magnum Ireland* (London: Thames & Hudson, 2005)

Lloyd, James, *My Circus Life* (London: Noel Douglas, 1927)

Longley, Michael, *Collected Poems* (London: Jonathan Cape, 2006)

Mateer, James, *A Life on the Open Road* (Bangor: Edyplus Publications, 1996)

Meadmore, G.F., and W.S. Meadmore (eds), *The King Pole*, no. 5, Winter 1948

Merriman, Brian, *The Midnight Court and the Adventures of a Luckless Fellow*, trans. Percy Arland Ussher (London: Jonathan Cape, 1926)

Moore, George, *The Untilled Field* (Gerrards Cross: Colin Smythe, 1976)

Muldoon, Paul, *Poems 1968–1998* (London: Faber & Faber, 2001)

O'Brien, Flann, *At Swim-Two-Birds* (London: Penguin Classics, 2001)

—, *Plays and Teleplays*, ed. Daniel Keith Jernigan (Champaign, London and Dublin: Dalkey Archive Press, 2013)

Ó Conaire, Pádraic, *Deoraíocht*, 3rd edn (Dublin: Cló Talbot, 1973)

—, *Exile*, trans. Gearailt Mac Eoin (London and Chester Springs, PA: Peter Owen, 2009)

—, *Field and Fair*, trans. Cormac Breathnach (Cork: Mercier Press, 1966)

—, *The Woman at the Window*, trans. Eamonn O'Neill (Cork: Mercier Press, 1966)

O'Driscoll, Dennis, *Stepping Stones: interviews with Seamus Heaney* (London: Faber & Faber, 2009)

Parker, Stewart, *Dramatis Personae: a John Malone memorial lecture* (Belfast: John Malone Memorial Committee, 1986)

—, *Plays*, 2 vols (London: Methuen, 2000–2)

Pearse, Pádraic H., *Political Writings and Speeches* (Dublin: The Talbot Press Limited, 1952)

Reade, Amye, *Ruby; or how girls are trained for a circus life. Founded on fact*, revd edn (London: Trischler & Company, 1890)

Seago, Edward, *Circus Company* (London: Putnam, 1933)

—, *Sons of Sawdust with Paddy O'Flynn's Circus in Western Ireland* (London: Putnam, 1934)

Shakespeare, William, *The Norton Shakespeare*, ed. Stephen Greenblatt et al., 2nd edn (New York and London: W.W. Norton & Company, 1997; repr. 2008)

Simpson, Derek (ed.), *Circus*, Circus Association of Ireland, 17 vols, 1990–2000

Skeffington, F.J.C., and James Joyce, *Two Essays: 'A Forgotten Aspect of the University Question' and 'The Day of the Rabblement'* (Dublin: Gerrard Bros, 1901)

Synge, J.M., *Collected Works*, gen. ed. Robin Skelton, 4 vols (London: Oxford University Press, 1962–8)

—, *The Playboy of the Western World and Other Plays*, ed. Ann Saddlemyer (Oxford: Oxford University Press, 1998)

—, *Travels in Wicklow, West Kerry and Connemara*, revd edn (London: Serif, 2009)

Thackeray, William Makepeace, *The Irish Sketch Book, 1842* (Belfast and Dover, NH: The Blackstaff Press, 1985)

Tóibín, Colm (ed.), *The Penguin Book of Irish Fiction* (London: Penguin, 1999; repr. 2001)

Tristan, Flora, *London Journal: a survey of London life in the 1830s*, trans. Dennis Palmer and Giselle Pincetl (London: George Prior Publishers, 1980)

Trollope, Anthony, *An Autobiography*, ed. David Skilton (London: Penguin Books, 1996)

Yeats, Jack, *The Collected Plays of Jack B. Yeats*, ed. Robin Skelton (London: Secker & Warburg, 1971)

Yeats, W.B, *Autobiographies* (Dublin: Gill & Macmillan, 1955)

—, *Essays and Introductions* (New York: The Macmillan Press Ltd, 1961)

—, *Explorations* (London: Macmillan & Co. Ltd, 1962)

—, *The Poems*, ed. Daniel Albright (London: Everyman, 1992)

—, *Selected Plays*, ed. Richard Allen Cave (London: Penguin, 1997)

Manuscripts and Archive Material

Bailly, Auguste, 'L'Ulysse de James Joyce et le Monologue Intérieur', *Candide*, 23 May 1940, n.p., clipping in 'Archives Joyce d'Adrienne Monnier: articles sur Joyce et *Ulysses*', New York, New York Public Library Berg Collection

Banville, John, *Birchwood* Manuscript, Dublin, Trinity College Dublin Archives and Manuscripts MSS 10252/3/3: Banville Literary Papers

Barkentin, Marjorie, *James Joyce's Ulysses in Nighttown* (New York: s.n., 1934)

Brion, Marcel, 'Les Grandes Figures Européennes – James Joyce, Romancier', *Gazette des Nations*, 3 March 1928, no. 4, clipping in 'Archives Joyce d'Adrienne Monnier: articles sur Joyce et *Ulysses*', New York, New York Public Library Berg Collection

Carrère, Jean, 'Mussolini et La Littérature: Mussolini et Alessandro Manzoni', *Gazette des Nations*, 3 March 1928, no. 3, clipping in 'Archives Joyce d'Adrienne Monnier: articles sur Joyce et *Ulysses*', New York, New York Public Library Berg Collection

Clifton, Harry, 'Pulling Hard Against the Stream (Do Your Best For One Another)' (London: Hopwood & Crew, *c.*1867)

Demasy, P., 'Un Nouveau Rabelais', *Chronique de Paris*, 14 February 1930, n.p., clipping in 'Archives Joyce d'Adrienne Monnier: articles sur Joyce et *Ulysses*', New York, New York Public Library Berg Collection

Farrer, David, Letter to John Banville, 18 April 1972, Dublin, Trinity College Dublin Archives and Manuscripts, MSS 10252/3/10: Banville Literary Papers

Gibson, Barbara, *Oral History of the Circus*, 39 entries (audio and print) (London: British Library, 2000–3)

Goldstone, Patricia, 'Director's Notes', in the programme for *The Circus Animals' Desertion*, Dublin, Trinity College Dublin Archives and Manuscripts, Mun/Soc/Players/9/140

Heaney, Seamus, 'Wheels within Wheels', Dublin, National Library of Ireland MS 49,493/95 (Folder 1): MS drafts for poems included in *Seeing Things*, Sheet A

—, 'Wheels within Wheels', Dublin, National Library of Ireland MS 49,493/95 (Folder 1) (cont.): MS drafts for poems included in *Seeing Things*, Sheet C

Johnny Patterson's Great London Circus Songster: only original Irish clown, DeWitt's Song and Joke Book Series, no. 241, 1878

MacCarthy, Desmond, 'Le Roman Anglais d'Après-Guerre (1919–1929): Joyce', *Revue de Paris*, 7 May 1932, pp. 145–8, clipping in 'Archives Joyce d'Adrienne Monnier: articles sur Joyce et *Ulysses*', New York, New York Public Library Berg Collection

Moore, James (ed.), *The Anti-Union*, 2 vols (Dublin: James Moore, 45 College Green, 1798–9)

O'Sullivan, Thaddeus, Letter to John Banville, 17 November 1981, Dublin, Trinity College Dublin Archives and Manuscripts, MSS 10252/3/13/2: Banville Literary Papers

Walsh, Townsend, 'Love of the Circus', unpublished manuscript draft (*c.*1900), New York, New York Public Library Manuscripts and Archives Division, MSS Col 3213

Yeats, Jack B., Letter to Thomas MacGreevy, 21 March 1927, Dublin, Trinity College Dublin Archives and Manuscripts, MSS 10381/84/1-2

—, Letter to Thomas MacGreevy, 12 September 1933, Dublin, Trinity College Dublin Archives and Manuscripts, MSS 10381/119

Secondary Sources

A Century of Fairground Memories, Sheffield University Television, 2000

Alexander, Ian W., *Bergson: philosopher of reflection* (London: Bowes & Bowes, 1957)

Allen, Nicholas, *Modernism, Ireland and Civil War* (Cambridge: Cambridge University Press, 2009)

Anderson, Benedict, *Imagined Communities*, revd ed. (London and New York: Verso, 2006)

Andrews, Elmer, *The Art of Brian Friel: neither reality nor dreams* (New York: St Martin's Press, Inc., 1995)

Apt Russell, Sharman, *Hunger: an unnatural history* (New York: Basic Books, 2005)

Arensberg, Conrad M., and Solon T. Kimball, *Family and Community in Ireland*, 3rd edn (Ennis, Co. Clare: Clasp Press, 2001)

Armstrong, Isobel (ed.), *New Feminist Discourses: critical essays on theories and texts* (New York: Routledge, 1992)

Arnold, Bruce, *Jack Yeats* (New Haven, CT and London: Yale University Press, 1998)

Austin, J.L., *How To Do Things with Words* (Oxford: The Clarendon Press, 1962)

Bachelard, Gaston, *The Poetics of Space*, trans. Maria Jolas (Boston, MA: Beacon Press, 1994)

Bailly, Auguste, 'L'Ulysse de James Joyce et le Monologue Intérieur', *Candide*, 23 May 1940

Bakhtin, Mikhail, *Rabelais and His World*, trans. Hélène Iswolsky (Bloomington, IL and Indianapolis, ID: Indiana University Press, 1984)

Barthes, Roland, *Camera Lucida: reflections on photography*, trans. Richard Howard (London: Vintage, 1993; repr. 2000)

Becker, Jared, *Nationalism and Culture: Gabriele D'Annunzio and Italy after the Risorgimento* (New York: Peter Lang, 1995)

Bedient, Calvin, *The Yeats Brothers and Modernism's Love of Motion* (Notre Dame, ID: University of Notre Dame Press, 2009)

Benjamin, Walter, *Reflections: essays, aphorisms, autobiographical writings*, ed. Peter Demetz, trans. Edmund Jephcott (New York: Schocken Books, 1986)

—, *Selected Writings of Walter Benjamin*, gen. ed. Michael Jennings, trans. Rodney Livingston et al., 4 vols (Cambridge, MA and London: The Belknap Press, 2001–3)

Berger, John, *Ways of Seeing* (London: BBC and Penguin Books, 1972; repr. 2008)

Bergson, Henri, *Laughter: an essay on the meaning of the comic*, trans. Cloudesley Brereton and Fred Rothwell (London: Macmillan, 1911)

Boltwood, Scott, *Brian Friel, Ireland, and the North* (Cambridge: Cambridge University Press, 2007)

Booth, John, *Jack B. Yeats: a vision of Ireland* (Newton Abbot: David St John Thomas, 1993)

Bouissac, Paul, *Semiotics at the Circus* (Berlin and New York: de Gruyter Mouton, 2010)

Bradshaw, Harry, 'Johnny Patterson, the Rambler from Clare', *Dal gCais*, vol. 2, 1986, http://www.clarelibrary.ie/eolas/coclare/music/johnny_patterson_bradshaw2.htm [accessed 15 October 2012]

Burke, Helen, 'Jacobin Revolutionary Theatre and the Early Circus: Astley's Dublin Amphitheatre in the 1790s', *Theatre Research International*, vol. 31, no. 1, March 2006, http://dx.doi.org/10.1017/S0307883305001859 [accessed 15 October 2012]

Butler Cullingford, Elizabeth, *Ireland's Others: ethnicity and gender in Irish literature and popular culture* (Cork: Cork University Press, 2001)

Cairns, David, and Shaun Richards, *Writing Ireland: colonialism, nationalism and culture* (Manchester: Manchester University Press, 1988)

Carville, Justin (ed.), *Early Popular Visual Culture*, vol. 5, no. 3, October 2007

Casey, Daniel J., and Robert E. Rhodes (eds), *Views of the Irish Peasantry, 1800–1916* (Hamden, CT: Archon Books, 1977)

Cliff, Brian, and Nicholas Grene (eds), *Synge and Edwardian Ireland* (Oxford: Oxford University Press, 2012)

Coogan, Tim Pat, *Ireland in the Twentieth Century* (London: Hutchinson, 2003)

Corbin, Alain, *Women for Hire: prostitution and sexuality in France after 1850*, trans. Alan Sheridan (Boston, MA: Harvard University Press, 1990)

Corcoran, Neil, *The Poetry of Seamus Heaney: a critical study* (London: Faber & Faber, 1998)

Croft-Cooke, Rupert (ed.), *The Circus Book* (London: Sampson Low, Marston & Co. Ltd, 1948)

Croft-Cooke, Rupert, and Peter Cotes, *Circus: a world history* (London: Paul Elek Ltd, 1976)

Crompton, Sarah, 'Samuel Johnson Prize 2013: Lucy Hughes-Hallett is a revelation', *Telegraph*, 4 November 2013, http://www.telegraph.co.uk/culture/books booknews/10425909/Samuel-Johnson-Prize-2013-Lucy-Hughes-Hallett-is-a-revelation.html [accessed 5 November 2013]

Cronin, Denis A., Jim Gilligan and Karina Holton (eds), *Irish Fairs and Markets: studies in local history* (Dublin: Four Courts Press, 2001)

Cronin, Mike, *A History of Ireland* (Basingstoke: Palgrave Macmillan, 2003)

Crowley, Ronan, '"Between contemporaneity and antiquity": Katie Lawrence and the music hall scaffold of "Circe"', *Hypermedia Joyce Studies*, vol. 9, no. 2, 2008, http://hjs.ff.cuni.cz/archives/v9_2/essays/crowley.htm [accessed 16 July 2014]

Curtis, Liz, *Nothing But the Same Old Story: the roots of anti-Irish racism* (London: on Ireland, 1984)

Davis, Janet M., *The Circus Age: culture & society under the American big top* (Chapel Hill, NC and London: The University of North Carolina Press, 2002)

Davison, Neil R., *James Joyce, Ulysses and the Construction of Jewish Identity: culture, biography and "the Jew" in modernist Europe* (Cambridge: Cambridge University Press, 1996)

Dawe, Gerald, 'A Hard Act: Stewart Parker's *Pentecost*', in Gerald Dawe, *The Rest Is History* (Newry: Abbey Press, 1998)

Deane, Seamus, 'Masked with Matthew Arnold's Face: Joyce and liberalism', *Canadian Journal for Irish Studies*, vol. 12, June 1986, www.jstor.org/stable/25512660 [accessed 1 September 2014]

—, *Strange Country: modernity and nationhood in Irish writing since 1790* (Oxford: Clarendon Press, 1997)

Deleuze, Gilles, *Bergsonism*, trans. Hugh Tomlinson and Barbara Habberjam (New York: Zone Books, 1991)

—, *Francis Bacon: the logic of sensation*, trans. Daniel W. Smith (London and New York: Continuum, 2003; repr. 2012)

Douglas, Alfred, and David Sheridan, *The Tarot: the origins, meaning and uses of the cards* (Harmondsworth: Penguin, 1974)

Douglas, Roy, Liam Harte and Jim O'Hara, *Drawing Conclusions: a cartoon history of Anglo-Irish relations 1798–1998* (Belfast: The Blackstaff Press, 1998)

Eagleton, Terry, *Heathcliff and the Great Hunger: studies in Irish culture* (London and New York: Verso, 1995)

—, *Walter Benjamin, or, Towards a Revolutionary Criticism* (London: Verso, 1981)

Ellmann, Maud, *The Hunger Artists: starving, writing & imprisonment* (London: Virago Press, 1993)

—, *The Nets of Modernism: Henry James, Virginia Woolf, James Joyce, and Sigmund Freud* (Cambridge: Cambridge University Press, 2010)

Ellmann, Richard, *The Consciousness of Joyce* (Toronto and New York: Oxford University Press, 1977)

Fairhill, James, *James Joyce and the Question of History* (Cambridge: Cambridge University Press, 1993)

Fairley, James, *Fun Is Our Business: the story of Barry's Amusements* (Newtownards: Colourpoint Books, 2006)

Fanning, Charles (ed.), *Selected Writings of John V. Kelleher on Ireland and Irish America* (Carbondale, IL and Edwardsville, IL: Southern Illinois University Press, 2002)

Felstead, S. Theodore, *Stars Who Made the Halls: a hundred years of English humour, harmony and hilarity* (London: T. Werner Laurie Ltd, 1947)

Fitzgerald, Patrick, and Brian Lambkin, *Migration in Irish History, 1607–2007* (Basingstoke: Palgrave Macmillan, 2008)

Foley, Declan J. (ed.), *The Only Art of Jack B. Yeats* (Dublin: The Lilliput Press, 2009)

Foster, Roy, *Paddy and Mr Punch: connections in Irish and English history* (London: Allen Lane/Penguin, 1993)

—, 'We Are All Revisionists Now', *The Irish Review*, vol. 1, 1986

Frankcom, G., and J.H. Musgrave, *The Irish Giant* (London: Gerald Duckworth & Co. Ltd, 1976)

French, Philip, 'The Best of 1991: ghosts of high returns', *Observer*, 29 December 1991

Freud, Sigmund, *The Penguin Freud Library*, vol. 7, ed. Angela Richards, trans. James Strachey (London: Penguin Books, 1991)

Frost, Thomas, *Circus Life and Circus Celebrity* (London: Tinsley Brothers, 1875)

Froula, Christine, *Modernism's Body: sex, culture, and Joyce* (New York: Columbia University Press, 1996)

Gallagher Winarski, Kathleen, 'Neil Jordan's *Miracle*: from fiction to film', in *Contemporary Irish Cinema: from The Quiet Man to Dancing at Lughnasa*, ed. James MacKillop (Syracuse, NY: Syracuse University Press, 1999)

Gibbon, Peter, 'Arensberg and Kimball Revisited', *Economy and Society*, vol. 2, no. 4, 1973

Gibbons, Luke, *Transformations in Irish Culture* (Cork: Cork University Press, 1996)

Gifford, Don, with Robert J. Seidman, *Ulysses Annotated: notes for Joyce's Ulysses* (Berkeley and Los Angeles, CA: University of California Press, 1988)

Gleadell, Colin, 'Seago Rides Again', *Telegraph*, 3 June 2014, http://www.telegraph. co.uk/luxury/art/35292/art-sales-royal-favourite-edward-seago-rides-again.html [accessed 27 January 2015]

Goodby, John, *Irish Poetry Since 1950: from stillness into history* (Manchester: Manchester University Press, 2000)

Graham, Colin, *Deconstructing Ireland: identity, theory, culture* (Edinburgh: Edinburgh University Press, 2001)

Graham, Colin, and Richard Kirkland (eds), *Ireland and Cultural Theory: the mechanics of authenticity* (London: Macmillan Press Ltd, 1999)

Greeley, Andrew, *The Catholic Imagination* (Berkeley: University of California Press, 2001)

Gryta, Caroline Nobile, 'Who Is Signor Maffei? And Has *Ruby: the Pride of the Ring* Really Been Located?', *James Joyce Quarterly*, vol. 21, no. 4, Summer 1984, http:// www.jstor.org/stable/25476612 [accessed 30 September 2014]

Gunn, Ian, and Clive Hart, with Harald Beck, *James Joyce's Dublin: a topographical guide to the Dublin of Ulysses* (London: Thames & Hudson, 2004)

Haslam, Richard, 'Neil Jordan and the ABC of Narratology: "Stories to do with love are mathematical"', *New Hibernia Review*, vol. 3, no. 2, Summer 1999, www.jstor. org/stable/20557552 [accessed 24 January 2014]

Higham, Nick, 'The 2013 Samuel Johnson Prize', *Today*, BBC Radio 4, 5 November 2013

Herr, Cheryl, *Joyce's Anatomy of Culture* (Urbana and Chicago, IL: University of Illinois Press, 1986)

Herlihy, Daniel, 'The Making of the Medieval Family: symmetry, structure, and sentiment', *Journal of Family History*, vol. 8, no. 2, 1983), 10.1177/ 03631990830080202 [accessed 28 July 2014]

Higgins, Geraldine, *Brian Friel* (Tavistock: Northcote House Publishers Ltd, 2010)

—, *Heroic Revivals from Carlyle to Yeats* (New York: Palgrave Macmillan, 2012)

Hinson, Hal, 'The "Miracle" of Neil Jordan', *Washington Post*, 14 July 1991

Hogan, Robert, and James Kilroy, *The Modern Irish Drama II: laying the foundations: 1902–1904* (Dublin: The Dolmen Press, 1974)

Hooper, Glenn, and Colin Graham (eds), *Irish and Postcolonial Writing: history, theory, practice* (Basingstoke: Palgrave Macmillan, 2002)

Houen, Alex (ed.), *Textual Practice: affects, text, and performativity*, vol. 25, no. 2, April 2011

Howe, Desson, 'No Cure for "Miracle"', *Washington Post*, 19 July 1991

Huber, Werner, and Seán Crosson (eds), *Contemporary Irish Film: new perspectives on a national cinema* (Vienna: Braumüller, 2011)

Hughes, Kevin (dir.), *The Political Circus: the paintings of Ramie Leahy*, Wallslough Studios, 2011

Kappeler, Susanne, *The Pornography of Representation* (Cambridge: The Polity Press, 1986)

Kendall, Tim, *Paul Muldoon* (Bridgend: Seren, 1996)

Kennedy, Róisín (ed.), *Masquerade and Spectacle: the circus and the travelling fair in the work of Jack B. Yeats* (Dublin: National Gallery of Ireland, 2007)

Kenner, Hugh, *Joyce's Voices* (Berkeley: University of California Press, 1978)

Keogh, Dermot, *Twentieth-Century Ireland: nation and state* (Dublin: Gill & Macmillan, 1994)

Kermode, Frank, *Romantic Image* (London and New York: Routledge Classics, 2002)

Kern Paster, Gail, *The Body Embarrassed: drama and the disciplines of shame in early modern England* (Ithaca, NY: Cornell University Press, 1993)

Kershner, R. Brandon, *Joyce, Bakhtin, and Popular Literature: chronicles of disorder* (Chapel Hill, NC and London: The University of North Carolina Press, 1989)

—, 'The World's Strongest Man: Joyce or Sandow?', *James Joyce Quarterly*, vol. 30, no. 4, Summer–Fall 1993, www.jstor.org/stable/25515763 [accessed 15 October 2012]

Kiberd, Declan, *Inventing Ireland: the literature of the modern nation* (London: Vintage, 1996)

—, Ulysses *and Us: the art of everyday life in Joyce's masterpiece* (New York and London: W.W. Norton & Company, 2009)

Killen, John, *John Bull's Famous Circus* (Dublin: O'Brien Press, 1985)

King, Philip (dir.), *Bringing It All Back Home: the influence of Irish music*, BBC/ Hummingbird Productions, 1991

Kirby, Peadar, Luke Gibbons and Michael Cronin (eds), *Reinventing Ireland: culture, society and the global economy* (London and Sterling, VA: Pluto Press, 2002)

Kwint, Marius, 'Astley's Amphitheatre and the Early Circus in England, 1768–1830', unpublished doctoral thesis, University of Oxford, 1994

Lang, Frederick K., *Ulysses and the Irish God* (London: Associated University Press, 1993)

Lavan, Rosamund, 'Seamus Heaney and Society, 1964–1994', unpublished doctoral thesis, University of Oxford, 2014

Lee, Joseph, *The Modernisation of Irish Society: 1848–1918* (Dublin: Gill & Macmillan, 1973)

Levin, Jennifer Burns, '"Ruby pride of the on the floor naked": fetishizing the circus girl in Joyce's *Ulysses*', *Joyce Studies Annual*, 2009, 10.1353/joy.0.0016 [accessed 16 July 2014]

Lloyd, David, *Anomalous States: Irish writing and the post-colonial moment* (Dublin: The Lilliput Press, 1993)

—, 'Republics of Difference: Yeats, MacGreevy, Beckett', *Third Text*, vol. 19, no. 5, 2005

Lloyd, Matthew, 'The Royal Hippodrome, Victoria Street, Belfast', *Arthur Lloyd: the music hall and theatre history site*, http://www.arthurlloyd.co.uk/BelfastTheatres.htm#hippodrome [accessed 17 November 2014]

Longley, Edna, *Yeats and Modern Poetry* (Cambridge: Cambridge University Press, 2013)

Lynam, Shevawn, *Humanity Dick: a biography of Richard Martin, 1754–1834* (London: Hamish Hamilton, 1975)

Lyons, F.S.L., *Ireland Since the Famine* (London: Fontana, 1973)

Koch, John T. (ed.), *Celtic Culture: a historical encyclopedia*, 5 vols (Santa Barbara, CA and Oxford: ABC-CLIO, 2006)

M.W.D., '"The Circus": the new adventures of Charlie Chaplin', *Observer*, 18 March 1928

MacRaild, Donald M., *The Irish Diaspora in Britain, 1750–1939*, 2nd edn (Basingstoke: Palgrave Macmillan, 2011)

Managh, Ray, 'Fossett's Circus Faces "Uphill Struggle To Survive"', *Irish Examiner*, 13 February 2015, http://www.irishexaminer.com/business/fossetts-circus-faces-uphill-struggle-to-survive-312383.html [accessed 24 March 2015]

Marx, Karl, and Friedrich Engels, *Articles on Britain*, ed. and trans. not known (Moscow: Progress Publishers, 1971)

Mathews, P.J., *Revival: the Abbey Theatre, Sinn Féin, the Gaelic League and the Co-operative Movement* (Cork: Cork University Press, 2003)

McCafferty, Nell, *A Woman to Blame* (Cork: Attic Press, 1985)

McCarthy, Conor, *Modernisation, Crisis and Culture in Ireland, 1969–1992* (Dublin: Four Courts Press, 2000)

McCourt, John (ed.), *Roll Away the Reel World: Joyce and cinema* (Cork: Cork University Press, 2010)

McDonald, Marianne, and J. Michael Walton (eds), *Amid Our Troubles: Irish versions of Greek tragedy* (London: Methuen, 2002)

McGee, Patrick, *Paperspace: style as ideology in Joyce's Ulysses* (Lincoln, NE and London: University of Nebraska Press, 1988)

McGrath, F.C., 'Friel and the Irish Art of Lying', in *Brian Friel's (Post)Colonial Drama: language, illusion, and politics* (Syracuse, NY: Syracuse University Press, 1999)

McIlroy, Brian, 'Interview with Neil Jordan', *World Cinema 4: Ireland* (Trowbridge: Flicks Books, 1989)

McKinven, John, *The Hanlon Brothers: their amazing acrobatics, pantomimes, and stage spectacles* (Glenwood, IL: David Meyer Magic Books, 1998)

Meehan, Ciara, *The Cosgrave Party: a history of Cumann na nGaedheal, 1923–33* (Dublin: Royal Irish Academy, 2010)

Mercier, Vivien, *The Irish Comic Tradition* (London: Souvenir Press, 1991)

Monnier, Adrienne, 'Joyce's *Ulysses* and the French Public', trans. Sylvia Beach (1931), *Kenyon Review*, vol. 8, no. 3, Summer 1946, http://www.jstor.org/stable/4332775?seq=1 [accessed 1 September 2014]

Ní Mhunghaile, Lesa, 'Pádraic Ó Conaire', *Dictionary of Irish Biography*, eds James McGuire and James Quinn (Cambridge: Cambridge University Press, 2009), http://dib.cambridge.org/viewReadPage.do?articleId=a6314 [accessed 21 July 2014]

Norman, Edward, *A History of Modern Ireland* (London: Allen Lane/The Penguin Press, 1971)

Norris, Margot, *Virgin and Veteran Readings of Ulysses* (New York: Palgrave Macmillan, 2011)

O'Brien Johnson, Toni, *Synge: the medieval and the grotesque* (Gerrards Cross: Colin Smythe, 1982)

O'Donoghue, Bernard, *Seamus Heaney and the Language of Poetry* (Hemel Hempstead: Harvester Wheatsheaf, 1994)

Ó Gráda, Cormac, *Black '47 and Beyond: the Great Irish Famine in history, economy, and memory* (Princeton, NJ: Princeton University Press, 1999)

O'Toole, Fintan, 'How Poetry Joins Dramatic Action', *Guardian*, 29 November 1990

—, *The Ex-Isle of Erin: images of a global Ireland* (Dublin: New Island Books, 1997)

Ó Tuathaigh, Gearóid, *Ireland Before the Famine: 1798–1848* (Dublin: Gill & Macmillan, 1972)

Palma, Brian, 'Bonfire of the Inanities', *Guardian*, 11 April 1991

Parker, Lynne, 'Showtime: the strategy of mischief in the plays of Stewart Parker', in *The Dreaming Body: contemporary Irish theatre*, ed. Melissa Shira and Paul Murphy (Gerrards Cross: Colin Smythe, 2009)

Pernot-Deschamps, Marguerite, *The Fictional Imagination of Neil Jordan, Irish Novelist and Film Maker: a study of literary style* (Lewiston, NY: The Edwin Mellen Press, 2009)

Perry, L. Curtis, *Apes and Angels: the Irishman in Victorian caricature* (Newton Abbot: David & Clark, 1971)

Power, Mary, 'The Discovery of *Ruby*', *James Joyce Quarterly*, vol. 18, no. 2, Winter 1981, https://www.jstor.org/stable/25476349 [accessed 16 July 2014]

Pramaggiore, Maria, 'The Celtic Blue Note: jazz in Neil Jordan's "Night in Tunisia", *Angel* and *The Miracle*', *Screen*, vol. 39, no. 3, Autumn 1998

Pyle, Hilary, *Jack B. Yeats: a biography* (London: Routledge & Kegan Paul, 1970)

Rabaté, Jean-Michel, 'A Clown's Inquest into Paternity: fathers, dead or alive, in *Ulysses* and *Finnegans Wake*', in *The Fictional Father: Lacanian readings of the text*, ed. Robert Con Davis (Amherst, MA: University of Massachusetts Press, 1981)

Read, Alan, *Theatre, Intimacy and Engagement: the last human venue* (Basingstoke: Palgrave Macmillan, 2008)

—, *Theatre in the Expanded Field* (London: Bloomsbury, 2013)

Redmond, Craig, *Ring of Cruelty II: the use of animals in circuses in Ireland*, Captive Animals Protection Society, 2012, www.irishcircuses.org/ringofcruelty2 [accessed 11 October 2012]

Renan, Ernest, *The Poetry of the Celtic Races*, trans. William G. Hutchinson (Port Washington, NY: Kennikat Press, 1970)

Restuccia, Frances L., *Joyce and the Law of the Father* (New Haven, CT and London: Yale University Press, 1989)

Reynolds, Paige, *Modernism, Drama, and the Audience for Irish Spectacle* (Cambridge: Cambridge University Press, 2007)

Richtarik, Marilynn, *Stewart Parker: a life* (Oxford: Oxford University Press, 2012)

Riggs, Pádraigín, 'Pádraic Ó Conaire's London: a real or imaginary place?', in *The Irish Writing London: Volume 1: Revival to the Second World War*, ed. Tom Heron (London: Bloomsbury, 2013)

Riggs, Pádraigín, and Norman Vance, 'Irish Prose Fiction', in *The Cambridge Companion to Modern Irish Culture*, eds Joe Cleary and Claire Connolly (Cambridge: Cambridge University Press, 2005)

Robinson, David, *Chaplin: his life and art* (London: Grafton, 1992)

Roche, Anthony, *Contemporary Irish Drama* (Basingstoke: Palgrave Macmillan, 2009)

Rockett, Kevin, Luke Gibbons and John Hill (eds), *Cinema and Ireland* (London: Routledge, 1988)

Russell, James, *Edward Seago* (Farnham: Lund Humphries and Portland Gallery, 2014)

Ryle Dwyer, T., *The Rose of Tralee: fifty years a' blooming* (Dublin: O'Brien Press, 2009)

Salamon, Julie, 'Film: when real life exceeds teens' dreams', *Wall Street Journal*, 1 August 1991

Sheedy, Kieran (prod.), 'Fossett's Circus', *Documentary on One*, RTÉ, 30 March 1975, http://www.rte.ie/radio1/doconone/2011/0715/646808-documentary-podcast-fossetts-circus-national-ireland-history [accessed 9 August 2018]

Shipp, Horace, *Edward Seago: a painter in the English tradition* (London: Collins, 1952)

Smith, Eleanor (ed.), *British Circus Life* (London: George G. Harrap & Co. Ltd, 1948)

Snoddy, Theo, *Dictionary of Irish Artists: 20th century* (Dublin: Wolfhound Press, 1996)

Sontag, Susan, *On Photography* (London: Penguin Books, 1979)

Speaight, George, *The Book of Clowns* (London: Sidgwick & Jackson, 1980)

—, *A History of the Circus* (London: The Tantivy Press, 1980)

Stafford, Fiona, *Local Attachments: the province of poetry* (Oxford: Oxford University Press, 2010)

—, *Starting Lines in Scottish, Irish, and English Poetry: from Burns to Heaney* (Oxford: Oxford University Press, 2000)

Steinberger, Rebecca, *Shakespeare and Twentieth-Century Irish Drama: conceptualizing identity and staging boundaries* (Aldershot: Ashgate, 2008)

Stoddart, Helen, *Angela Carter's Nights at the Circus* (Abingdon: Routledge, 2007)

—, *Rings of Desire: circus history and representation* (Manchester and New York: Manchester University Press/St Martin's Press, 2000)

Stokes, John, '"Lion Griefs": the wild animal act as theatre', *New Theatre Quarterly*, vol. 20, no. 2, May 2004, 10.1017/S0266464X04000041 [accessed 30 June 2011]

Swift, Roger (ed.), *Irish Migrants in Britain, 1815–1914: a documentary history* (Cork: Cork University Press, 2002)

Takagami, Shin-Ichi, 'The Fenian Rising in Dublin, March 1867', *Irish Historical Studies*, vol. 29, no. 115, May 1995

Tait, Peta, 'Feminine Free Fall: a fantasy of freedom', *Theatre Journal*, vol. 48, no. 1, March 1996, www.jstor.org/stable/3208712 [accessed 18 August 2014]

Towsen, John H., *Clowns: a panoramic history* (New York: Hawthorn Books Inc., 1976)

Trotter, Mary, *Ireland's National Theaters: political performance and the origins of the Irish dramatic movement* (Syracuse, NY: Syracuse University Press, 2001)

Turner, John, *Historical Hengler's Circus* (Formby: Lingdales Press, 1989)

—, *Victorian Arena: the performers; a dictionary of British circus biography*, 2 vols (Formby: Lingdales Press, 1995–2000)

Vernon, James, *Hunger: a modern history* (Cambridge, MA and London: The Belknap Press, 2007)

Walsh, Ian R., *Irish Experimental Theatre: after W.B. Yeats* (Basingstoke: Palgrave Macmillan, 2012)

Ward, Patrick, *Exile, Emigration and Irish Writing* (Dublin and Portland, OR: Irish Academic Press, 2002)

Waters, John, *Jiving at the Crossroads* (London: Transworld Ireland, 2011)

Watts, Jennifer A., 'Strangers in a Strange Land', in Jennifer A. Watts and Scott Wilcox, *Bruce Davidson/Paul Capanigro: two American photographers in Britain and Ireland* (New Haven, CT: Yale University Press, 2014)

Wills, Clair, *Reading Paul Muldoon* (Newcastle upon Tyne: Bloodaxe Books, 1998)

Youngs, Tim (ed.), *Travel Writing in the Nineteenth Century: filling in the blank spaces* (Cambridge: Cambridge University Press, 2012)

Zucker, Carole, *The Cinema of Neil Jordan: dark carnival* (London: Wallflower Press, 2008)

Index

Illustrations are indicated by page numbers in **bold**.

Abbey Experimental Theatre Company, 99

Abbey Theatre, 7, 98, 99, 118, 121, 129–30

abortion, 154, 181

'Acushla Machree' (Patterson), 20–21

adultery, 6, 25, 30, 33

advertisements, 2, 34, 82

'Air and Angels' (Donne), 138

Albert Courtney's Big Top Circus, 2

All For Their Country (pantomime), 97

Alone (Yeats), 80

American circus companies, 3, 19, 128

American Three Ring Circus, 3

'Amhrán an Ghorta' (Ó Gráda), 72

'Among School Children' (Yeats), 167–8, 174

'Among Schoolchildren' (Heaney), 167–8, 174

anarchy, 8, 58, 64, 141, 142, 145, 153

Anderson, Benedict, 53

Andrews, Elmer, 113, 114–15, 116

animal performers, 2, 31, 50, 64–5, 68, 160–61, 164, 168, 175–6

animal welfare, 2, 6, 34

anticlimax, 9–10

anti-performance, 10, 27–8

Arensberg, Conrad, 12, 52–3, 59–62, 65, 74, 83, 85, 88, 90, 91

Arlen, Harold, 22

Arnold, Bruce, 100

Arts Council Ireland, 178

Astley, Philip, 96–7, 98, 101, 112

Astley's Amphitheatre (Dublin), 3, 97

Astley's Amphitheatre (London), 96–7, 124

At Swim-Two-Birds (O'Brien), 124

attendant figures, 117, 125

Audience with Hal Roach, 123

authority, 10–11, 18, 28, 43, 115, 148–50

Autobiography (Trollope), 85

backstage spaces, 7, 108, 114

Bacon, Francis, 117

Bakhtin, Mikhail, 4, 43, 44, 177

Ballymun, Dublin, 181

Banville, John
    Birchwood, 6, 13–14, 127, 135–48, 151, 154, 156, 161, 167, 169, 170, 181, 185
    interview with, 7–8, 135–6, 137–8, 139, 159

Barnum, P.T., 22

Barnum and Bailey's Circus, 22, 39

Barry, Tom, 19, 124

Baskin, Bibi, 112

BBC, 114, 182

'Bearded Woman, by Ribera' (Muldoon), 147–8

Becker, Jared, 45–6

Beckett, Samuel
    and attendant figures, 117
    Deleuze's analysis of, 117
    Durcan's poem on, 110–11
    echoes of in *Crystal and Fox*, 96, 113, 119
    echoes of in *Heavenly Bodies*, 96, 125–6

Beckett, Samuel (*continued*)
    and Jack B. Yeats, 96, 101
    Krapp's Last Tape, 173
    McGovern's interpretations of, 110
    Molloy, 68–9
    quoted by Tumble Circus, 177
    The Unnamable, 105
    Waiting for Godot, 13, 94
    and W.B. Yeats, 96
'Beckett at the Gate, The' (Durcan),
    110–11
Belfast, 49–50, 111, 126, 130, 177–80,
    182–3, 184
Belfast Community Circus, 184
Belfast Festival, 178–80
Benjamin, Walter, 131, 140, 155, 172
Bergson, Henri, 103, 105, 107
Berthoff, Warner, 120
Bertram Mills' Circus, 2
Between the Acts (Woolf), 81
bicycles, 68–9, 165–6, 169–71
Big Top, The (RTÉ), 112, 153
Birchwood (Banville), 6, 13–14, 127,
    135–48, 151, 154, 156, 161, 167, 169,
    170, 181, 185
Birrell, Augustine, 58
'Blackberry Picking' (Heaney), 145
Blake, William, 84
Blarney Castle, 75
Bleak House (Dickens), 62
Boland, Eavan, 119, 122
Boltwood, Scott, 118
Booth, Charles, 55
Booth, William, 55, 56
Bostock, Frank, 161
Boucicault, Dion
    depiction of in *Heavenly Bodies*, 6, 7,
        24, 25, 95, 125–30
    influence on Jack Yeats, 99–100, 126
    referenced in *Faustus Kelly*, 121, 125
    The Shaugraun, 7, 100, 129–30
Bouissac, Paul, 10, 27–8, 34, 134, 159
Boyd, John, 114
Bradley, James, 25
Bradshaw, Harry, 21, 23, 24, 25

Brady, Paul, 124
Brallaghan, Barney, 19, 124
Bray, Co. Wicklow, 155–7, 159
Breathnach, Cormac, 54
Brecht, Bertolt, 122, 125, 177
Brennan, Patrick, 11
Bridges, Madlyne, 25
Bringing It All Back Home
    (Hummingbird Productions), 124
Brion, Marcel, 45
British Circus Life (Smith), 49, 92
Browning, Robert: *Sordello*, 137
Browning, Tod: *Freaks*, 158
Buff Bill's Menagerie, 75, 111
bureaucracy, 2, 112
Burke, Edmund, 8–9
Burke, Helen, 97
Burnand, F.C., 32
Burns, Ursula, 177, 180, 181, 182
Butler Cullingford, Elizabeth, 157
Byrne, Anne, 88

caricature, 57, 85, 124, 125; *see also*
    cartoons; stereotypes
Carleton, William, 125
Carlyle, Thomas, 55, 62, 87
Carmichael, Hoagy: 'Stardust', 158, 159
carnivalesque, 4, 43, 177
Carrère, Jean, 45
cartoons, 57–8, 75–9, 76, 78
Cash Converters, 182
'Castles in the Air' (Patterson), 19
Cathleen ni Houlihan (Yeats), 153
Catholic iconography, 6, 14, 64, 134–5,
    140, 143–4, 147–9, 152, 156–8, 161,
    163–5, 168, 172
Catholicism, 22, 64, 67, 85–6, 91–2,
    135–6, 153–5, 161, 163–4
CBC International, 3
Celtic Tiger, 153, 178
Celtic Twilight (Yeats), 52, 81
'Centaur's, (Muldoon), 185
chaos, 4, 142, 145
Chaplin, Charlie, 41–2
'Chartism' (Carlyle), 55, 62

child welfare, 6, 34

Chipperfield's Circus, 2

Christian imagery *see* Catholic iconography

Chronique de Paris, 44

Cider with Rosie (Laurie Lee), 145

cinema, 49, 81, 101, 114, 130, 158

Circorama, 49, 81

Circus, The (Chaplin), 41–2

Circus: a delightful day with the circus folk (Nemo), 79

circus animals *see* animal performers

'Circus Animals' Desertion' (Yeats), 14–15, 95–6, 104, 106–9, 115–16, 126, 135–7, 150, 160, 166, 184–5

Circus Association of Ireland, 1

Circus Company (Seago), 79, 80–81, 84, 88

Circus Dwarf, The (Yeats), 79–80

Circus Has Come, The (Yeats), 5, 10

Circus magazine, 1–3, 111, 112, 153

circus posters, **17**, 39, 58, 75–9, **78**, 83

circus women *see* gender; women

Civil War, 14, 50, 138

Clare Journal, 23

Clifton, 'Handsome Harry', 25–7, 39, 44

clowns, 3, 7, 8, 10–11, 16–30, 38, 81, 86, 94–5, 103, 124–9, 141, 175, 182–3, 185

colonialism, 6, 57, 70–71, 82–3, 98, 138, 145–6

colour, 49, 61, 65, 115

comedy, 42, 123, 128, 163, 181–2

'Comic Cosgrave' (Markievicz), **76**, 76–7

community, 11, 12, 52–3, 59–64, 67, 74, 88, 92–3

Connemara, 54, 83, 86, 87

Constable, John, 79

Constitution of Ireland, 11, 90, 154

Cooper and Bailey's Circus, 19

Corcoran, Neil, 173

Cork, 75, 111

Cosgrave, W.T., 76–7

Cotes, Peter, 75

Cotter, Patrick, 183

Courtney, Wayne, 3

Cowper, William, 84

Cranitch, Ellen, 129

Croft-Cooke, Rupert, 75

Crowley, Ronan, 10, 39

Crystal and Fox (Friel), 6, 7, 13, 60, 95–6, 112–18, 181, 184–5

Cullen, Paul, 180

cultural exchange, 12, 55

'Cultural History of Toys' (Benjamin), 140

cultural nationalism, 11, 52, 56, 73, 143–4, 171

Culture Ireland, 178

Cumann na nGaedheal, 76–9, 88

Cure at Troy, The (Heaney), 169

Dacre, Harry, 25

Daily Telegraph, 69–70

'Daisy Bell' (Dacre), 25

Dale family, 80–81, 88

D'Angelo, Beverly, 157–8

D'Annunzio, Gabriele, 46

Damn the Circus (Tumble), 177, 181–3

'Danny, Go After Your Father' (Patterson), 21, 25, 30

Dante: *Purgatorio*, 137

Davidson, Bruce, 131–5, 143, 147, 148, 151, 157, 158, 168, 174, 181

Davis, Janet, M., 22, 39–40, 46

Dawe, Gerald, 12–13, 96, 129

de Faoite, Diarmuid, 54

de Valera, Éamon, 52, 72, 75, 77–9, 90

Deane, Seamus

  essays on Friel, 119

  Reading in the Dark, 135, 136, 148–9, 151–3, 154, 157, 173

  Strange Country, 8–9

  on Synge's *Playboy*, 42–3

Death of a Naturalist (Heaney), 145

Death or Circus (Tumble), 177–81, **179**

Deconstructing Ireland (Graham), 8, 13

Deleuze, Gilles, 117, 125

Demasy, P., 44

Deoraíocht see *Exile* (Ó Conaire)

Destry Rides Again, 159, 171

'Devvy's Circus' (poster), 77, **78**, 88

Dibdin, Charles, 97, 98, 108

Dickens, Charles

    Bleak House, 62

    Hard Times, 62–3, 87, 114

Dingle, Co. Kerry, 18, 29, 72, 86, 87, 89

discontinuity, 9, 101, 103, 185

disinheritance, 119–20

'Do Your Best for One Another'

    (Patterson), 23–8, 76–7, 129

Donne, John: 'Air and Angels', 138

Donnelly, Ignatius, 9

Double Jockey Act, The (Yeats), **102**,

    102–3, 107, 116

doubling, 7, 139–40, 143

Dramatis Personae (Parker), 125–6

'Dramatis Personae' (Yeats), 98, 111

dreams, 27–8, 45, 64, 103, 115–16, 158–60

Dublin, 3, 16, 18, 33, 42, 49–50, 54, 73, 75,

    95, 97, 99, 111, 123, 154, 180, 181

Dublin Zoo, 50

Duffy, Arthur, 111

Duffy, James, 111

Duffy, John, 111

Duffy, John James, 111

Duffy's Circus, 1, 3, 49, 96, 111, 113, 121,

    131–4, **132**, **133**, 148–9

'Duffy's Circus' (Muldoon), 6, 13–14, 135,

    136, 149–51, 152–3, 161, 171

Durcan, Paul, 110–11

Eagleton, Terry, 43, 45, 47

Easter Rising, 176

Eglinton, John, 22

Ellmann, Maud, 68, 70, 167, 168

emigration, 11, 19–21, 53–60, 62, 65–71,

    72–3, 90, 121, 124

End of the Affair (Jordan), 162

English circus companies, 2, 49–50, 75,

    128

English literature, 11–12, 51, 55, 62–3, 81,

    83–4

eroticism, 7–8, 13–14, 35–6, 134, 141, 159;

    see also sexuality

Esquire magazine, 134

European circus companies, 3, 112

European Union (EU), 3, 112

Everyman, 125–6

Exile (Ó Conaire), 4, 6, 7, 11–12, 50–73,

    82–3, 93, 115, 124, 140, 177, 184

Ex-Isle of Erin (O'Toole), 11, 178

fables, 55–6, 100

Faith Healer (Friel), 116, 122, 125

family, 6, 11, 25, 30, 33, 37–8, 51–3, 59–67,

    74, 88–93, 96, 114–16, 131–2, 147–8,

    155–60; *see also* father figures

Family and Community in Ireland

    (Arensberg & Kimball), 12, 52–3,

    59–62, 65, 74, 83, 85, 88, 90, 91

Famine, 71–3, 129, 138, 145

'Famine Song' *see* 'Amhrán an Ghorta'

    (Ó Gráda), 72

Fanning, Kenneth, 176, 177–83, **179**

Fanque, Pablo, 19

fantasy, 13, 25–6, 38–9, 42, 43, 64, 65, 89,

    110, 140–42, 145, 151–2, 156–60

Farrer, David, 138

father figures, 10, 16–18, 21–2, 37–8,

    47–8, 63–6, 115–16, 147–50, 159–60,

    178–80; *see also* family

Faust and Marguerite (Lutz), 127

Faustus Kelly (O'Brien), 121, 122, 125

'Feeling into Words' (Heaney), 172

Fellini, Federico: *La Strada*, 158

Felstead, S. Theoore, 26

Festival of Fools, Belfast, 184

Fianna Fáil, 76–9

'Fianna Fallacy Puppet Show' (poster)

    77, **78**

Field and Fair (Ó Conaire), 54

Field Day Theatre Company, 119, 129

financial crisis, 175, 176

Finnegans Wake (Joyce), 10, 18, 19, 40–41,

    45, 151

First World War, 50, 89–90

fit-up shows, 113–18

fly-posting, 2–3, 112; *see also* circus

    posters

food, 51, 55, 69, 88; *see also* hunger

'For the Commander of the *Eliza*' (Heaney), 145
Fossett, Bobby, 111–12
Fossett, Johnny, 111–12
Fossett, Marion, 175–6
Fossett, Ted, 111
Fossett, Teddy, 2–3, 111–13
Fossett's Circus, 1–2, 3, 15, 92–3, 96, 111–13, 136, 153, 156–62, 175–6, 178, 182, 183
Foster, Roy, 146
fragmentation, 9, 185
Frawley, Oona, 176
Freaks (Browning), 158
Freeman's Journal, 54
French, Philip, 155
French Revolution, 8–9, 97
Freud, Sigmund, 66
Friel, Brian
    Crystal and Fox, 6, 7, 13, 60, 95–6, 112–18, 181, 184–5
    Faith Healer, 116, 122, 125
    and the Field Day Theatre Company, 119, 129
    'The Illusionists', 120–21
    The Mundy Scheme, 122–3
    Philadelphia, Here I Come!, 122
    'The Theatre of Hope and Despair', 118–19, 122
Frost, Thomas, 75
Froula, Christine, 42

Gaelic League, 11, 54
Gaiety Theatre, Dublin, 98
Gallagher Winarski, Kathleen, 136–7
Galway, 54–5, 59–61
Gate Theatre, Dublin, 110
Gavan, D.K., 25
Gazette des Nations, 45
gender
    as performative, 6, 33–4, 42–3
    re-gendering, 33–4, 42–3
    as socially-constructed, 6
    see also women
George VI, 84

Gibbons, Luke, 8, 49, 51, 185
Gibson, Barbara, 90
Go-Between, The (Hartley), 142–3
Goldstone, Patricia, 109
Good Friday Agreement, 3
Graham, Colin, 8, 9, 10, 12, 13, 185
Gray, Peter, 176
'Great Hunger, The' (Kavanagh), 62
Gregory, Augusta, Lady, 98
Groarke, Raymond, 176
grotesque, 6, 39–44, 64, 66, 85–6, 87, 145–6, 163
Gryta, Caroline Nobile, 36
Guardian, 113

Halappanavar, Savita, 180–81
Hanlon Lees Brothers, 183–4
'Hard Act, A' (Kiberd), 11–12
Hard Times (Dickens), 62–3, 87, 114
Harlequin's Positions (Yeats), 99
Hartley, L.P.: *The Go-Between*, 142–3
Harvard Irish Study, 12, 52–3, 59–62, 65, 74, 83, 85, 88, 90, 91
Hayes, Joanne, 154–5
Heaney, Seamus
    'Among Schoolchildren', 167–8, 174
    'Blackberry Picking', 145
    The Cure at Troy, 169
    Death of a Naturalist, 145
    'Feeling into Words', 172
    'For the Commander of the *Eliza*', 145
    'The Makings of a Music', 137
    The Midnight Verdict, 171
    'Mossbawn', 167, 171, 174
    'Omphalos', 167
    Preoccupations, 167
    'Reading', 167
    review of *Mules*, 185
    'Rhymes', 167
    Seeing Things, 165, 168–9, 173
    Stepping Stones, 14–15
    'Wheels within Wheels', 6, 7, 13–14, 135, 164–74, 185
'Hearing Things' (Dawe), 96

Heavenly Bodies (Parker), 6, 7, 13, 24–5,
    72, 94–6, 125–30, 182, 185
Heckler, Margaret, 123
Hengler's Circus, 16–18, **17**, 33–4, 39,
    40–41, 42
Herlihy, David, 88
Herr, Cheryl, 10
heteroglossia, 43
Higgins, Geraldine, 41, 114
'High Talk' (Yeats), 96, 104–5, 108, 116,
    136, 150
Higham, Nick, 46
Hilliard, Nicholas, 79
Hinde, John, 49–50, 73, 81, 92, 130
Hippodrome Cinema, Belfast, 49, 130
history, 12–13, 51, 72, 123–4, 129, 135,
    138–42, 145–6, 155, 172, 178
Hogarth, William, 79
Holiday magazine, 131
Holland, Kitty, 180
Holloway, Joseph, 110–11
Hughes-Hallett, Lucy, 46
Hugo, Victor, 163
'Humanism of Joyce, The' (Monnier),
    44, 182
humanitarianism, 23, 44, 71
hunger, 55, 68–73
'Hunger Artist, A' (Kafka), 68, 72, 73, 81
hunger marches, 70
hunger strikes, 70, 71
hybridity, 13, 56, 152

illegitimacy, 4, 43, 89; *see also* legitimacy
'Illusionists, The' (Friel), 120–21
Imagined Communities (Anderson), 53
In Darkest England (Booth), 55, 56
incest, 66–7, 137, 139–40
Independent, 160–61
India, 82
industrialisation, 52
infanticide, 154–5
infantile sexuality, 66
Inghinidhe na hÉireann, 41
inheritance, 61–2, 74
intergenerational dynamics, 73, 74, 161–2

Into the West (Sheridan), 157
Inventing Ireland (Kiberd), 8, 12–13, 118,
    129
inversion, 4, 35, 43, 44, 182
Ireland Since the Famine (Lyons), 72
Irish Countryman, The (Arensberg), 52
Irish Film Institute, 184
Irish identity, 1, 8–9, 13–14, 51, 73, 91–2
Irish language, 4, 11–12, 51, 54–7, 59, 73,
    82–3
Irish Literary Theatre (ILT), 98, 99, 120;
    see also Abbey Theatre
'Irish National Theatre, An' (Yeats), 98,
    122
Irish Parliamentary Party, 24, 58
Irish Privy Council, 97
Irish Review, 146
Irish Sketch Book 1842 (Thackeray),
    85–6
Irish Stage Act, 97
'Irish Studies and the Dynamics of
    Memory' conference, 176
Irish Times, 177, 180
Irish universal see universality
'It's Only a Paper Moon' (Arlen), 22

James, Henry, 168
James Joyce Quarterly, 36
Jem Casey's Historical Tour of Ireland
    (Wet Paint), 123–4
Jiving at the Crossroads (Waters), 143–4,
    154, 155, 157, 163, 170
John, Augustus, 79
'John Bull's Famous Circus' (Lynd), **57**,
    57–8, 76
Johnny Patterson the Singing Irish Clown
    (Barabbas Theatre), 10–11
*Johnny Patterson's Great London Circus
    Songster*, 19–21, **20**, 25–6
Johnson, Henry T., 36
Jordan, Neil
    The End of the Affair, 162
    interviews, 7, 155–6, 158, 160–61
    The Miracle, 4, 6, 13–14, 135, 136–7,
        153–64, 168, 171, 174, 178, 181

Joyce, James
  Finnegans Wake, 10, 18, 19, 40–41, 45, 151
  influence on Heaney, 167, 174
  A Portrait of the Artist as a Young Man, 85
  Stephen Hero, 21–2, 29
  'Subjugation', 31, 36
  Ulysses, 6, 7, 10–11, 16–18, 22, 25–8, 31–48, 61, 95, 116, 125, 127, 141, 174, 181, 182, 184, 185

Kafka, Franz: 'A Hunger Artist', 68, 72, 73, 81
Kavanagh, Patrick, 62
Kendall, Tim, 150, 153
Kennedy, Róisín, 5
Kerry Babies Case, 154–5
Kiberd, Declan, 8, 10, 12–13, 118, 129, 185
Kilcolgan, Co. Galway, 86
Kilkenny Beer Festival, 112
Kimball, Solon, 12, 52–3, 59–60, 61–2, 65, 74, 83, 85, 88, 90, 91
Knight, Laura, 79
Koch, John T., 51
Krapp's Last Tape (Beckett), 173
Krause, A.S., 69–70

Labour movement, 77
'Lake Isle of Innisfree' (Yeats), 181
'Land of Starvation' series (*Daily Telegraph*), 69–70
Last Poems (Yeats), 95, 106–7, 117, 136, 163
laughter, 103, 107–8, 110, 123, 142
Laughter (Bergson), 103
Lee, Laurie: *Cider with Rosie*, 145
legitimacy, 24, 28, 126–7
Lemass, Seán, 77
Levin, Jennifer Burns, 35–6, 44
Life and Labour of the People of London (Booth), 55
Life on the Open Road (Mateer), 114
Limerick, 111
'Lion Tamer, The' (Durcan), 110

Listowel, Co. Kerry, 85–6
'Little Marcus's Nora' (Ó Conaire), 67
Lloyd, David, 56, 62, 96, 101–4, 108
Lloyd, James, 23
local authorities, 2, 112
Logic of Sensation, The (Deleuze), 117
London, 11–12, 51, 53–9, 62, 65–73, 82–3, 96–7
London Nights (Symons), 108
'Long-legged Fly' (Yeats), 105, 137, 173
Longley, Edna, 108–9, 115, 135–6
Longley, Michael, 136, 150
Love of the Circus (Walsh), 71
Lovett, Ann, 154
Lutz, Wilhelm Meyer, 127
Lynd, Robert: 'John Bull's Famous Circus', **57**, 57–8, 76
Lyons, F.S.L., 72

Mac Theatre, Belfast, 177–8
McCafferty, Nell, 155
McCarthy, Conor, 142
MacCarthy, Desmond, 46
McColgan, John, 130
McCourt, John, 10
McCracken, Henry Joy, 125
MacDonnell, Antony, 58
Mac Eoin, Gearailt, 11–12, 50–58, 62, 63, 68, 69, 72–3
McErlane, Paul, 178
McGovern, Barry, 110
McGowan, Brendan, 54
McGrath, F.C., 118
MacGreevy, Thomas, 99, 101
McKendry, Donal, 184
McMahon, Joseph, 74
McMinn, Richard, 111
MacSwiney, Terence, 70, 71
magic, 131, 134, 147, 148–9, 160, 183
magic realism, 7, 139
Maguire, Donal, 28
'Makings of a Music' (Heaney), 137
Malone, John, 125
'Manifesto for the Irish Literary Theatre' (Yeats, Gregory & Martyn), 98

'Many Can Help One' (Patterson), 22–3
Manzoni, Alessandro, 45–6
Mark-FitzGerald, Emily, 176
Markievicz, Constance, 76–7
Martyn, Edward, 98
martyrdom, 28, 44–5, 71
Marxism, 70
Mary, Virgin, 154, 155
Masefield, John, 80
Mateer, James, 114
melodrama, 99–100, 101, 114, 126–7, 139
memory, 10, 17–18, 53, 64–5, 71–2, 89–91,
    103–9, 147, 151, 163, 167, 170, 172–3,
    176
Meredith, George, 84
Merriman, Brian, 171
metempsychosis, 31–3, **32**, 47
Midnight Verdict, The (Heaney), 171
mime, 124
Miracle, The (Jordan), 4, 6, 13–14, 135,
    136–7, 153–64, 168, 171, 174, 178, 181
modernism, 81, 142
modernity, 9, 11, 51, 52, 63, 71, 92
Molloy (Beckett), 68–9
Moloney, Mike, 184
Molyneux, Capel, 97
Monnier, Adrienne, 44, 182
Montague, Helen, 129
Moore, George
    'A Play-House in the West', 121–2,
        124, 125
    The Untilled Field, 59, 62, 121–2
'Mossbawn' (Heaney), 167, 171, 174
Muir, Edwin, 68
Muldoon, Paul
    'The Bearded Woman, by Ribera',
        147–8
    'Centaurs', 185
    'Duffy's Circus', 6, 13–14, 135, 136,
        149–51, 152–3, 161, 171
    interview with, 7, 136
    Mules, 6, 135, 147–51, 153, 185
    'Yeats and the Afterlife' lecture, 95
Mules (Muldoon), 6, 135, 147–51, 153, 185
Mundy Scheme, The (Friel), 122–3

music hall, 19, 25–8, 39, 94, 95, 106, 109,
    127, 128
Mussolini, Benito, 45

Nation, 54
National Gallery, London, 109
National League, 77
nationalism, 41, 53, 56, 70, 71, 73; *see also*
    cultural nationalism
navels, 143, 167, 172
Nemo: *The Circus: a delightful day with*
    the circus folk, 79
Nets of Modernism (Ellmann), 167
New Ireland, 54
New Irelanders, 24
Nicholson, William, 109
'Nineteen Hundred and Nineteen'
    (Yeats), 172
Norris, Margot, 35, 36
Northern Ireland, 3, 4, 13, 14, 112, 126,
    130, 136, 141–2, 150, 153, 182–3, 184
Northern Star (Parker), 13, 125, 129
nostalgia, 9–10, 72–3, 146, 167, 176
'Nothing But the Same Old Story'
    (Brady), 124
Nothing But the Same Old Story
    (Information on Ireland), 124, 125

O'Brien, Flann
    At Swim-Two-Birds, 124
    Faustus Kelly, 121, 122, 125
    influence on Parker, 125
O'Brien Johnson, Toni, 161–2, 163
Observer, 155
Ó Conaire, Pádraic
    Exile (Deoraíocht), 4, 6, 7, 11–12,
        50–73, 82–3, 93, 115, 124, 140,
        177, 184
    Field and Fair, 54
    life, 53–5
    'Little Marcus's Nora', 67
    'Seanlitríocht na hÉireann agus
        Nualitríocht na hEorpa', 59
    Seven Virtues of the Rising (Seacht
        mBua an Éirí Amach), 54

O'Donnel, 19, 124
O'Driscoll, Dennis, 14
Oedipus complex, 135, 156–9, 161
Ó Faoláin, Seán, 122
O'Flaherty, Liam, 55
O'Flynn, Paddy, 79, 80, 81–3, 86, 87–8, 89, 181
Ó Gráda, Cormac, 72
'Old Log Cabin in the Dell' (Patterson), 25
O'Leary, Sean, 81, 82, 83, 87, 89, 90–92
Olympia Theatre, Dublin, 159–60
'Omphalos' (Heaney), 167
On the Boiler (Yeats), 136
'On the Concept of History' (Benjamin), 131, 172
Onct More's Circus (Yeats), 99, 100
Oral History of the Circus (Gibson), 90
Oscar Mime Company, 124
Ó Séaghdha, Barra, 153–4
O'Sullivan, Thaddeus, 14, 138–9, 156, 183
otherness, 12, 41, 56–7, 60–61, 70–71, 158
O'Toole, Fintan, 11, 113, 153, 178
Our Irish Theatre (Gregory), 98

Paddington, Pablo, 19
pantomime, 3, 13, 94, 97, 109, 111
Parish, Mitchell, 158
Parker, Jim, 25
Parker, Lynne, 7, 94, 126, 129–30, 182
Parker, Stewart
  absence from *Inventing Ireland*, 12–13, 129
  Dramatis Personae, 125–6
  Heavenly Bodies, 6, 7, 13, 24–5, 71, 94–6, 125–30, 182, 185
  Northern Star, 13, 125, 129
  Pentecost, 13
  Spokesong, 25
Parnell, Charles Stewart, 24, 41
Parnell, John Howard, 41
partition, 50, 150
paternity, 24, 28, 30, 178–80; *see also* father figures
pathetic fallacy, 34, 62

Patterson, Johnny, 7, 10–11, 18–28, **20**, 30, 39, 44, 71–2, 76–7, 81, 181
  depiction of in *Heavenly Bodies*, 24–5, 72, 94–5, 125–9, 185
Pattman, Andrew, 138–9
Paulo, Clara, 75
Paulo, Frank, 75
Peacock Theatre, 7, 94–5, 99, 129–30, 182
Pentecost (Parker), 13
Philadelphia, Here I Come! (Friel), 122
photography, 49, 131–5, 147, 157, 174
Pike, The (Hughes-Hallett), 46
Pinter, Harold, 113
Planet Circus, 3
Playboy of the Western World (Synge), 42, 88, 161–2, 181
'Play-House in the West, A' (Moore), 121–2, 124, 125
Pollexfen, George, 98
pony races, 75, 81
popular culture, 8, 9, 10–11, 96, 119
Portrait of the Artist as a Young Man (Joyce), 85
postcards, 49
postcolonial theory, 12
poverty, 22–3, 50, 53–5, 59, 64–5, 68–73, 75, 86–7, 93
Power, Mary, 34, 36
pregnancy, 154, 155–6, 178–80
Preoccupations (Heaney), 167
Press, 97
Pride of the Ring (Johnson), 36
Promessi Sposi, I (Manzoni), 45
prostitution, 40, 42, 67
Protestantism, 23, 137
psychoanalytic theory, 66, 113, 143, 160
'Pulling Hard Against the Stream' (Clifton), 25–7, 44
Punch magazine, 32, 58, **58**, 70, 124, 125, 142
Purgatorio (Dante), 137
Purser, John, 99–100, 101, 121, 126
Pyle, Hilary, 103

quests, 100, 168–9

Rabelais, François, 43–4, 45, 46
Rabelais and His World (Bakhtin), 44
race, 12, 70, 73, 77, 82–3
Read, Alan, 47–8
Reade, Amye: *Ruby: a novel founded on the life of a circus girl*, 34–8, 47, 184
'Reading' (Heaney), 167
Reading in the Dark (Deane), 135, 136, 148–9, 151–3, 154, 157, 173
realism, 118, 142
rebellion, 7–8, 64, 97, 141
Reco's Circus, 49–50, 73, 92, 130
Redmond, John, 58
Reed, Carol: *Trapeze*, 158
re-gendering, 33–4, 42–3
Renaissance festival, 43
Renan, Ernest, 53
'Republics of Difference' (Lloyd), 96, 101–4
revisionism, 71, 120, 125, 129, 142, 144, 146
Reynolds, Joshua, 79
Reynolds, Paige, 71
'Rhymes' (Heaney), 167
Richtarik, Marilynn, 24, 25, 129
Riggs, Pádraigín, 51, 57
ringmasters, 2, 43, 58, 108–9, 112, 114–15, 135–6, 140, 172
Rings of Desire (Stoddart), 4–5
Risorgimento, 45–6
Riverdance, 130, 182
Roach, Hal, 123–4, 126
Roche, Anthony, 100–101
'Rocky Road to Dublin' (Gavan), 25
Roe, Owen, 94–5, 123–4, 125, 127–30
romanticism, 9, 21, 28, 80, 144–5, 159
Romanticism, 87, 163
Rose of Tralee Festival, 112
Rotunda, Dublin, 16, 18, 42
Rough Magic theatre company, 7, 94–5, 125
Rousselot, Philippe, 159
Royal Circus, London, 97
RTÉ, 24, 112, 153, 184

Ruby: a novel founded on the life of a circus girl (Reade), 34–8, 47, 184
Ruby: the Pride of the Ring (in *Ulysses*), 6, 31–8, 44, 116
Rushe, Desmond, 113, 122

Sandow, Violet, 90
Sanger's Circus, 80, 88
satire, 41, 45, 75–9, 130
Seacht mBua an Éirí Amach see *Seven Virtues of the Rising* (Ó Conaire)
Seago, Edward
    Circus Company, 79, 80–81, 84, 88
    paintings and illustrations, 79–80, 80
    Sons of Sawdust, 6, 12, 50–53, 79–93, 140, 177, 185
'Seanlitríocht na hÉireann agus Nualitríocht na hEorpa' (Ó Conaire), 59
Second World War, 50
Seeing Things (Heaney), 165, 168–9, 173
Segner, Tina, 176, 177–83, **179**
Semiotics at the Circus (Bouissac), 10
Seven Virtues of the Rising (Ó Conaire), 54
sexuality, 6, 7–8, 13–14, 35–6, 42, 52, 66–7, 134–5, 141–6, 150–53, 158–65, 167, 169, 171–3, 180
Shakespeare, William: *The Tempest*, 138, 140, 152, 160
Shanachie, The, 29
Shaugraun, The (Boucicault), 7, 100, 129–30
Shaw, George Bernard, 125
Sheridan, Jim: *Into the West*, 157
Shipp, Horace, 79
Sickert, Walter, 109
Singing Clown, The (Yeats), 28–9, **29**
Sinn Féin, 57
Sligo (Yeats), 100, 101, 103, 109, 117
Smith, Eleanor, 49, 92
social class, 27, 65, 77, 82
social commentary, 36, 51, 55, 59, 62
socialism, 23, 44, 45

Sons of Sawdust (Seago), 6, 12, 50–53, 79–93, 140, 177, 185
Sordello (Browning), 137
Speaight, George, 130
Spencer, Theodore, 21–2
'Spinning Song' (Bridges), 25
split personalities, 7, 113
Spokesong (Parker), 25
Spurrier, Steven, 79
Stafford, Fiona, 166, 168, 169, 173
stage Irishmen, 13, 19, 96, 98, 128–9
staged failure, 28, 34
'Stardust' (Carmichael), 158, 159
Starving London (Krause), 69–70
'Statues, The' (Yeats), 163
Stephen Hero (Joyce), 21–2, 29
Stepping Stones (Heaney), 14–15
stereotypes, 19, 21, 58–9, 123–4, 125, 127–8
Stewart Parker: a life (Richtarik), 25
'Stilts' (Longley), 136
Stoddart, Helen, 4–5, 9, 43, 63, 97, 103, 176
'Stolen Child, The' (Yeats), 47
Strada, La (Fellini), 158
Strange Country (Deane), 8–9
String of Pearls, The, 114
'Subjugation' (Joyce), 31, 36
sublimity, 163
subversion, 4–5
Sullivan, Agnes, 3
Sun, 26
superstition, 91–3, 122
Swallow's Circus, 19
Symons, Arthur: *London Nights*, 108
Synge, John Millington
    attends circus performances with Yeats, 11, 18, 28–30, 86
    and heroic figures, 41
    influence on Friel, 119
    The Playboy of the Western World, 42, 88, 161–2, 181
    The Well of Saints, 163

Tallone, Giovanna, 116
teenage motherhood, 154, 155–6

television, 2, 112, 113–14, 117–18
Tempest, The (Shakespeare), 138, 140, 152, 160
Tenniel, John: 'Two Forces', **58**, 58–9, 67, 77, 142
Thackeray, William Makepeace, 85–6
theatre, 5, 7, 12–13, 94–130, 139, 156, 159–60, 163, 164, 177–8
'Theatre, The Pulpit, and The Newspapers' (Yeats), 120, 122, 135, 153, 160, 164
Theatre Licensing Act, 97
'Theatre of Hope and Despair, The' (Friel), 118–19, 122
Theatre Royal, Dublin, 97, 98
Theatres Act, 97
'Three Essays on the Theory of Sexuality' (Freud), 66
Tír na nÓg, 157
Tóibín, Colm, 142, 144
Tone, Theobald Wolfe, 3
Toronto Daily Leader, 128
tradition, 52, 61–2, 63, 71, 92
tragic modernism, 47
'Tragic Theatre, The' (Yeats), 100–101
Tralee, Co. Kerry, 23–4, 85
Transformations in Irish Culture (Gibbons), 8
Trapeze (Reed), 158
travel writing, 12, 49–52, 84–7
Tristan, Flora, 59
Trollope, Anthony, 84–5
Troubles, 4, 13, 14, 112, 126, 130, 141–2
Tumble Circus, 15, 175, 176–83, **179**
Turner, John, 33–4
'Two Forces' (Tenniel), **58**, 58–9, 67, 77, 142

Ulysses (Joyce), 6, 7, 10–11, 16–18, 22, 25–8, 31–48, 61, 95, 116, 125, 127, 141, 174, 181, 182, 184, 185
    'Calypso', 6, 11, 18, 31–8, 44
    'Circe', 6, 7, 11, 18, 22, 25–6, 30, 31, 33, 38–48, 61, 127, 185
    'Cyclops', 28

Ulysses (Joyce) (*continued*)
  'Eumaeus', 18, 41
  'Hades', 38, 40
  'Ithaca', 16–18, 27, 33, 38, 42, 45
  'Nausicaa', 33, 42, 141
  'Nestor', 25
  'Oxen of the Sun', 125
  'Proteus', 95
  'Sirens', 39
Ulysses and Us (Kiberd), 10
uncanny, 66, 139–40
United Irishmen, 125
United States, 19–23, 121–4
universality, 14–15, 23, 28, 139, 156,
  183
Unnamble, The (Beckett), 105
Untilled Field, The (Moore), 59, 121–2
utopias, 13–14, 27

Vance, Norman, 51
variety acts, 110–12
Vernon, James, 70
violence, 6, 8, 28, 31, 46, 65, 89, 91, 140,
  141–2, 150–52
voices off, 7, 92, 173

Waiting for Godot (Beckett), 13, 94
Walls, Barry, 2
Walsh, Ian, 99
Walsh, Townsend, 71
War of Independence, 50
Wasgate, Samuel ('Lulu'), 33–4
Washington Post, 155–6
Waters, John: *Jiving at the Crossroads*,
  143–4, 154, 155, 157, 163, 170
Watts, Jennifer, 131
Well of Saints, The (Synge), 163
Westerns, 2, 81, 112, 159, 171–2
Wet Paint theatre company, 123–4
'What is a Nation?' (Renan), 53
'Wheels within Wheels' (Heaney), 6, 7,
  13–14, 135, 164–74, 185
White, C.A., 25, 39
Whitelaw, William, 14, 150
Williams, Gus, 25, 39

women
  absence of female texts/perspectives, 5
  and Catholic iconography, 6, 134–5,
    143–4, 157–8, 161, 172
  and Catholicism, 154–5, 161
  and pregnancy, 154, 155–6, 178–80
  representations of, 5–7, 133–5, **134**,
    143–6, 154–63, 171–2, 178–80
  as representative of land/Ireland, 6,
    66–7, 143–4, 150, 152–3, 171
  role within the circus, 6, 29–30
  and sexuality, 6, 7–8, 13–14, 35–6,
    66–7, 134–5, 143–6, 150–53,
    158–65, 167, 171–2, 180
  state attitudes towards, 154–6,
    180–81
  see also gender; family
Wonderful Traveller, The (Yeats), 108
Woolf, Virginia: *Between the Acts*, 81
Word, The, 113
Words Upon the Window Pane (Yeats),
  105
Wordsworth, William, 166
Work in Progress see *Finnegans Wake*
  (Joyce)

Yeats, Jack B.
  Alone, 80
  attends circus performances with
    Synge, 11, 18, 28–30, 86
  Boucicault's influence upon, 99–100,
    126
  The Circus Dwarf, 79–80
  The Circus Has Come, 5, 10
  The Double Jockey Act, **102**, 102–3, 107,
    116
  Harlequin's Positions, 99
  letters, 99
  miniature theatre, 99, 100
  National Gallery exhibition, 109
  Onct More's Circus, 99, 100
  paintings of Patterson, 18
  The Singing Clown, 28–9, **29**
  Sligo, 100, 101, 103, 109, 117
  The Wonderful Traveller, 108

Yeats, W.B.
  'Among School Children', 167–8, 174
  Cathleen ni Houlihan, 153
  The Celtic Twilight, 52, 81
  'The Circus Animals' Desertion',
    14–15, 95–6, 104, 106–9, 115–16,
    126, 135–7, 150, 160, 166, 184–5
  'Dramatis Personae', 98, 111
  and heroic figures, 41
  'High Talk', 96, 104–5, 108, 116, 136,
    150
  influence on Beckett, 96
  influence on Heaney, 7, 166, 167–8
  introduction to *The Well of Saints*, 163
  and the Irish Literary Theatre, 98, 99,
    120
  'An Irish National Theatre', 98, 122
  'The Lake Isle of Innisfree', 181
  Last Poems, 95, 96, 104–9, 117, 136, 163

  'Long-legged Fly', 105, 137, 173
  'Nineteen Hundred and Nineteen',
    172
  On the Boiler, 136
  plans for travelling theatre company,
    118
  'The Statues', 163
  'The Stolen Child', 47
  'The Theatre, The Pulpit, and The
    Newspapers', 120, 122, 135, 153,
    160, 164
  'The Tragic Theatre', 100–101
  The Words Upon the Window Pane, 105
Yeats and Modern Poetry (Longley),
  108–9
'Yeats and the Afterlife' (Muldoon), 95
Youngs, Tim, 12

Zucker, Carole, 161, 162